YALE STUDIES IN POLITICAL SCIENCE, 28

CONGRESS AND
THE BUREAUCRACY

A THEORY OF INFLUENCE

R. DOUGLAS ARNOLD

NEW HAVEN AND LONDON
YALE UNIVERSITY PRESS
1979

Published with assistance from
the Mary Cady Tew Memorial Fund.

Designed by Sally Harris
and set in VIP Electra type.
Printed in the United States of America by
Halliday Lithograph, West Hanover, Mass.

Published in Great Britain, Europe, Africa, and
Asia (except Japan) by Yale University Press,
Ltd., London. Distributed in Australia and
New Zealand by Book & Film Services, Artarmon,
N.S.W., Australia; and in Japan by Harper & Row,
Publishers, Tokyo Office.

Library of Congress Cataloging in Publication Data

Arnold, R. Douglas, 1950–
    Congress and the bureaucracy.

    (Yale studies in political science; 28)
    Includes index.
    1. Government spending policy—United States.
2. Administrative agencies—United States—Management.
3. Public administration—Decision making.   4. United
States. Congress. I. Title. II. Series.
JK585.A78   353.007'21   78-65493
ISBN 0-300-02345-6

To My Parents

CONTENTS

List of Figures   ix
List of Tables   xi
Acknowledgments   xiii

PART ONE: A THEORY OF INFLUENCE

1 Politics and Geography   3
2 Political Goals   19
3 Building Coalitions   37
4 Allocating Benefits   55
5 Measuring Influence   72

PART TWO: THE THEORY APPLIED

6 Military Employment   95
7 Water and Sewer Grants   129
8 Model Cities Grants   165
9 Coalitions and Public Policy   207

Appendix A: Methodological Problems in Five Previous Studies   217
Appendix B: Fluctuations in Military Employment   225
Index   229

FIGURES

4.1   Range of General-Benefit Preferences   57

4.2   Consensus Distribution   59

4.3   Indifference   61

4.4   Polarized Distribution   63

5.1   Sample Probit Function   80

6.1   Attitudes Toward the Defense Budget   97

6.2   Mean Army and Air Force Employment for Districts on
Armed Services Committee   105

6.3   Proportion of Districts on Armed Services with at Least One
Army or Air Force Installation   105

6.4   Proportion of Armed Services Members Coming from Districts in Top Decile and Top Quartile of All Districts,
Ranked by Army and Air Force Employment   106

6.5   Mean Army and Air Force Employment for Districts on
Military Subcommittees of Appropriations Committee   107

7.1   Hypothetical Function of Age and Acceptance   143

7.2   Probability of Acceptance as a Function of Age for Three
Classes of Applications (1970)   148

TABLES

6.1 Effects of Military Committee Membership on Decisions to
     Close Major Air Force Installations (1952–74)   108
6.2 Effects of Military Committee Membership on Decisions to
     Close Major Army Installations (1952–74)   109
6.3 Probit Analysis: Effects of Committee Membership on
     Decisions to Close Major Air Force Installations   113
6.4 Probit Analysis: Effects of Committee Membership on
     Decisions to Close Major Army Installations   114
7.1 Effects of Committee Membership on Project Selection,
     1970   139
7.2 Effects of Congressman's Ideology (and Party) on Project
     Selection, 1970   140
7.3 Effect of Project Size on Project Selection, 1970   141
7.4 Probit Analysis: Effects of Political Variables on Project
     Selection, 1970   145
7.5 Effect of Congressman's Position on Overriding Veto on
     Project Selection, 1971   153
7.6 Effects of Committee Membership on Project Selection,
     1971   154
7.7 Effect of Project Size on Project Selection, 1971   155
7.8 Probit Analysis: Effects of Political Variables on Project
     Selection, 1971   156
7.9 Probability of Acceptance for Applications Located in
     Districts that Were, Either in 1970 or 1971, Represented
     on the Subcommittee on Agriculture of House
     Appropriations   160
7.10 Probability of Acceptance for Applications Located in
     Districts Represented on the Independent Offices Sub-
     committee between 1966 and 1971   161

8.1   Comparison of Freshman's Position on Funding in 1967
         with Predecessor's Position in 1966   171
8.2   Opponents in 1966 Who Became Supporters in 1967
         When Their Districts First Applied for Benefits   172
8.3   Appropriations Committee Members' Support for Model
         Cities in 1966 and 1967   173
8.4   Acceptance Rate for Multiple-District Cities Compared with
         That for Single-District Cities (Round One)   177
8.5   Effect of 1967 Vote on District Selection (Round One)   179
8.6   Effects of Committee Membership (and 1967 Vote) on
         District Selection (Round One)   180
8.7   Number of Cities Accepted per District (Round One)   182
8.8   Probit Analysis: Effects of Political Variables on District
         Selection (Round One)   184
8.9   Acceptance Rates for Multiple-District and Single-District
         Cities (Round Two and Both Rounds Together)   189
8.10 Effects of 1967 Vote on District Selection (Round Two and
         Both Rounds Together)   190
8.11 Effects of Committee Membership (and 1967 Vote) on
         District Selection (Round Two and Both Rounds
         Together)   191
8.12 Acceptance Rates for Opponents of Funding in 1967
         (Round Two)   194
8.13 Number of Cities Accepted per District (Both Rounds)   195
8.14 Probit Analysis: Effects of Political Variables on District
         Selection (Round Two)   196
8.15 Probit Analysis: Effects of Political Variables on District
         Selection (Both Rounds)   198
8.16 Effect of Congressman's Party on District Selection
         (Both Rounds)   199
8.17 Acceptance Rates for Cities with Populations between
         100,000 and 415,000 (Both Rounds)   201
B.1   Regression Analysis: Effects of Committee Membership on
         Employment Fluctuations at Army Installations   226
B.2   Regression Analysis: Effects of Committee Membership on
         Employment Fluctuations at Air Force Installations   227

ACKNOWLEDGMENTS

My greatest debt is to my good friend David Mayhew, who has given me endless encouragement and superb advice throughout three years of research and writing. I am also indebted to my wife, Helen, first for sharing her fellowship so that we could both spend a delightful year in Bourges, France, and then for being my most severe critic during that year as I attempted to formulate a theory of congressional influence and a methodology adequate to test it.

I am grateful to James Fesler, Joseph LaPalombara, David Mayhew, and Eric Peterson, who read and commented on the entire manuscript, as well as to Herbert Kaufman and Bruce Russett, who commented on portions of it. Gerald Kramer was helpful when I was first struggling with the many theoretical and methodological problems. Chris Achen and Suzanne Weaver also offered valuable advice at the design stage. The Brookings Institution supported me as a research fellow for the final year of writing.

PART ONE
A THEORY OF INFLUENCE

1: POLITICS AND GEOGRAPHY

The central objective of this book is to determine the extent to which American congressmen influence bureaucratic decisions concerning the geographic allocation of expenditures. My more general interest is congressional-bureaucratic relationships, particularly the responsiveness of bureaucrats to congressional influence and the conditions that cause this responsiveness to vary. A study of geographic allocation merely provides a convenient vantage point for observing these relationships. Three reasons account for the focus on geographic allocation rather than on some other bureaucratic decisions. First, decisions about where funds will be spent are made regularly, so one might expect institutionalized patterns of behavior to have developed. Second, virtually all congressmen are interested in decisions about geographic allocation and, more important, their allocational preferences are well known. Finally, decisions about expenditures are easily quantifiable, which allows one to use quantitative methods to infer the extent of congressional influence.

Although my principal interest is in the study of congressional-bureaucratic relationships, there are other pertinent reasons for investigating the politics of geographic allocation. First, an understanding of the politics of allocation is crucial for those who seek to design effective public policy. The effectiveness of any expenditure program hinges on various decisions: the suitability of the chosen remedy, the total amount of resources employed, the nature of administrative organization. These are the traditional concerns of the policy analyst. But effectiveness also depends on where these resources are deployed, whether in areas of greatest need or in other areas as a consequence of standards unrelated to need. To design effective programs, policy analysts must understand *beforehand* how a program's benefits will be allocated, because even the "best" remedy, combined with abundant resources and good administration, may turn out to be ineffective by the time resources are allocated. A "lesser" remedy might actually be superior after allowance is made for the way in which benefits will be allocated.

Second, decisions about geographic allocation can have a substantial impact on the health of local or regional economies.[1] Opening or closing military installations, awarding new defense contracts or canceling old ones, or constructing large federal facilities of any type can make or break local economies. In explaining differences in the performance of local or regional economies, one needs some understanding of how allocational decisions are made. Moreover, precisely because federal spending has such an enormous effect on local economies, some have argued that economic impact should be seriously considered when these decisions are made.[2] But changes in the allocational system cannot be prescribed without first understanding how it operates and what political factors might hamper change.

ALLOCATIONAL PROCESSES

Three different procedures are employed to make decisions about the geographic allocation of federal expenditures: allocation by Congress on a project basis, allocation by Congress on a formula basis, and allocation by administrative agency. In the first method, Congress specifies by name each project to be funded and how much each shall receive. This specification is accomplished at either the authorization stage or the appropriations stage, occasionally during both. In the second procedure, Congress writes a general formula into law which delineates precisely how expenditures are to be allocated. In the third, Congress delegates allocational authority to an administrative agency. Although

1. For evidence concerning the impact of federal expenditures on regional economies, see Roger E. Bolton, *Defense Purchases and Regional Growth* (Washington, D.C.: Brookings, 1966).

2. There is disagreement, however, about which areas should receive consideration. On matters of defense spending, for example, some have argued that preference should be given to depressed areas, others suggest that each state deserves a "fair-share" of spending, and still others assert that federal spending should not be diminished or discontinued in areas that have become dependent on it. See Bolton, *Defense Purchases and Regional Growth*, pp. 2, 140–47, and James L. Sundquist, *Politics and Policy* (Washington, D.C.: Brookings, 1968), p. 61.

guidelines for the allocation of expenditures frequently accompany this delegation, agencies still have considerable discretion.

Actually, the division of labor between Congress and the agencies is not as simple as these three descriptions imply. Agencies are involved in many allocational decisions supposedly made by Congress, and congressmen are important even when decision-making authority has been delegated to agencies. To analyze the individual roles of congressmen and agencies in allocational decision making, it is useful to conceive of the decision making as a two-stage process. *Agenda setting* is the first stage. At this stage requests for a share of federal funds are received and placed on a list from which decision makers will select projects to be funded. Agenda are prepared in a variety of ways: at times formal applications by local communities are required; at times congressmen sponsor projects for their districts; and at other times agencies themselves prepare agenda. *Choice* is the final stage of the process, where decision makers, either in Congress or the agencies, select certain projects for funding. Occasionally it is useful to conceive an intermediate stage during which some alternatives are eliminated from the agenda before it reaches the final stage.

Division of labor between Congress and administrative agencies differs for various types of government expenditures. Congress is most directly involved in decisions about construction of federal facilities. Virtually all construction projects require either a specific congressional authorization or a specific appropriation; that is to say, Congress participates in the final stage of decision making: choice. Congressional involvement in previous stages varies according to construction type. For example, Congress participates in every stage of the process that selects rivers and harbors projects: congressmen sponsor projects for their constituencies, legislative committees authorize construction of some but not all of these, and appropriations committees choose projects to be funded. The agency responsible for rivers and harbors, the Army Corps of Engineers, has a more limited role to play. On the other hand, Congress is generally not involved in early stages of decision making when the question concerns where federal laboratories or military installations should be constructed. Usually an agency determines what type of facility should be constructed, prepares a list of localities suitable for such facilities, and selects one for the construction of a new facility;

Congress is then asked to approve the agency's selection and provide funds. In this case, Congress makes the final decision about construction—to build or not to build—but unlike the rivers and harbors example, it does not actually select which of the competing localities shall be the beneficiary. This does not imply that Congress has any less influence, for influence over outcomes does not require direct participation in decision making.

In contrast, most decisions about the geographic allocation of federal employment are made by administrative agencies. An agency can, within certain boundaries, determine where its employees shall work. One of these limits is the availability of adequate facilities, whether office buildings, laboratories, or military installations. Generally, an agency with spare facilities is free to transfer personnel among them— for example, from one military installation to another; but, of course, it cannot transfer personnel to nonexistent facilities! In the latter case, allocation of employment is really a question of constructing new facilities, and Congress is, as we have just seen, very much involved in such questions.

The authority to make decisions about the allocation of contracts has also been delegated to administrative agencies. Although agencies always make the final decisions about where contracts shall be allocated, there are significant differences in how each agency's agenda is prepared and in the extent to which its choices are confined. When goods or services to be procured are either commonly available or relatively uncomplicated, an agency generally advertises for bids; its agenda is the list of bids received. Agencies have little discretion in such cases, because they cannot control their agendas and because they are usually required to award contracts to organizations submitting the lowest bids. However, when the item to be procured is extremely complex—for example, a new weapons system—agencies need not advertise; instead, they negotiate with potential contractors until they reach an agreement with one of them. Negotiation gives the agency considerable latitude in matters of choice, even though its agenda of alternatives is restricted, because few organizations have the capacity to provide such complex items.

Grants to state and local governments are allocated either on a formula basis by Congress or on a project basis by administrative agencies—never on a project basis by Congress. The difference between allocation by formula and allocation on a project basis is sharp. When Congress establishes a formula program it specifies what types of jurisdictions will be eligible for assistance and according to what objective criteria funds will be allocated. Jurisdictions that fit these eligibility requirements know in advance the size of the grant to which they are entitled. But when Congress establishes a program to dispense project grants, it merely defines goals and sets minimum standards of eligibility, leaving to an administrative agency the task of developing more complete eligibility criteria. Jurisdictions that meet these criteria may apply for grants, but none knows in advance whether it will be awarded a grant or how large that grant might be. Agencies select or reject applications as they see fit and determine the size of each grant.

There has been a gradual shift over time in the way federal grants have been allocated.[3] When federal assistance programs were first established, states were usually the beneficiaries, and formulas were used invariably. But as federal assistance began to be channeled directly to local governments, project grants became increasingly important. This transition from the primacy of one allocational method to that of another reflects not only a shift in the type of beneficiary but also a change in the philosophy of federal assistance. Early grant programs were designed to help state governments perform their traditional functions, ranging from highway construction to public assistance. Formulas were considered an appropriate means for allocating funds, because such programs were intended to provide financial assistance to all states so that they might better solve their *own* problems. Later, when many of these same problems were recognized as *national* problems, allocation by formula seemed less attractive. Efficient solutions to national problems required that funds flow to areas of greatest need and to organizations that promised effective solutions. Project grants, unlike formula grants, could easily be channeled to the most needy areas and could be used to encourage innovation, or so it was thought. During the 1960s there was a tremendous increase in the number of grant programs, most of which involved project rather than formula grants. Since

3. For discussions concerning the development of the federal grant system, see James L. Sundquist, *Making Federalism Work* (Washington, D.C.: Brookings, 1969), pp. 1–13; Martha Derthick, *The Influence of Federal Grants* (Cambridge, Mass.: Harvard University Press, 1970), pp. 5–15; or Donald M. Haider, *When Governments Come to Washington* (New York: Free Press, 1974), pp. 54–57.

then, allocation by project has been the dominant allocational strategy, though many grants are still allocated by formula. The Nixon and Ford Administrations demonstrated a preference for formula rather than project grants. They terminated some grant programs and substituted new formula programs, notably general revenue sharing, which dispenses funds for recipient-determined purposes, and special revenue sharing, which restricts the purposes to which recipients may put the funds.

These, then, are the ways the federal government makes decisions about the geographic allocation of construction projects, federal employment, contracts, and grants to state and local governments. There are also a few expenditure programs that never require formal decisions about geographic allocation. Social security is the most conspicuous example. These programs typically give benefits directly to individuals or organizations without any regard to where the beneficiaries may be located. This study is not concerned with such programs.

THEORIES OF GEOGRAPHIC ALLOCATION

Most decisions about geographic allocation are bureaucratic decisions. Yet most studies of the politics of allocation have concentrated on Congress and devoted little attention to questions of bureaucratic behavior. In this book the emphasis is reversed; analysis is centered on bureaucratic decisions. The analysis includes an extensive examination of Congress's role, but it focuses on how congressmen influence bureaucratic decision making rather than on how Congress makes allocational decisions itself.

The following chapters develop a theory of how bureaucrats make decisions concerning the geographic allocation of expenditures. But before turning to that task, a detailed examination of previous theories is in order, for their inadequacies have prompted the development of this theory. Three theories merit attention. Each scrutinizes the manner in which a legislative assembly with geographic representation might handle the geographic allocation of benefits. Two are deductive theories developed without any particular representative assemblies in mind; they are of interest because, though based on similar premises, they reach completely opposite conclusions. The third theory, the distributive, has been developed specifically to explain aspects of policy making in the American political system.

BUCHANAN, TULLOCK, AND THE EXCLUSIVE-COALITION MODEL

Buchanan and Tullock were the first to construct a theoretical model of geographic allocation.[4] Their simple model of logrolling is based on the hypothetical example of farmers deciding about the maintenance of town highways. Consider a township inhabited by one hundred farmers with two systems of roads: a system of major highways maintained by the state and a system of locally maintained roads, each of which connects a few farms to the main highways. Decisions about the maintenance of local roads are made by majority vote of the farmers, with costs assessed against all farmers by means of a property tax. Buchanan and Tullock then seek to determine which roads would be maintained and at what general level of quality. They argue that if farmers are rational, minimum winning coalitions of fifty-one farmers would form and approve the maintenance of only the roads passing their farms and reject any maintenance for the other local roads.[5] Because all farmers share the costs, while only fifty-one share the benefits, these roads would be maintained at a higher level of quality than would be the case if the farmers had to choose a general level of quality for all roads in the town. However, the minimum winning coalitions that form are unstable; new coalitions of fifty-one can form at any time to reap the benefits while denying a share to nonmembers.

Buchanan and Tullock's theoretical model can be examined from two perspectives. First, one can question the underlying logic of the model and inquire whether rational actors in the situation posited by the authors are likely to behave in the way they predict. This is the approach

4. James M. Buchanan and Gordon Tullock, *The Calculus of Consent* (Ann Arbor: University of Michigan Press, 1962), pp. 135–45.
5. Riker's theory, published at about the same time, leads to a similar conclusion. Riker predicts that coalitions larger than the minimum needed to win would cast off their excess members, so that there would be fewer claimants for the resulting benefits. See William H. Riker, *The Theory of Political Coalitions* (New Haven: Yale University Press, 1962).

of Barry, and his critique will be discussed shortly. Second, one can examine how closely their model comes to representing real-world phenomena. To what extent are the motivations of legislators (or voters) similar to those of the one hundred farmers? To what extent are most questions of government spending similar to their example of rural road maintenance? And to what extent are legislatures that handle hundreds of different issues similar to their little legislature, which handles only one? Their model may be logically sound but still not give us any insight into the nature of empirical reality if it is based on false or highly unlikely assumptions.

Buchanan and Tullock's theory has, in my opinion, little relevance to empirical reality. The real world differs from their hypothetical world in at least two important respects. First, most government programs have spillover effects; they benefit others besides their most direct beneficiaries. Consequently, voters and legislators are concerned both with expenditures made in their front yards and with those made elsewhere. This concern stems not from any altruism, but from a broader conception of self-interest than the one Buchanan and Tullock employ. Buchanan and Tullock attempt to create a situation in which no farmer would have an interest in maintaining any local roads except the one passing his farm. Even with their carefully constructed example, however, they fail to make a case for such a narrow conception of self-interest. Would not most farmers have some interest in the maintenance of other roads if only because they use them to visit friends or because they want the local volunteer fire company to be able to assemble quickly in an emergency? A farmer may have a greater interest in the road on which he lives, but he still has *some* interest in the others. He is unlikely to want his road well maintained while others deteriorate, because he too would suffer from that deterioration. Once one admits a broader conception of self-interest, the model breaks down, because it is wholly dependent on voters who see their interests furthered by denying any benefits to those outside the winning coalition. The model might still be applicable to programs without any spillover effects; it is difficult, however, to think of many actual government programs in this category.

Second, real-world legislatures allocate a multitude of different expenditures, not just a single type.[6] Even if Buchanan and Tullock's

6. Strictly speaking, Buchanan and Tullock have developed a model for a referendum, not a legislature. But it has commonly been extended to include legislatures, and I have followed that tradition.

model could explain the behavior of legislatures that allocate only one type, it breaks down when confronted with legislatures allocating a wide range of expenditures. Consider, for example, a state legislature allocating all the various expenditures in the annual budget. Two possible courses are implied by Buchanan and Tullock's model. First, a single, minimum winning coalition might form for the entire budget, leaving the constituencies of excluded members without any share of state expenditures; the inevitable result would be an immense taxpayer's revolt. Alternatively, different coalitions could form for each expenditure item; so one group of constituencies would receive highway aid but not education aid, while another received education but not highway assistance. However, if this were to happen (and if one assumes diminishing marginal utility for both education and highway aid), members of both coalitions would then exchange with each other some education aid for some highway aid in order to improve the general welfare of their constituencies. Members of the two coalitions might not trade education and highway funds until all had equal shares of each, because tastes for the two undoubtedly vary from constituency to constituency; but the rational legislators postulated by Buchanan and Tullock would trade, just as rational economic men trade goods in the marketplace. Clearly, the exclusive-coalition model breaks down when confronted with a legislature allocating many different benefits. Either it implies a single coalition denying any benefits to excluded minorities, or it implies multiple coalitions for the various expenditure programs, followed by further trades between members of these coalitions until a more even distribution of expenditures eventually results.

BARRY AND THE UNIVERSALISTIC MODEL

Barry's extensive critique of Buchanan and Tullock's model provides a second theoretical treatment of the politics of geographic allocation.[7] Barry's basic argument is that rational actors in the situation posited by Buchanan and Tullock are unlikely to behave in the way they predict. He asserts that after forming a winning coalition, legislators would contract to stick together in order to make the formation of new coali-

7. Brian Barry, *Political Argument* (London: Routledge and Kegan Paul, 1965), pp. 250–56.

tions impossible. If such a permanent coalition did form and persistently vote in its members' interests alone, civil war or secession by the excluded minority would follow. On the other hand, if majorities did not make antidefection contracts, a different and unpredictable coalition would form each year serving only the interests of those who happened to be included in a given year. Barry suggests that this would be unsatisfactory to all concerned, for everyone would expect to be in the minority at least part of the time, and rational legislators consequently would prefer some "reasonable solution" to the problem so that minorities would never be deprived of a share of benefits. Two possible solutions are mentioned: spending the same amount on each road or maintaining all roads at some customary standard of repair.

Although both models rest on similar assumptions, they lead to very different conclusions. The fundamental difference between them is the legislators' outlook; Buchanan and Tullock's have a short-run mentality, while Barry's look beyond tomorrow. The former see a single play of the allocation game as the whole game; the latter realize that pursuing maximum short-term gains can make them big winners half of the time but big losers the other half. Barry's legislators regard their self-interest as maximized when some maintenance is done on their roads each year rather than suffering the feast-or-famine consequences implied by Buchanan and Tullock's model.

In fact, most American legislators probably have an outlook closer to Barry's legislators than to Buchanan and Tullock's. Legislators who regularly seek reelection generally prefer bringing home a modest amount of bacon each year to acquiring nothing some years and subsequently facing their opponents' charges of powerlessness. But this does not necessarily imply that such legislators will seek one of Barry's "reasonable" solutions; all it means is that they are unlikely to exclude minorities from a share of the benefits. Schemes can easily be devised which give some weight to objective criteria and some weight to criteria of coalition membership. The New York State Legislature has developed such a scheme for allocating salary and expense money ("lulus") among its members. Every legislator receives a statutory salary of $23,500 plus a fixed expense allowance, but legislative leaders and those who "cooperate" with the leadership receive extra lulus of up to $21,000.[8] There

8. See Francis X. Clines, "Party Faithful and the Favored Count Bonuses and Blessings," *New York Times*, 12 July, 1975, p. 12.

are no losers in this game, though some winners do considerably better than others.

Probably neither theoretical model accurately represents political reality for American legislatures. Nevertheless, both are useful for analysis if we consider them as representing endpoints of a continuum rather than as alternative models to be tested. The continuum runs from Barry's universalistic model, where objective criteria are the only determinants of allocation, to Buchanan and Tullock's exclusive-coalition model, where criteria of coalition membership completely determine allocations. Most American legislatures probably lie somewhere in between; they allocate benefits according to some combination of objective and "political" criteria. The precise location of a particular legislature on this continuum is difficult to determine. This book attempts to make such a determination for one legislature, the American Congress.

FEREJOHN, RUNDQUIST, AND THE DISTRIBUTIVE THEORY

The third theory of geographic allocation is the distributive theory.[9] Although there are various versions of this general theory, only one will be examined here, the version presented by Ferejohn and Rundquist.[10]

9. There is little consensus about what the term *distributive* should mean. The word was first used by Lowi in his threefold classification of policies as either distributive, regulatory, or redistributive. Lowi defined distributive policies as those characterized by "the ease with which they can be disaggregated and dispensed unit by small unit, each unit more or less in isolation from other units and from any general rule. . . . These are policies that are virtually not policies at all but are highly individualized decisions that only by accumulation can be called a policy" (p. 690). The class includes such diverse benefits as tax exemptions, the traditional tariff, and labor, business, and agricultural clientele services, as well as most matters of geographic allocation, excepting only formula programs and those that cannot be sufficiently disaggregated. Ferejohn and Rundquist adopt a narrower definition than Lowi's, including only matters of geographic allocation, again excepting formula and nondivisible programs. Strom uses a much broader definition that includes all matters of geographic allocation, including formula programs. In order not to add to the confusion, I avoid using the term *distributive* except when referring to the particular theory put forth by Ferejohn and Rundquist. See Theodore J. Lowi, "American Business, Public Policy, Case Studies, and Political Theory," *World Politics* 16 (1964): 677–715; Barry S. Rundquist and John A. Ferejohn, "Observations on a Distributive Theory of Policy-Making," in Craig Liske, William Loehr, and John McCamant (eds.), *Comparative Public Policy* (New York: John Wiley, 1975), p. 88; Gerald S. Strom, "Congressional Policy-Making and the Federal Waste Treatment Construction Grant Program" (Ph.D. dissertation, University of Illinois, 1973), p. 2.

10. Rundquist and Ferejohn, "Observations on a Distributive Theory of Policy-

According to these authors, the distributive theory concerns how "the institutional structure of decision-making in Washington relates to the geographic distribution of federal expenditures."[11] The theory rests on the assumption that congressmen are motivated by a desire to serve the economic interests of their constituencies. It suggests that because congressional decision making is committee-centered, congressmen are better able to serve these interests if they sit on the proper committees. Three hypotheses devolve from the theory. The *recruitment* hypothesis states that congressmen seek seats on those committees having jurisdiction over programs that directly affect their constituencies. The *overrepresentation* hypothesis asserts that as a consequence both of this differential recruitment and of the assignment process itself, committees overrepresent constituencies having an important stake in those programs under their jurisdiction. The *benefit* hypothesis declares that committee members' constituencies receive a disproportionate amount of benefits from those programs under their jurisdiction, because members have a disproportionate amount of influence over the formulation, administration, and funding of these programs.

Seven studies have attempted to test the validity of one or more of the distributive theory's hypotheses. Five of these have been case studies of particular expenditure programs: military contracts,[12] military employment,[13] rivers and harbor projects,[14] urban renewal expenditures,[15] and formula grants to states under a waste treatment construction program.[16] The other two studies examined spending patterns for seven large federal agencies.[17] Results have been mixed; some evidence tends

Making," pp. 87–108. For another version of the basic theory, see William A. Niskanen, Jr., *Bureaucracy and Representative Government* (Chicago: Aldine-Atherton, 1971).

11. Rundquist and Ferejohn, "Observations on a Distributive Theory of Policy-Making," p. 88.

12. Barry S. Rundquist, "Congressional Influences on the Distribution of Prime Military Contracts" (Ph.D. dissertation, Stanford University, 1973).

13. Carol F. Goss, "Military Committee Membership and Defense-Related Benefits in the House of Representatives," *Western Political Quarterly* 25 (1972): 215–33.

14. John A. Ferejohn, *Pork Barrel Politics* (Stanford: Stanford University Press, 1974).

15. Charles R. Plott, "Some Organizational Influences on Urban Renewal Decisions," *American Economic Review* 58 (May 1968): 306–21.

16. Strom, "Congressional Policy-Making."

17. Leonard G. Ritt, "Committee Position, Seniority, and the Distribution of Government Expenditures," *Public Policy* 24 (1976): 469; and Bruce A. Ray, "Investigating the Myth of Congressional Influence: The Geographic Distribution of Federal Spending," paper delivered at the 1976 Annual Meeting of the American Political Science Association.

to support the theory, while some clearly does not. Ferejohn and Rundquist provide a good description of the status of the theory in an article that compares the findings of their separate studies on rivers and harbors projects and military contracts.

Our analysis suggests that the distributive theory provides a rather inadequate explanation of policy-making in our two expenditure areas. . . . We found some conditions under which one hypothesis is supported and other conditions under which another hypothesis is supported. . . . These findings raise considerable doubt about the validity of the distributive theory in our policy areas. They suggest that parts of the theory are valid under some well-defined circumstances; however, the theory's basic assumption that congressmen seek to serve their constituencies' economies by becoming members of relevant standing committees is not reflected in our data. Instead we find a complex set of institutional constraints that interfere with straightforward predictions of the theory.[18]

The distributive theory is an attractive, intuitively appealing theory of geographic allocation. Yet it fails, at least for these five programs and seven agencies, to explain adequately the geographic patterns of committee membership and program expenditures. There are two possible explanations for this failure. First, the theory may be valid but the tests inadequate, either because of poor data or poor methods. Alternatively, the tests may be correct, in which case the theory needs revision or replacement. Probably it is a little of both—inadequate methods and an overly simplistic theory. A discussion of their methodological problems is postponed until chapter 5, while matters of theory are explored.

The distributive theory's main problem is that it oversimplifies the politics of geographic allocation. Simplification is, of course, necessary in order to make general statements about the political world. But whenever one attempts to generalize about a complex political process there is an ever-present danger that one may strip away its barest essentials along with less important features. The distributive theory oversimplifies the politics of allocation by speaking of congressmen, committees, and benefits as if all congressmen share the same single goal, all committees operate in more or less identical fashion, and all benefits are

18. Rundquist and Ferejohn, "Observations on a Distributive Theory of Policy-Making," pp. 106–07.

so similar that differentiation between them is unnecessary. But there are very real differences among congressmen, committees, programs, and allocational processes, and these differences have important implications for the way in which various expenditures are allocated geographically.

First, the process of allocation varies from program to program. Variations in agenda preparation and project selection have already been discussed. Preparing an agenda may depend on the initiative of congressmen or agency officials, or it may simply be a collection of all applications received from local communities. Selection of projects may be performed by a congressional committee, or the task may be delegated to an administrative agency. These variations in process affect the politics of allocation, because they determine where and how congressmen have the opportunity to influence decision making. Opportunities for influence are very different when an agency, rather than a congressional committee, prepares the agenda or selects projects to be funded. In both cases certain congressmen may be in a position to affect allocational decisions, but the congressmen influential in one instance may have little influence in the other. For example, a congressman may be very effective inside Congress in persuading other congressmen to do all sorts of favors for him,[19] but he may be unable to obtain similar favors from administrative officials even when he sits on the "proper" committees. Influence inside Congress need not be related to influence over administrative agencies.

Second, there are significant differences between various types of government benefits, even within the broad class of benefits known as "distributive policies." Lowi's classification of policies as distributive, regulatory, or redistributive may be useful for simply analyzing gross differences between the "arenas of power" one believes are associated with each. An intensive analysis of one of these policy types, however, requires further differentiation, because the policy types are too broad. Distributive policies are defined to include everything from defense contracting to public works. Yet the evidence from Ferejohn and Rundquist's work suggests that the two are not allocated in anywhere

19. For an amusing characterization of one congressman with this talent, D. R. (Billy) Matthews (D., Fla.), see Clem Miller, *Member of the House* (New York: Charles Scribner, 1962), pp. 39–41.

near the same fashion. One hint that there might be differences in the politics of allocation for the two issues is that congressmen look at them in very different ways. Congressmen see defense issues primarily in ideological terms; their support for the defense establishment has very little to do with how their districts benefit from defense spending.[20] Conversely, they see public works issues more in terms of how their own constituencies are affected.[21] Since congressmen view these two issues from such different perspectives, one might expect that those who allocate benefits would operate within very different constraints. Those who allocate public works benefits are likely to feel constrained by congressmen's allocational preferences, because those denied fair shares are more likely to become opponents of the program. Those who allocate defense contracts operate in another world, because congressional support is much less dependent on where contracts are awarded.

Finally, congressional committees differ in the types of congressmen they attract, their ability to retain members, and the particular functions they choose to perform.[22] Some committees attract congressmen primarily interested in constituency service; others attract congressmen for which this is only a secondary interest.[23] Some lose few members except by death, retirement, or defeat; others are merely way stations for those awaiting better assignments.[24] Some diligently oversee the performance of administrative agencies; others tend to look the other way.[25] Some annually authorize funds for the programs under their jurisdiction; others make huge long-term authorizations far above what they might reasonably expect would be funded. With all these dif-

20. See Wayne Moyer, "House Voting on Defense: An Ideological Explanation," in Bruce M. Russett and Alfred Stepan (eds.), *Military Force and American Society* (New York: Harper and Row, 1973), pp. 106–41.

21. This inference is supported by various studies of constituency influence on roll-call voting. See, for example, David R. Mayhew, *Party Loyalty Among Congressmen* (Cambridge, Mass.: Harvard University Press, 1966), esp. chapter 5; and Julius Turner, *Party and Constituency Pressures on Congress*, revised edition by Edward V. Schneier, Jr. (Baltimore: The Johns Hopkins Press, 1951, 1970), esp. chapter 4.

22. See Richard F. Fenno, Jr., *Congressmen in Committees* (Boston: Little, Brown and Company, 1973).

23. Ibid., pp. 1–14.

24. For evidence on specific committees, see George Goodwin, Jr., *The Little Legislatures* (Amherst: University of Massachusetts Press, 1970), pp. 114–15.

25. See Seymour Scher, "Conditions for Legislative Control," *Journal of Politics* 25 (1963): 526–51, for an excellent discussion of the conditions that affect legislative oversight of administrative agencies.

ferences in the recruitment, attractiveness, and operations of committees, one should not really expect that members of the various committees would be equally able to affect the allocation of expenditures.

THE NEED FOR BETTER THEORY

Currently there are three theories of geographic allocation: Buchanan
and Tullock's exclusive-coalition model, Barry's universalistic model,
and Ferejohn and Rundquist's distributive theory. Probably each has a
grain of truth, though none adequately explains the similarities and
differences in the politics of geographic allocation for hundreds of different expenditure programs. For this task a more elaborate theory is
needed, one that explicitly takes into account differences in allocational
processes, differences in the nature of government programs, and differences in congressional committees. This book begins to develop such
a theory. The theory is concerned exclusively with how *bureaucrats*
make decisions concerning the allocation of expenditures; it does not
attempt to explain how congressional committees make such decisions.

Chapters 2 through 4 present my theory of congressional influence in
bureaucratic decision making. Chapter 5 discusses how one should go
about testing the validity of this or any other theory of geographic
allocation and comments on the methodology employed by those who
attempted to test the distributive theory. Chapters 6 through 8 analyze
three different expenditure programs in an effort to test the validity of
the theory. The programs are military employment from 1952 to 1974,
model cities grants in 1967 and 1968, and water and sewer grants in
1970 and 1971. The three programs were not selected randomly, but
because they offer interesting differences in allocational process, and
because theory suggests that bureaucrats should adopt very different
allocational strategies for each. If the theory has any validity at all, it
should explain not only allocational decisions for a single program, but
also the different patterns of decisions for a diverse set of programs such
as these.

2: POLITICAL GOALS

THEORETICAL APPROACH

Ideally, a complete theory of bureaucratic decision making in matters of geographic allocation would have to incorporate a diverse set of variables reflecting three general forces that appear to affect decision making: the preferences and actions of significant political actors outside bureaucratic organizations—for example, members of Congress, the president, and his staff; the internal politics of organizations as well as the standard operating procedures that have evolved over time for making routine decisions; and the decision makers' own personal preferences and prejudices concerning the allocation of resources. The theory developed here is more limited. It has been constructed almost exclusively with elements of the first type, and in fact centers on the influence of just a single group of actors, members of the House of Representatives.[1] The theory's limited scope does not imply either that the other forces are inconsequential or that the best single explanation of geographic allocation must be centered on the House of Representatives. Its orientation merely reflects my principal purpose: to explore congressional-bureaucratic relationships by examining how congressmen influence allocation decisions. To restate the point in statistical terms: my goal is not to discover a model that maximizes the explained variance in the geographical distribution of expenditures. Instead, I seek to develop a precise model that relates congressional preferences about allocation to bureaucratic decisions, and to estimate the coefficients associated with each variable in the model—in other words, to determine just *how* influential certain types of congressmen are.[2]

1. In part two, however, where actual expenditure programs are examined, some of the other factors affecting allocational decisions are discussed briefly.
2. The purpose of the theory has been discussed at some length in order to avoid misunderstandings about what I am attempting to accomplish. A critic of a previous paper

My general approach to theory construction is that of economics. This method, once unknown to most political scientists, is now so common in political theory that it requires neither a lengthy introduction nor a defense of its virtues.[3] It has been employed, for example, to develop theories of parties, interest groups, committees, bureaucracies, and legislatures.[4] Theorists who use the approach begin by postulating the existence of certain individual actors with well-defined goals. Then, on the assumption that these actors will pursue their goals rationally, theorists deduce how they will behave in certain situations, specifically, how they will make choices when faced with alternative courses of action. These predictions may be expressed in the form of hypotheses and tested with empirical evidence.

BUREAUCRAT'S GOALS

Only a small fraction of all officials in a large bureaucratic organization are in a position to affect decisions about geographic allocation: those assigned the function of making such decisions, and their superiors in the organizational hierarchy. It is this small group to which reference is made when the term *bureaucrat* is used in this book.

As do most other political and social actors, bureaucrats have various goals. Those that relate to this study can be divided into two groups:

---

on the subject found the results of the empirical analyses to be "singularly unimpressive" because only 26 percent of the variance had been explained. But it is unclear, given the nature of the enterprise, why the amount of variance explained should be a criterion for judgment. It may, of course, be true that the results presented either in the previous paper or in the present work are unimpressive; but the reason for that judgment should not be that an insufficient amount of variance has been explained.

3. For a review of a portion of the literature employing this approach, see Michael Taylor, "Review Article: Mathematical Political Theory," *British Journal of Political Science* 1 (1971): 339–82. For discussions of the advantages of the economic approach, see John C. Harsanyi, "Rational-Choice Models of Political Behavior vs. Functionalist and Conformist Theories," *World Politics* 22 (1969): 513–38; or Brian Barry, *Sociologists, Economists, and Democracy* (London: Collier-Macmillan, 1970).

4. For an example of each, see Anthony Downs, *An Economic Theory of Democracy* (New York: Harper and Row, 1957); Mancur Olson, *The Logic of Collective Action* (Cambridge, Mass.: Harvard University Press, 1965); Duncan Black, *The Theory of Committees and Elections* (Cambridge: The University Press, 1958); Anthony Downs, *Inside Bureaucracy* (Boston: Little, Brown, 1967); and David R. Mayhew, *Congress: The Electoral Connection* (New Haven: Yale University Press, 1974).

occupational goals, which are an outgrowth of bureaucrats' roles in organizations and which serve as intermediate means to their more ultimate ends; and *personal* goals—for example, income, power, and prestige—products of socialization, but whose realization depends on the successful pursuit of occupational goals. In this theory bureaucrats are motivated by only three occupational goals.[5]

Their first occupational goal is budgetary security. Specifically, bureaucrats seek to reduce to a very low level the probability of significant declines in their total budget during the following few years. Three phrases in the definition require further elaboration. "A very low level" implies that bureaucrats are anxious to avoid risk, though they may not be obsessed with eliminating it altogether. "Significant declines" suggests that they are relatively unconcerned by token cuts in their budget, but are very agitated by cuts that require personnel or program changes of any magnitude. "The following few years" implies that bureaucrats have a time frame extending beyond the current year. They are unlikely, for example, to adopt a budgetary strategy that is very productive in the short run but threatens their long-run budgetary security.

Second, bureaucrats pursue budgetary growth. They seek to increase the size of their budget during the succeeding year.

Third, they are motivated by a sense of public service. Specifically, each bureaucrat serves his own conception of the public interest. Notice that I do not assume that bureaucrats *do* serve the public interest, or even that it is possible to define objectively what the public interest requires. Additionally, in order to simplify analysis, I assume that all

5. There are only three works in which the economic approach has been used to analyze bureaucratic behavior: Downs, *Inside Bureaucracy*; William A. Niskanen, Jr., *Bureaucracy and Representative Government* (Chicago: Aldine, 1971); and Gordon Tullock, *The Politics of Bureaucracy* (Washington, D.C.: Public Affairs Press, 1965). Downs's work, a general theory of bureaucratic decision making, is based on a complex set of motivational assumptions. First, he assumes that all bureaucrats have multiple goals drawn from a list of nine possible goals (power, prestige, income, convenience, security, loyalty, pride in excellent work, commitment to a program, and desire to serve the public interest), and then he postulates five different "ideal types" of bureaucrats, each of which pursues a different combination of these goals. Niskanen attempts to develop a theory explaining the output behavior of bureaucracies—i.e., what level of public services will bureaucratic organizations tend to supply. His only motivational assumption is that bureaucrats maximize the total budget of their bureaus during their tenure. Tullock's work is a theory of how the individual bureaucrat behaves in an organization. He assumes that bureaucrats are motivated by a desire for career advancement—i.e., each seeks to move up the organizational hierarchy.

bureaucrats administering a particular expenditure program have the *same* conception of the public interest, at least insofar as such a conception affects their decisions concerning allocational and budgetary strategies.

Because the preceding three goals frequently conflict, a *hierarchy of goals* is created. (Conflict occurs when actions designed to achieve one goal impede the achievement of another.) The primary goal of budgetary security always takes precedence over the secondary goals of budgetary growth and public service. That is, bureaucrats will not adopt strategies designed to increase the size of their budgets or further their conceptions of the public interest if, by doing so, they also endanger the security of their budgets. Neither of the two secondary goals takes precedence over the other. Instead, bureaucrats are willing to make trade-offs between them. They are willing to sacrifice small increases in their budgets in order to advance significantly the public interest, and they are willing for the public interest to suffer slightly in return for large increases in their budgets.

JUSTIFICATION OF ASSUMPTIONS

Although I do not seek to prove that these four motivational assumptions are correct, it is important to demonstrate that they are at least reasonable assumptions given the world in which bureaucrats live and the personal goals which they share. The income incentive is probably their most important personal goal. Their jobs are, after all, primarily a means of support; accordingly, it seems reasonable that all bureaucrats attempt to maintain at least their present levels of income. This objective gives every bureaucrat a potent interest in the organization's survival, and since survival requires the budget's annual approval, it is in everyone's self-interest to work for its adoption. In addition, many bureaucrats are not satisfied with their present incomes and work to increase them, principally through promotions. Ordinarily, promotions can be obtained only when others resign or retire; however, they are considerably easier to obtain if the organization grows and new positions are created. It is, therefore, in the bureaucrat's self-interest to promote organizational growth by working for budgetary increases.

As a motivating force, desire for power and prestige is probably less universal than income. Nevertheless, most bureaucrats assiduously attempt to avoid losses in either, and many strive to increase their shares of both. The amount of power and prestige a bureaucrat enjoys is largely a function of his position in the organizational hierarchy. Those nearer the top generally enjoy greater prestige, have more subordinates subject to their influence, and control more resources important to those outside the organization. Bureaucrats struggle for budgetary security because it helps them maintain their present power and prestige. A nondiminishing budget not only guarantees a bureaucrat's current position; it also insures that he will continue to have the same number of subordinates under his influence and control the same amount of resources. Bureaucrats battle for budgetary growth because it helps them to increase their present levels of power and prestige by facilitating both promotions and aggrandizement.[6] Promotions, as I have already noted, are facilitated by organizational growth, which in turn requires budgetary growth. Aggrandizement refers to increasing the power and prestige of one's existing position by acquiring either new functions, more subordinates, or control over more resources. All such additions require money, and once again the bureaucrat's self-interest impels him to scramble for budgetary growth.

Most bureaucrats do not act exclusively in a self-interested search for income, power, and prestige; usually each has a conception of the public interest which affects his behavior.[7] Bureaucrats' notions about the public interest typically include a set of expectations about how certain benefits should be allocated: urban planners have opinions about the proper allocation of redevelopment funds, admirals about the location of naval facilities, transportation analysts about the placement of new roads. These expectations can have important effects on allocational decisions, at least when they do not conflict with bureaucrats' other goals. For various reasons, bureaucrats tend to develop narrow conceptions of the public interest, conceptions that place disproportionate emphasis on problems associated with the programs they administer. One reason is that they are intimately acquainted with these problems, but only dimly aware of the range and magnitude of those facing others; this constant contact with the same problems cannot help but enhance

6. The concept of aggrandizement is from Downs, *Inside Bureaucracy*, pp. 93–95.
7. The reader should recall that I am concerned only with a small group of middle level and upper-level bureaucrats. I do not necessarily attribute the same motivation to those outside this group.

their importance to those charged with solving them. Another reason is that many of the upper-level bureaucrats who work for a specific agency were originally attracted to it because they had a strong interest in the social functions it performs. This narrow conception, however acquired, impels bureaucrats to advocate increased funding for the programs they administer. Thus, a bureaucrat's goal of budgetary growth stems not only from his personal goals of income, power, and prestige, but also from his public-service goal.

Bureaucrats are assumed to have a hierarchy of goals, with the goal of budgetary security taking precedence over the goal of budgetary growth. Bureaucrats place a higher priority on security because their basic attitudes towards change are asymmetrical: their preferences against budgetary reductions are much more intense than those in favor of budgetary increases. This reflects the fact that decreases impose considerable costs on the present members of an organization, whereas increases benefit them to a much lesser degree. For example, if an agency's budget is cut by 50 percent, many of its present employees will lose their positions, and those who do not will lose a considerable amount of power and prestige. On the other hand, if its budget is increased by 50 percent, most benefits will go to new employees, with only a small portion affecting present employees. A second reason for this asymmetrical attitude is that bureaucrats become accustomed to receiving a certain utility income; generally, the threat of losing part of what one already has is a more powerful motivating force than the prospect of gaining something one never before enjoyed.[8] My assumptions about

8. A bureaucrat's attitude toward budgetary change can be illustrated with a graph of expected utility as a function of budget size. The graph uses hypothetical data, with "Agency's Total Budget" measured along the x-axis and "Bureaucrat's Expected Total

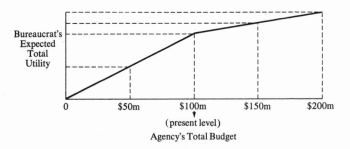

Bureaucrat's Asymmetrical Attitude Toward Budgetary Change

bureaucrats' budgetary goals are *not* equivalent to the assumption that
they seek to maximize their total budget, the principal motivational
assumption of Niskanen's theory of bureaucratic behavior.[9] Bureaucrats
who seek budget maximization will, under certain circumstances, select
strategies different from those that officials motivated by a primary goal
of budgetary security and a secondary goal of budgetary growth would
choose. The alternative assumptions are not equivalent, because bureaucrats in this theory are averse to risk, whereas those who seek budget
maximization are not.[10]

Although I have assumed that bureaucrats are motivated by three
goals, my theory of bureaucratic decision making rests principally on
the two budgetary goals. The argument will be made that bureaucrats
make certain allocational decisions in order to further their goals of
budgetary security and budgetary growth. The public-service goal has
two relatively minor functions. First, it prevents bureaucrats from

Utility" on the y-axis. Notice that the bureaucrat's expected utility curve contains a corner
at the level of the current budget ($100m). Below this corner marginal utility is relatively
high, reflecting the considerable losses in utility income associated with budget cuts; above
the corner it is much lower, suggesting that large increases in the budget yield only modest
additions to utility income. The interesting feature of this type of utility function is that it
shifts over time. If, for example, the budget were increased substantially, bureaucrats' utility
incomes would also rise. Gradually they would become accustomed to this new income,
and they would begin to consider any declines in this level to be extremely undesirable;
consequently, the corner in their utility function would drift upwards. Such a corner is
analogous to Wildavsky's concept of any agency's *base*, the portion of any agency's budget
which it expects will be funded each year without intensive scrutiny. Additions to the base
one year do, in a year or two, become part of a new base line of expectations. See Aaron
Wildavsky, *The Politics of the Budgetary Process* (Boston: Little, Brown, 1964), pp. 17,
102–23.

9. Niskanen, *Bureaucracy and Representative Government*, pp. 36–42.

10. An example illustrates the different behavior implied by the two alternative specifi-
cations of goals. Suppose for a moment, that a bureaucrat in an agency with a current
budget of $500 million faces a choice between two budgetary strategies: one strategy (S_1)
yields a future budget of $500 million with certainty; the other (S_2) yields either a budget
of $800 million with a probability of .6 or a budget of $200 million with a probability
of .4. A bureaucrat who seeks to maximize the budget would select S_2, because the
expected value of this strategy is $560 million as compared with $500 million for S_1. But a
bureaucrat who seeks budgetary security would select S_1 because he considers unacceptable a 40 percent chance of a $300 million reduction in his budget. (This particular
example includes only a single year's budget, whereas both my motivational assumptions
and Niskanen's assumption of budget maximization suggest that bureaucrats compare the
consequences of various strategies over a number of years. A more complex example
could be constructed, however, to demonstrate that the lack of equivalence between the
two sets of goals does not depend on the time perspective chosen. It is wholly dependent
on the aversion to risk which bureaucrats are assumed to have.)

selecting strategies that are productive in terms of budgetary growth but that also produce consequences seriously at variance with their conceptions of the public interest. Second, it breaks ties (a frequent occurrence given the number of congressmen in an agency's environment with nearly equal influence) when many equally productive strategies are available. The assumption that all bureaucrats who administer a particular program share the same goals allows one to treat the bureau administering it as if it were a single person (or, if you prefer, as if it were wholly governed by a single individual).

CONGRESSMEN'S GOALS

Although members of both the House and Senate are interested in the geographic allocation of federal expenditures, this theory is concerned exclusively with members of the House. This restriction has been made to simplify both the theory and its subsequent analysis. Many of the assumptions and generalizations made about House members could also be applied to senators; however, some clearly do not apply.[11] Throughout this work the term *congressman* refers to members of the House of Representatives only.

The congressmen in this model are motivated by two goals.[12] The

11. The principal difference between the House and Senate which prevents one form making (and testing) generalizations applicable to both is the nature of their constituencies. House members represent constituencies of nearly equal size; senators represent whole states, the largest of which is nearly seventy times more populous than the smallest. These variations complicate the problem of measuring influence. It is further complicated by the fact that states are represented by two senators apiece, and there is no good method for separating the independent effects of each on allocational decisions.

12. Two important works on Congress analyze how the pursuit of individual goals affects the behavior of congressmen: Richard F. Fenno, Jr., *Congressmen in Committees* (Boston: Little, Brown, 1973) and Mayhew, *Congress: The Electoral Connection*. Mayhew assumes that congressmen are single-minded seekers of reelection, and then explores how the pursuit of this goal affects the kinds of activities in which they engage, the organization and operation of congressional institutions, and the nature of public policy. Fenno assumes that congressmen have three basic goals: achieving influence within the House, making good public policy, and helping their constituents and thereby insuring their reelection. He analyzes how congressmen differ in the importance they attach to each of these goals, how these differences are reflected in the membership of six House committees, and how the goals associated with committee members affect the decision-making processes of these committees. Mayhew's reelection goal and Fenno's three goals are related to the two goals postulated in this work. Some of these relations are discussed at various points in the text.

first is constituency service. Specifically, I assume that each congressman seeks to obtain for his constituency a portion of each program's expenditures. Second, they are concerned with the acceptability of their voting records. Each congressman seeks to maintain a voting record acceptable both to his constituency and to himself. No hierarchy of goals is assumed as it was for bureaucrats. Instead, I suppose that when the two goals conflict, congressmen calculate[13] the relative importance of each and act accordingly.

VOTING RECORDS

The principal reason why congressmen seek to maintain an acceptable voting record is that it serves their more fundamental goal of reelection.[14] At least some constituents make decisions about which candidate to support in an election and how intense that support should be on the basis of the candidates' positions on the "issues." A roll-call vote is the one instance in which congressmen are forced to take public positions, and they usually proceed with caution to insure that the positions they do take are not far out of line with the expectations of those in their reelection constituencies.[15] It is true, of course, that most voters haven't the vaguest idea how their representatives vote on specific roll calls. Nevertheless, a congressman must take care, because an opponent in a future election might unearth potentially unpopular votes and fabricate a campaign issue out of them. Frequently the problem is to anticipate how one's constituents might react in some future election rather than to discern where they might stand on the issue today.

Certain groups of constituents *do* follow roll-call activity. Those who have a direct financial interest in a particular policy usually keep themselves informed, or at least their leaders do. Labor leaders know how a congressman votes on labor issues, educational groups know where he stands on aid to education, and highway contractors know his position

13. In a manner described later.
14. For discussions of the relationships between roll-call voting and elections, see John W. Kingdon, *Congressmen's Voting Decisions* (New York: Harper and Row, 1973), pp. 29–68; Mayhew, *Congress: The Electoral Connection*; and the references cited in each.
15. The term *reelection constituency*, referring to the people in a congressman's district he thinks vote for him, is from Richard F. Fenno, Jr., "Congressmen In Their Constituencies: An Exploration," paper presented at the annual convention of the American Political Science Association, 1975, p. 5.

on the highway trust fund. Furthermore, these groups are not only more knowledgeable about their congressman's positions, they also have more intense preferences about the proper positions for him to take. A congressman must pay special heed to their preferences, because they are more likely to provide or withhold their support on the basis of his stand on a single issue.

Although congressmen certainly must consider constituency opinion, it is seldom determinative. Constituents may have no opinions at all on some issues, or their preferences may be so weak that they can safely be ignored, or they may be so evenly divided that no position could possibly "reflect" their wishes. When constituency opinion is absent, weak, or divided, congressmen can hardly be confined by it; they may, therefore, vote according to their own personal preferences.

A congressman also seeks to maintain a voting record acceptable to himself. That is to say, the average congressman (like his counterpart in the bureaucracy) has some conception of what the public interest requires, and whenever possible, he uses his vote in Congress to advance it. As part of this conception, he has a set of attitudes towards public policy issues. He has preferences, for example, concerning the proper role of government in society, the desirability of budget deficits, the responsibility of the fortunate to the less fortunate, and the relative dangers of inflation and unemployment. Through various mechanisms (described later), these general policy attitudes then serve as a decision-making guide on roll-call votes.

CONSTITUENCY SERVICE

Congressmen pursue the goal of constituency service because it helps them achieve their more fundamental goal: reelection. Allocation of federal expenditures to a congressman's district can affect his reelection prospects in at least three ways. First, if he can convince a program's direct beneficiaries that he was in some way responsible for the benefits they enjoy, they may have an incentive to support him in subsequent campaigns. The beneficiaries, of course, will never know for sure if their congressman was influential in obtaining benefits for them or whether they would have received them anyway. What is important, however, is whether they think it likely that he was in some way respon-

sible. Most congressmen devote a considerable amount of their resources (principally staff time) to creating that impression. Their activities include helping local groups prepare grant applications, arranging
conferences between applicants and agency officials, making inquiries
about an application's status or the reasons for delay, or appealing an
adverse decision to some higher authority. When a congressman performs one or more such services for a group and its application is subsequently accepted, the group members will be encouraged to believe
that his involvement in the allocational process was significant. But
even when congressmen perform none of these services, they frequently
attempt to take credit for favorable decisions. Virtually all congressmen
announce with great fanfare the awarding of grants and contracts to
groups in their constituencies, and few forget to have their own names
mentioned at the same time. If the beneficiaries of a program come to
believe that their congressman is responsible for the benefits they enjoy,
they may provide votes, money, or workers for his reelection campaign.
Their reasons for contributing may vary. They may simply believe that
they owe him a favor in return for his assistance, or they may want him
reelected so that he can continue to provide them with benefits. Finally, they may hope that by contributing to his campaign in a way he
cannot help but notice (e.g., money) he will be inspired to work hard
for their interests in the future and they will enjoy easy access to his
office.

Second, allocation of funds to a congressman's district allows him to
generate favorable publicity for himself. Congressmen search constantly
for ways in which they can publicize who they are and what they have
done, because they believe a well-known and well-respected incumbent
is more difficult to defeat than an unknown incumbent.[16] One way in
which publicity can be generated is to become associated with an event
considered newsworthy by local journalists; coverage of the event then
carries with it free publicity for the congressman. Since the announcement of federal money for even the smallest project is usually considered newsworthy in all but the largest American cities, it is not surprising that congressmen are eager to make such announcements them-

16. The empirical evidence tends to support their belief. See Donald E. Stokes and
Warren E. Miller, "Party Government and the Saliency of Congress," in Raymond E.
Wolfinger (ed.), *Readings on Congress* (Englewood Cliffs, N.J.: Prentice-Hall, 1971), pp.
14–18.

selves. They are intended as much for nonbeneficiaries as for those who will receive direct benefits from a project. To illustrate, a congressman who announces a new central air-conditioning system for the local veteran's hospital is not merely interested in informing the direct beneficiaries of their good fortune (after all, most of the cooler veterans will come from outside the district); he is principally interested in getting a simple message to his constituents. The most important part of such a message is his name; it will be repeated every time he announces a grant until, eventually, even the least attentive constituents have a dim awareness of who he is. The second part of the message is that their congressman has done something good for the district. The public at large may not long remember precisely what their congressman claims to have done, but the important point is that they attach good deeds to his name. Construction projects are particularly attractive to congressmen because they offer so many opportunities for publicity. A simple grant announcement may generate only a single news story, but construction projects involve a whole series of events after the announcement: ground breakings, cornerstone layings, ribbon cuttings, grand openings, and dedications. Each event is covered by the news media, and each will find the congressman front and center.

Finally, the allocation of federal expenditures can affect the prosperity of local economies, and the prosperity of a district's economy can influence a congressman's prospects for reelection—or at least so it is thought. Most federal expenditures are too small to have a significant effect on local economies and, therefore, need not concern us. Large expenditures, however, such as those for military installations, defense contracts, or major federal facilities, can make the difference between a prosperous economy and a depressed one. A congressman must be concerned with the health of his district's economy to the extent that he expects he might be blamed for its poor performance. How local economic conditions affect congressional elections is an empirical question that has yet to be settled. There is good evidence to indicate that voting decisions are, in part, judgments about how well incumbents have managed the economy. At the national level, economic fluctuations are closely related to the proportion of votes in congressional elections going to the party that controls the presidency.[17] In other words, the incum-

17. See Gerald H. Kramer, "Short-Term Fluctuations in U.S. Voting Behavior, 1896–1964," *American Political Science Review* 65 (1971): 131–43; and Edward R. Tufte,

bent president and his congressional party are held responsible for good times and bad.

But who is held responsible for economic conditions of a more local nature? Who, for example, do voters blame when the economy as a whole is booming while their own local economy is declining? There is no simple answer. Probably in most situations voters continue to hold the president's party responsible; they react as they would if the whole economy were declining, because the only economic element in their voting calculus is a comparison of their well-being today with that of yesterday. But the answer may be very different if the performance of the local economy can be traced to a large decline in federal expenditures resulting, for example, from cancellation of a defense contract or closure of a military installation. In this case, the incumbent congressman himself may be blamed for economic decline, particularly if his opponent makes a campaign issue of his inability to protect his district's most fundamental interests.[18] Voters may not, on their own, make the connection between their economic well-being and their congressman's activities; however, if the connection is explained to them during a campaign, they may well respond by turning him out. As yet, there are no empirical studies that explore whether congressmen are, in fact, blamed for the economic consequences of large decreases in federal expenditures.[19] Nevertheless, congressmen *think* they might be blamed, and this fear impels them to protect, as best they can, the flow

"Determinants of the Outcomes of Midterm Congressional Elections," *American Political Science Review* 69 (1975): 812–26.

18. For example, after Glenn Davis (R., Wisc.) opposed continued development of the MBT-70 tank, there were layoffs at the General Motors plant in his district where part of it was to be produced. "One of the engineers laid off by GM because of the MBT-70 cancellation began campaigning for Davis's House seat on the grounds that Davis had failed to serve his constituency's needs. Although ultimately he failed to file as an official candidate by the August deadline and Davis was reelected in November, Davis admits that the challenger had him worried" (Craig Liske and Barry Rundquist, "The Politics of Weapons Procurement: The Role of Congress," *Monograph Series in World Affairs*, vol. 12, no. 1 [Denver: The Social Science Foundation and Graduate School of International Studies, University of Denver, 1974], p. 63).

19. There are, of course, individual cases in which local economic decline is thought to have contributed to a congressman's defeat, but there is no systematic evidence. For example, E. S. Johnny Walker (D., N.M.), a member of the Armed Services Committee, lost his seat in 1968 after the closure of Walker Air Force Base, an installation in his district with nearly six thousand military personnel. The economy of the surrounding county suffered badly, and for the first time Walker did not carry it. If he had, he would have been reelected. See Michael Barone, Grant Ujifusa, and Douglas Matthews, *The Almanac of American Politics* (Boston: Gambit, 1972), p. 506.

of expenditures to their districts. It may not be crucial that they succeed in preventing the cutoff of funds, but it is important that they fight hard and publicly. Senators Magnuson and Jackson (D., Wash.) spent two years trying to sustain government support for Boeing's supersonic transport. In the end they failed, and thousands of their constituents were thrown out of work; but no future opponent will ever accuse them of negligence, for they conducted a long, well-publicized campaign. One last point about the economic motivation for constituency service: Although congressmen must exert themselves to protect the flow of expenditures to their districts lest there be economic repercussions, they probably have no great incentive to acquire additional expenditures for their districts in order to improve their economies. Acquisition of such expenditures yields two important dividends for congressmen: electoral support from beneficiaries and publicity aimed at their less attentive constituents; whatever indirect effects there may be, based on improvements in local economies, are likely to be minor by comparison.

But even if pursuing the goal of constituency service can help congressmen achieve their more fundamental goal of reelection, is it reasonable to assume that all congressmen pursue this goal? There are, after all, various ways of getting reelected. Dexter argues that congressmen have considerable freedom in choosing how they will go about the task,[20] and Mayhew suggests that there are significant differences between the ways different types of congressmen attempt to build electoral followings.[21] So why assume that *all* congressmen seek to obtain program expenditures for their districts? An answer to the question requires a careful differentiation between two roles that congressmen can play in the allocational process: congressman as *entrepreneur* and congressman as *local agent*. The entrepreneur, on his own initiative, searches for ways to obtain funds for his district. If the funds require a formal application, he will find an appropriate community organization and encourage it to apply. If no formal application is required, he will suggest to the allocating agency that his district deserves a share. From beginning to end he is the prime mover. The local agent, on the other hand, does not take the initiative. He waits for a group of his con-

---

20. Lewis Anthony Dexter, "The Job of the Congressman," in Raymond E. Wolfinger (ed.), *Readings on Congress* (Englewood Cliffs, N.J.: Prentice-Hall, 1971), pp. 69–89.
21. Mayhew, *Congress: The Electoral Connection*, pp. 73–76.

stituents to request his assistance on some matter, and only then does he act. He helps them transact their business in Washington, but he does not search for new ways in which he can serve them.

Virtually all congressmen perform as local agents, but only a few become entrepreneurs. Congressmen are free to accept or reject the latter role depending on their own personal interests. They may adopt it if they are genuinely interested in acquiring constituency benefits or if they consider it the best or easiest means of insuring their reelection; but there are no pressures forcing it upon them. There are pressures, however, forcing congressmen to act as local agents. They come in the form of regular letters, phone calls, and personal visits asking for help in dealing with the bureaucracy on grant applications or similar matters. Requests for assistance come from representatives of municipalities, counties, school systems, universities, hospitals, water districts, housing authorities, businesses, and the like. Congressmen can no more ignore requests such as these than they can ignore the appeals of individual citizens involved in bureaucratic tangles. In fact, it would be particularly foolish to do so, because they usually come from the most politically active constituents. These constituents may not expect their congressmen to take the initiative in constituency service, but they most certainly expect assistance when they request it.

In this theory I am primarily interested in the final stage of the allocational process—choice—and only peripherally in previous stages. Consequently, there is no need to be too preoccupied with congressmen as entrepreneurs, because the principal effect of entrepreneurial activity is on the agenda-setting stage. It can have a significant effect at this stage, because generally only a small group of congressmen seek to place on the agenda alternatives of potential benefit to their constituencies; others are, by preference, uninvolved. At the final stage of the allocational process, many more congressmen participate; this is where congressmen as local agents first become important. Only at this point do I assume *all* congressmen seek to obtain shares of program's expenditures.

This assumption does not imply that congressmen engage in any complex sequence of activities designed to achieve this goal. The theory requires only that each congressman knows when his constituents are competing for a share and that each prefers that an application from his own district be accepted in preference to one from another district. Congressmen generally know when their constituents are competing, because the constituents tell them. Although there is incomplete evidence on the point, it appears that a significant proportion of those applying for grants ask their congressman for some form of assistance.[22] By requesting his services as local agent, they also insure that he is aware of their needs, just in case he finds himself in a position to help them.

I have already argued that congressmen prefer that expenditures flow into their own districts because it enhances their chances for reelection. One class of congressmen, however, tends to have less intense preferences about allocation because the acquisition of federal expenditures yields below-average electoral benefits for them: those who represent portions of very large cities. Big-city congressmen have a number of peculiar problems. First, it is considerably more difficult for them to generate personal publicity with federal grant announcements. Small-town papers are usually hungry for news and eager to publish grant announcements; big-city papers generally have more news than they can print, and grant announcements receive low priority. Second, it is difficult for big-city congressmen to obtain credit from a program's beneficiaries for their help in acquiring a share of expenditures. Federal programs frequently provide collective benefits for the whole community, not just for a single congressional district within it. This means that most of the beneficiaries are not even the constituents of a congressman who has worked diligently to acquire benefits. There is also an information problem. With twenty congressmen representing a city, voters cannot know which one actually deserves the credit for obtaining benefits; in a smaller city with only a single congressman, there are no competitors for credit. Third, big-city congressmen may fear less the economic and electoral consequences of large reductions in federal expenditures. Closing a military base in a small community can wreck the economy; closing the same-sized base in a big city will have less serious consequences, because the economy is so much larger. These arguments about big-city congressmen may not apply to those from

22. Kenneth E. Gray reports that in 1957 a fairly typical congressman handled sixty-one different requests from groups (local governments, businesses, etc.) for assistance in obtaining benefits, as well as 386 requests from individuals regarding their personal problems with the government ("Congressional Interference in Administration," in Daniel J. Elazar [ed.], *Cooperation and Conflict* [Itasca, Ill.: Peacock Publishers, 1969], pp. 521–42). These figures have undoubtedly multiplied in the past twenty years as both the number of grant programs and the size of a congressman's office staff have increased.

machine cities. Machine congressmen have a special enticement to work for constituency benefits, because machine leaders are looking over their shoulders. At least in large cities where the "Olson problem"[23] exists, machines provide the selective incentives necessary to induce congressmen to work for collective benefits that will be enjoyed throughout the whole city.[24] For purposes of this theory, distinctions on the basis of city size are not made; distinctions are made in Part Two, where empirical evidence is examined.

THE BASIS FOR EXCHANGE

Congressmen and bureaucrats are interdependent decision makers. Though each has authority to make certain decisions without consulting the other, each generally finds it in his own self-interest to consider the other's preferences. This is because the ability of each to attain his goals is at least partially dependent on the actions of the other. Bureaucrats pursue goals of budgetary security and budgetary growth, but attaining these goals depends on congressmen's decisions. Similarly, congressmen seek shares of government spending for their districts, but achieving this goal depends on bureaucrats' decisions. Both congressmen and bureaucrats tend to adjust their decisions to accommodate each other's preferences whenever they believe it might help them achieve their own goals. When bureaucrats make allocational decisions they consider the effects their own decisions might have on a congressman's decision about supporting their budgetary request. They suspect that the probability of a congressman supporting their budget might be slightly greater if they were to award a grant to his district. Similarly, when a congressman makes a decision about whether to support or oppose an agency's budgetary request, he considers the effect that his stand on the budget might have on the agency's allocational decisions. He suspects that the probability of his receiving a share of expenditures might be slightly greater if he were to support the agency's request.

23. The "Olson problem" refers to the fact that individuals in large groups are not motivated to work for collective benefits unless provided with selective incentives. See Olson, *The Logic of Collective Action.*

24. Evidence supporting this generalization for one machine city (Chicago) appears in Leo M. Snowiss, "Congressional Recruitment and Representation," *American Political Science Review* 60 (1966): 637.

The relationship between congressmen and bureaucrats is a type of exchange relationship. Under certain circumstances congressmen and bureaucrats trade support on budgetary matters for favorable consideration on allocational matters. But this exchange relationship is very different from that of the familiar economic market. The principal difference is that there are few agreed-upon trades between congressmen and bureaucrats. In the economic marketplace we are accustomed to negotiated trades between two parties: a producer supplies a particular good in exchange for a consumer's payment; a laborer works so many hours for an agreed-upon wage. But in this political marketplace it is the exception, not the rule, when a congressman and a bureaucrat explicitly agree to exchange support on a specific roll-call vote for a specific allocation of benefits. Instead, they trade speculatively and on credit; they are continually repaying past favors and building up a stock of credits useful for obtaining additional favors sometime in the future. Bureaucrats allocate expenditures both in gratitude for past support and in hopes of future congressional support; and congressmen support agencies both because they owe them for past allocations and because they desire future allocations.

This exchange relationship is complex for a number of other reasons. First, constituency benefits are only one of the factors that influence congressmen's decisions about whether to support budgetary requests. Some congressmen are predisposed to support the requests of certain agencies and require only small allocations to insure their continued support; others are strongly biased against these requests, and no allocation, no matter how large, can induce them to alter their positions. Second, bureaucrats and other coalition leaders are not totally dependent on constituency benefits to persuade congressmen to join coalitions; they have alternative strategies. Furthermore, they can employ mixed strategies, attracting some congressmen with constituency benefits and others by different means.

Before examining the conditions under which congressmen and bureaucrats find it in their interests to exchange budgetary support for constituency benefits, we need a better understanding of how congressmen make decisions on budgetary matters and an understanding of how bureaucrats and other coalition leaders attempt to build coalitions to pass budgets.

3: BUILDING COALITIONS

CONGRESSMEN'S VOTING DECISIONS

This section develops a framework for the analysis of congressmen's voting decisions which is quite different from those usually employed to analyze voting behavior. Generally, those who study roll-call voting seek to determine why congressmen voted as they did on a specific set of alternatives, a set consisting of those issues that actually reached the floor during a given time period. Their task is to identify the factors that influenced congressmen's decisions and to assess the relative impact of each. The factors most frequently identified are party, ideology, and constituency, though there are others. Here, however, I am primarily interested in the ways in which coalition leaders *anticipate* congressmen's voting decisions when they design new expenditure programs and select legislative strategies to enact them. Accordingly, the analytic framework is oriented towards the types of factors that coalition leaders can manipulate, rather than those they cannot, such as party, ideology, and constituency. Of course, these three variables appear in various parts of the framework, but they do not provide the organizing structure for it. Later the framework will prove useful for assessing the effectiveness of alternative strategies for building and expanding coalitions.

Congressmen are assumed to make three separate evaluations before deciding whether or not to support an expenditure program: a general-benefit evaluation, a local-benefit evaluation, and a support-trading evaluation. Each of the first two evaluations yields a preference concerning the program under consideration, a preference that has both direction (for or against) and intensity (ranging from very weak to very strong). A congressman's "true" preference for a particular program is assumed to be a weighted average of these two preferences, weighted according to the intensity of each. A congressman's final decision about whether to vote in accordance with this preference depends on his support-trading evaluation.

A *general-benefit evaluation* is defined as a congressman's appraisal of a program as a whole without regard to any expenditures that might be made in his district. It is a judgment about a program's worthiness, not about the value of its local benefits. Frequently it includes an appraisal of the collective benefits that his district, as well as others, would enjoy under a particular program (e.g., national defense), but it does not include calculations about the benefits that would accrue to his district alone (e.g., the benefits from defense spending in his district). A congressman's general-benefit evaluation is a decision about whether a program is consistent with his own policy attitudes as well as those of his constituents. (This follows from my assumption that a congressman seeks to maintain a voting record acceptable both to his constituency and to himself.) As such, it may be a judgment about whether a program's goals represent a proper activity for the federal government, whether the means employed to achieve these goals seem appropriate, and whether the benefits to be derived are worth the costs to be incurred.

Congressmen's policy attitudes affect their general-benefit evaluations in a variety of ways.[1] At times the connection between a congressman's attitude and the issue under consideration is so clear and direct that little deliberation is required. For example, a rural congressman opposed on principle to federal assistance to local governments hardly needs to consider the merits of a particular urban assistance program. But usually the connection between attitudes, issues, and decisions is less clear. Two mechanisms account for the influence of policy attitudes on voting decisions in such instances: selective perception and cue passing. Selective perception refers to the tendency of congressmen to notice and to find persuasive those arguments that emphasize their own general policy attitudes but to reject those based on assumptions they do not share. Cue passing refers to a congressman's reliance on his colleagues for advice on specific proposals. A congressman's own policy attitudes can still be said to influence his general-benefit evaluation, because he invariably turns for advice to those who share his general attitudes on the policy under consideration.[2]

1. This paragraph relies heavily on John W. Kingdon, *Congressmen's Voting Decisions* (New York: Harper and Row, 1973), pp. 72–79, 157–60, 245–54.

2. Ibid., p. 75.

A *local-benefit evaluation* is defined as a congressman's estimate of the expected benefits that he and his constituents would receive from a program's expenditures in his district. It is an evaluation of *expected* benefits, because no congressman can be certain whether his district will receive a share or, if so, how large that share might be. My assumption that congressmen pursue the goal of constituency service suggests that a congressman will have a positive local-benefit preference whenever he sees at least a small probability of receiving some share of a program's expenditures. But the intensity of this preference depends on his estimate of the probability of receiving an allocation and also on his estimate of the expected size of that allocation. These estimates are relatively easy to make when an established program is being considered, because a congressman knows the size of the shares that are usually allocated, the frequency with which his district has applied in the past, and the general patterns of agency decisions. The estimates are not as easy to make for a new program, because a congressman has no such history to guide him. A congressman will have a negative local-benefit preference whenever he sees virtually no possibility of receiving a share of expenditures. This negative preference may be very intense if a congressman feels his district has been (or will be) treated unfairly in the allocational process—for example, if communities in his district are ineligible for benefits or if he thinks those who allocate benefits would discriminate against competitors from his district.

A congressman's *true preference* for an expenditure program is assumed to be a weighted average of his general-benefit and local-benefit preferences, weighted according to the intensity of each. Usually, of course, the two preferences are of the same direction and reinforce one another. Occasionally, however, the two evaluations yield conflicting preferences, with one pointing towards support and the other towards opposition. In such cases, a congressman's true preference takes the direction of the more intense preference, but its intensity is moderated by the effect of the other preference.

A *support-trading evaluation* refers to a congressman's evaluation of the net benefits that would accrue to him if he were to vote against his true preference and according to the preference of some other political actor. A congressman sometimes votes against his true preference because he wishes to trade his support on the issue under consideration for another actor's support on some matter of greater concern to him. Actors with whom he might exchange support include his fellow congressmen, members of important congressional committees, party leaders, or the president. Matters on which he might seek their support include committee assignments, constituency projects, passage of favorite bills, publicity, patronage, or campaign assistance. Of course, support-trading involves both costs and benefits. Voting against one's own policy preferences involves personal costs, and voting against either the policy preferences of one's constituents or the interests of those competing for benefits may be electorally risky. The benefits to be derived depend on a congressman's assessment of how valuable the other actor's support is for the achievement of his objective and on how valuable the objective itself is to him. A congressman will engage in support trading if—and only if—the expected benefits of the trade exceed its expected costs. Consequently, if his true preference is extremely intense, a congressman will usually not find it in his interest to engage in support trading, because the potential costs are too great. It is only when preferences are weak that there is much opportunity for support trading.[3]

COALITION LEADERS

Winning coalitions do not form on their own. They are formed by diligent coalition leaders who invest their time and resources in an effort to persuade congressmen to join. Usually political actors choose to become coalition leaders because they have significantly more intense preferences concerning the program under consideration than do most other relevant actors, and because they believe the achievement of their own political goals depends, in part, on the fate of a particular program. The leadership for a particular program usually consists of both bureaucrats and congressmen; occasionally it includes the president.

3. In this work *support trading* refers to a broader range of activities than those generally implied by *logrolling*, the more familiar term. Logrolling usually refers to trades among politicians of equal status; seldom is it used to describe a relationship between, for example, a congressman and the president. Also, logrolling generally refers to *policy* trades but not to trades involving such diverse political commodities as campaign assistance or committee assignments.

Bureaucrats invariably become coalition leaders for programs they already administer. Their goal of budgetary security gives them such an intense interest in the continuation of these programs that they can hardly sit back and wait for others to handle the task of coalition building. Frequently, they become coalition leaders for proposed programs that, if passed, would be administered by them. This is particularly likely when the agency itself has formulated the program under consideration.

A president may choose to become a coalition leader under several circumstances. One is when he has adopted a proposed new expenditure program as part of his annual legislative program. He works to assemble a coalition, in part because he wants to claim credit for enactment. His intense interest in the fate of such a program generally wanes after it has been passed, and he has little incentive for continuing to act as a coalition leader in subsequent efforts to maintain or expand the coalition. A president also may choose to become a coalition leader when a program involves the nation's international power or prestige, traditional presidential concerns. Defense programs fall in this category, as did the space program in the early 1960s.

Congressmen find it in their interest to become coalition leaders under various circumstances. Some congressmen choose to become leaders because they have strong general-benefit preferences concerning the policy under consideration, others because they have strong local-benefit preferences owing to the fact their districts receive, or expect to receive, disproportionally large shares of a program's expenditures. Congressmen with intense preferences of either type frequently are, by choice, members of those committees with jurisdiction over the program being considered; consequently, they are in an excellent position to exercise leadership.

A third type of congressman becomes a coalition leader because it helps him maintain or increase his institutional power and prestige in the House. The pursuit of influence within the House was not one of my postulated goals, because only a small proportion of congressmen pursue it as an end itself (rather than as a means to policy or local-benefit ends), and because its only apparent effect on the politics of geographic allocation is to induce certain congressmen to become coalition leaders. Fenno ascribes this goal to members of the Appropriations and Ways and Means Committees;[4] in addition, it probably motivates party leaders. Members of these two committees usually work hard to attract supporters for the bills they report, because they fear defeat would diminish their influence in the House.[5] Leaders of the party that controls the presidency usually act as coalition leaders for new proposals that are part of the president's legislative program; the task comes with the job. Party leaders seldom act as coalition leaders for established programs, though occasionally they may help to arrange trades between blocs of their party's congressmen—for example, inducing rural congressmen to support urban programs in return for the support of urban congressmen on agricultural programs.

Coalition leaders attempt to build winning coalitions in various ways. Three broad classes of strategies are available to leaders for building and expanding coalitions, classes that parallel congressmen's three separate evaluations of expenditure programs. *General-benefit strategies* are designed to induce positive general-benefit evaluations; *allocational strategies* are designed to produce positive local-benefit evaluations; and *support-trading strategies* are intended to persuade opponents to vote against their true preferences in exchange for assistance on other matters. Although my principal interest is in allocational strategies, considerable space is devoted to the other two strategies, because all three are interrelated. Coalition leaders usually select strategies that complement one another. They select allocational strategies that compensate for the weaknesses of their general-benefit strategies, and they select support-trading strategies that compensate where the other two are unproductive.

In discussing strategies for coalition leaders, it will be useful to differentiate between *new* expenditure programs and *established* expenditure programs. New programs are defined as proposed programs that have yet to receive an initial authorization from Congress. Established programs are those for which funds have been appropriated one or more times. The two categories clearly are not exhaustive; they fail to include programs that have been authorized but have yet to receive their first appropriations. This intermediate category is examined briefly in chapter 8.

4. Richard F. Fenno, Jr., *Congressmen in Committees* (Boston: Little, Brown, 1973), p. 3.
5. Ibid., pp. 49, 55.

STRATEGIES FOR NEW PROGRAMS

How large a coalition do leaders generally seek to build for a new expenditure program? The answer to this question has important consequences for the strategies leaders select for attracting congressmen. At the very least, of course, they seek to form minimum winning coalitions, coalitions just large enough to ensure victory. At times these minimum winning coalitions are simply one half plus one; frequently, however, they are considerably larger because a whole series of majorities are required, one at each stage of the congressional process. Another reason leaders aim for coalitions slightly larger than a majority is that they want to minimize risks of miscalculation or last-minute changes.

But do coalition leaders care whether a supporting coalition is any larger than this? Specifically, are there incentives that either encourage leaders to build very large coalitions or motivate them to prevent the formation of very large coalitions? The second question is important in view of Riker's well-known theory of political coalitions. Riker assumes that American national politics is a zero-sum game and argues that participants in such a game make strenuous efforts to reduce oversized coalitions so the benefits of coalition membership can be divided among as few members as possible.[6] But Riker's analysis does not apply to the situation analyzed in this work, for it is not a zero-sum game and benefits are not restricted to members of winning coalitions. In fact, members of winning coalitions do not even acquire preferential rights to shares of benefits; they must compete both with each other and with nonmembers in a bureaucratic decision-making process subsequent to coalition formation. Thus, neither leaders nor members should care if a coalition approaches its maximum possible size, the total membership of the House. On the other hand, there is no reason why coalition leaders should endeavor to build such oversized coalitions for new programs. There are a few situations in which oversized coalitions are definitely preferred; for example, presidents commonly seek them when they want legitimating resolutions on foreign affairs issues such as the Tonkin Gulf Resolution.[7] But in the case of new expenditure programs,

6. William H. Riker, *The Theory of Political Coalitions* (New Haven: Yale University Press, 1962), pp. 54–55.
7. Fenno, *Congressmen in Committees*, p. 28.

coalition leaders gain no greater rewards from oversized coalitions than from minimum winning coalitions. Their rewards depend on getting programs passed, not on assembling large coalitions.

General-Benefit Strategies

Coalition leaders who devise general-benefit strategies are cognizant of the fact that congressmen's policy attitudes are usually fixed, at least in the short run. On occasion they do change, in response to gradual shifts in public opinion or as a consequence of dramatic, unforeseen events (e.g., Sputnik); however, they seldom change as a result of direct efforts at persuasion.[8] Consequently, coalition leaders interested in gaining immediate victories have as their principal task making both the proposed new programs and the arguments used to justify them compatible with the policy attitudes of a majority of congressmen. Only those with a long-term perspective can afford to wait for congressmen's policy attitudes to be brought into accord with their most preferred policy proposals, whether as a result of their own efforts at influencing public opinion or by events beyond their control, such as changes in the composition of Congress. In this section I am concerned only with short-term strategies, those that require no attitudinal changes. The discussion centers on three types of strategies: polarizing, issue-avoiding, and accommodating.

In *polarizing strategies* coalition leaders attempt to intensify any ideological or partisan cleavages associated with proposed expenditure programs so that congressmen can easily sort themselves into supporting and opposing camps. Leaders sometimes choose to intensify rather than reduce conflict because it helps congressmen to link their basic policy attitudes to the issues involved in specific programs, and because it helps to unify potential supporters by contriving an ideological foe to be overcome.[9] A polarizing strategy usually divides congressmen into two large groups, intense supporters and intense opponents, leaving few in between with weak preferences. Obviously, such a strategy can succeed only if the underlying distribution of attitudes favors a proposed program.

Polarizing strategies are most commonly employed for issues that do

8. On these points see Kingdon, *Congressmen's Voting Decisions*, pp. 251-54.
9. See Lewis A. Coser, *The Functions of Social Conflict* (Glencoe, Ill.: Free Press, 1956), pp. 87-110.

not involve local expenditures, for example, civil rights or labor-management relations; only occasionally are they used to build coalitions for expenditure programs.[10] There are at least two reasons for this. First, expenditure programs commonly involve multiple opinion cleavages, and polarization along two or more of these lines may produce a coalition of minorities large enough to block passage. This was the problem with educational assistance in the late 1950s and early 1960s, when racial and religious cleavages were intertwined with the already deep division over the desirability of any federal aid. Second, polarizing strategies reduce the effectiveness of local-benefit strategies; by increasing the intensity of opponents' general-benefit preferences, they make them less susceptible to the enticements of local benefits.

In *issue-avoiding strategies* coalition leaders attempt to steer clear of any major opinion cleavages in Congress when formulating and promoting new expenditure programs. Such strategies are designed to eliminate, or at least reduce, potential conflict so that few congressmen will have intense negative preferences. Minimizing the intensity of general-benefit preferences has two important effects. First, it reduces the number of congressmen with sufficient motivation to organize coalitions in opposition to programs. Without leaders who can counter the arguments put forth in favor of a program, congressmen are less likely to oppose it. Second, it increases congressmen's susceptibility to coalition leaders' allocational and support-trading strategies. Of course, it is not always possible to avoid *every* major cleavage in Congress; but the success of such a strategy probably depends as much on the ingenuity of the coalition leaders as on the nature of the underlying cleavages. For example, after the House refused in 1963 to authorize additional funds for the Area Redevelopment Administration (an agency that made direct grants and loans to businesses in economically depressed areas) because of serious conflicts between labor and business interests, and between depressed and nondepressed areas, coalition leaders responded with a new program consisting of grants for public works infrastructure projects

10. An example of an expenditure program advanced by a polarizing strategy is the area redevelopment program passed in 1958 and 1960, though both times vetoed by the president. Coalition leaders intensified the division between labor and rural groups supporting action and business groups opposing action by refusing to make any compromises. The strategy was only partly inspired by legislative politics; by "forcing" Republicans to oppose it, Democratic leaders generated a convenient issue to take to the people in the 1960 election. See James L. Sundquist, *Politics and Policy: The Eisenhower, Kennedy, and Johnson Years* (Washington, D.C.: Brookings, 1968), pp. 63–73.

in the same areas. The new program sailed through Congress, for virtually no congressmen oppose public works.[11] Sometimes a successful issue-avoiding strategy merely requires a clever repackaging of an old idea, both to avoid divisions in Congress and to give former opponents a rationalization for shifting their positions. Consider, for example, the National *Defense* Education Act, a proposal supported, after Sputnik, by many who had long opposed any aid to education.[12]

Polarizing and issue-avoiding strategies represent opposite approaches to coalition building; one attempts to exacerbate underlying opinion cleavages, the other to bridge them. In between lie *accommodating strategies*, those which moderate conflict. Coalition leaders who employ such strategies commence by proposing new expenditure programs that approximate what they consider ideal; then, during the course of the legislative process, they modify the programs to secure the acquiescence of at least some of those opposed to the original proposals. Most modifications take place at the committee stage in response to objections from groups affected by the proposals or from congressmen sitting on the committee. By ironing out serious conflict at the committee stage, a relatively united front can be presented on the floor so that few congressmen will receive negative cues. Of course, the modifications adopted may not suffice to make all congressmen supporters, but they may reduce the intensity of opposition so that allocational and support-trading strategies can be effective.

Polarizing, accommodating, and issue-avoiding strategies should be considered as ideal types, not exhaustive categories. There are no sharp lines separating them, and, in fact, *mixed* strategies, which combine elements either of the first with the second or of the second with the third, are probably more common than the three pure types. For my purposes, however, these three categories will be adequate.

Allocational Strategies

Coalition leaders have only a few allocational strategies available for promoting *new* programs, since they do not yet have any benefits to allocate. No doubt some coalition leaders, particularly those destined to administer a program if it passes, could make contingent promises of

11. Ibid., pp. 105–10.
12. Ibid., pp. 173–80.

benefits in exchange for support. Usually, however, they do not. Such bargains would be especially difficult to make for programs requiring local initiative, for neither congressmen nor bureaucrats know in advance which communities might apply.

Though coalition leaders cannot at this stage bargain with individual congressmen, they can affect the expectations of broad classes of congressmen. First, they can enlarge a program's *geographic scope* so that more localities will be eligible for benefits and, as a consequence, more congressmen will see opportunities for acquiring district benefits. Eligibility requirements for an urban program can be defined so that even the most rural district will have at least one large town that qualifies for benefits. Such concepts as "economically depressed regions," "educationally disadvantaged children," or "federally impacted areas" are equally slippery and can be fashioned to fit nearly any political situation. Second, they can multiply the number of shares to be allocated so that the probability of each individual congressman obtaining a share will increase. Congressmen can better afford to remain indifferent when only a few shares are to be allocated than when there are a few hundred. There are, however, limitations to the use of these two techniques. It is impossible to broaden the geographic scope for some programs because potential beneficiaries live in circumscribed areas—for example, miners or Indians. For others, leaders can enlarge geographic scope without limit, but they cannot significantly increase the number of shares to be allocated without interfering with other public functions. NASA could have constructed its various administrative, research, assembly, training, and control facilities almost anywhere, but it probably could not have split them into 435 packages and still have accomplished its missions. Finally, unless agencies can increase their budgets at the same rate with which they increase the number of shares to be allocated, the value of each local share to a congressman will decline. There is, after all, a substantial difference between procuring a one-twentieth share of a $10 million program and procuring a one-four-hundredth share of the same program.

Support-Trading Strategies

For attracting congressmen, general-benefit and allocational strategies are considerably more productive than support-trading strategies. Leaders can, and frequently do, build winning coalitions by using only general-benefit and allocational strategies; however, they usually cannot assemble winning coalitions exclusively on the basis of support-trading strategies, for they have but a limited stock of favors available for exchange. The value of support-trading strategies rests not on the number of coalition members they can produce but rather on their ability to attract, at a relatively low cost, the last few members necessary to transform losing coalitions into winning ones. General-benefit and allocational strategies are, at least for new programs, strategies for dealing with *blocs* of congressmen; leaders think in terms of how to attract liberals or conservatives, or how to appeal to those from cities or the hinterlands. Support-trading strategies differ in that they usually have more specific targets—individual congressmen.

Coalition leaders have a limited stock of resources available for support trading, a stock that must serve other purposes besides building a coalition for a single program. Since coalition leaders are assumed to be rational, they attempt to minimize the expenditure of these scarce resources. One consequence of this is that they employ support-trading strategies only if they believe that their general-benefit and allocational strategies are inadequate to insure a winning coalition. Another consequence is that they choose support-trading strategies that produce coalitions large enough to win, but no larger. A final consequence is that coalition leaders prefer to exchange support with congressmen who have relatively weak preferences about the program under consideration, because, in general, fewer resources are required to convince them to vote against their true preferences.

Coalition leaders can perform various favors for congressmen in an effort to persuade them to support a program they might otherwise oppose. Some are in a position to assist congressmen in their quest for constituency benefits. (Here I am concerned exclusively with those benefits *not* included in the expenditure program under consideration.) A coalition leader who sits on a committee that itself allocates constituency benefits (e.g., Public Works or Interior) may promise favorable consideration for a congressman's pet project in exchange for the congressman's support of the program for which he is assembling a coalition. A president may use what influence he has with the bureaucracy to expedite a project of special concern to a congressman.

Some coalition leaders are also in a position to provide or withhold various electoral resources. A president can, with very little effort, help a congressman gain valuable publicity (as long as the president himself remains popular). Invitations to bill signings, pictures of a congressman in "serious" discussion with the president, and campaign appearances in a congressman's district are highly valued commodities, and not just for their therapeutic effects on the congressman's ego. Congressional leaders, both party and committee, also control electorally important resources: disbursements from the Congressional Campaign Committees, appointments to regular and special committees, or designations as subcommittee chairmen. All of these can be used to persuade reluctant congressmen of the wisdom of supporting a new expenditure program.

In addition to constituency benefits and electoral resources, support-trading strategies may include policy trades, either between pairs of individuals or groups of congressmen. When two groups of congressmen have opposite preferences on a pair of issues and when they also differ in the intensity with which they hold these preferences, it is frequently mutually advantageous for them to exchange support on the two issues so that the members of each group prevail on the issue more important to them. For example, rural congressmen may agree to support an urban assistance program in return for the support of urban congressmen when agricultural programs are on the agenda. Pairs of congressmen may negotiate such trades, though their net contribution to a winning coalition is usually slight. More important are policy trades arranged between blocs of congressmen, for these trades can sustain programs that enjoy the support of but a small minority. Party leaders once performed as central brokers in arranging such trades, but this role appears to be less common today.

These relationships have been described as if they involved agreed-upon trades between leaders and congressmen, with the former explicitly promising to provide specific favors in return for the latter's support. In fact, carefully negotiated agreements that delineate the obligations of each party are probably as rare here as they are between congressmen and bureaucrats over questions of allocation. Instead, coalition leaders constantly perform favors for others, either because they owe them for past support or because they hope to create obligations they may call in sometime in the future. Similarly, congressmen agree to leaders' requests for support either to discharge existing obligations or to create new ones. Indeed, much of congressional activity can be interpreted as an effort on the part of both leaders and followers to create such obligations, even though they may not know precisely when or on what issue they will call them in.

Coalition leaders have considerable freedom in how they assemble coalitions for new programs. Occasionally there may be a program for which only a single grand strategy could possibly succeed, but this is surely the exception. More common are various combinations of general-benefit, allocational, and support-trading strategies equally capable of producing a winning coalition. Leaders can choose between making further modifications in a proposed program in order to reduce conflict, broadening its geographic scope and multiplying its benefits in order to attract congressmen eager for local benefits, calling in existing obligations and creating new ones to induce congressmen to vote against their true preferences, or doing a little of each. The particular choices they make may, at the time, seem unimportant, especially if the alternative strategies are equally productive. Their long term consequences, however, may be very different, for as we shall see, some initial strategies facilitate coalition formation in subsequent years, while others hinder it.

STRATEGIES FOR ESTABLISHED PROGRAMS

Established programs are those that have been through the budgetary cycle of authorization, appropriation, and expenditure at least once. Since most of these programs periodically require new authorizations and appropriations if they are to continue, coalition leaders need strategies for maintaining and enlarging each program's supporting coalition. Usually the strategies employed are considerably different from those used to build the original coalitions. In fact, the coalition leadership itself is likely to be quite different.

After a program has been in operation for a short time, those who administer it usually emerge as its principal coalition leaders because they have the most to gain by its continuance and the most to lose by its demise. Others, for example congressmen or the president, may still be interested in a program's survival, but it is probably just one of their many competing interests, and it may not be strong enough to command their full attention or to impel them to invest their time and resources in the maintenance of the supporting coalition. Program administrators, on the other hand, have no more important interest than the continuance of the programs they administer, for the realization of many of their personal goals depends on it.

Bureaucrats, then, are the principal coalition leaders for established programs. But congressmen also play a role, though it is considerably less significant than their role for new programs. Usually members of the legislative committee with jurisdiction over a particular expenditure program constitute the core of a program's congressional support. This reflects both the committee-recruitment and committee-assignment processes, which tend to produce legislative committees filled with congressmen favorably disposed towards the programs they supervise. In addition, members of the corresponding appropriations subcommittees may act as coalition leaders, though they play a peculiar leadership role. Subcommittee members do, in a sense, act as coalition leaders whenever they attempt to attract supporters for the funding levels they have recommended. But since it is known that they shape these recommendations in anticipation of floor action, considerable "followership" hides behind their leadership.[13] In fact, their most strenuous efforts at genuine leadership probably occur when they have miscalculated their colleagues' reaction and they must scramble to avoid being "rolled" on the floor. Although at times subcommittee members may be motivated to work for the maintenance of a program's supporting coalition, on other occasions they work for its breakup. In general, the Appropriations Committee provides a poor source of coalition leaders for expenditure programs, because its subcommittees are deliberately stacked with members indifferent or even hostile to the programs they review,[14] and because its members tend to be motivated more by a desire to maintain their institutional power and prestige than by a desire to promote particular policies.[15]

13. Manley, in his analysis of Wilbur Mill's influence, has written that the paradox of leadership is that it always involves followmanship. See John F. Manley, "Wilbur D. Mills: A Study in Congressional Influence," American Political Science Review 63 (1969); 442–43.

14. Richard F. Fenno, Jr., The Power of the Purse (Boston: Little, Brown, 1966), pp. 138–43.

15. Fenno, Congressmen in Committees, pp. 2–5.

Coalition Size

Previously I argued that coalition leaders for *new* programs have no incentives to assemble anything larger than minimum winning coalitions. The situation is different, however, for established programs, principally because of the change in coalition leaders. Bureaucrats generally seek to build very large coalitions for the programs they administer because large coalitions help to insure that their budgets will be approved in subsequent years. If their only interest were to obtain approval for the current budget, a minimum winning coalition would do very nicely. But their search for long-term budgetary security makes such a coalition a risky choice. It is risky, first of all, because the composition of both Congress and its committees changes periodically. This year's supporters may not return after the next election, and this year's opponents may eventually gain seats on those committees with jurisdiction over the program's budget. Even without membership changes, the "mood" of Congress may fluctuate, with, for example, an economy mood replacing a spending spree. Such a shift can convert a portion of a program's supporters into opponents. Bureaucrats attempt to anticipate and counteract such changes by building oversized coalitions that provide a large reservoir of supporters.

The job of coalition leaders is facilitated by the fact that congressmen tend to vote at least partially according to habit.[16] Those who favored a program's creation are likely to support its continuance, though, of course, their support is far from certain. Coalition leaders, therefore, begin with a collection of congressmen predisposed towards continuing a program; their job is to prevent anything from altering these predispositions. On the other hand, these same voting habits impede coalition leaders' attempts to expand a program's supporting coalition. Those who opposed a program's creation are likely to be opposed to additional appropriations for its continuance or expansion.

General-Benefit Strategies

Coalition leaders have available a wide range of general-benefit strategies suitable for established programs. An extensive review of these

16. Kingdon, *Congressmen's Voting Decisions*, pp. 254–57.

strategies seems unnecessary in this work, for there is little connection between the particular general-benefit strategies employed and the allocational strategies adopted. I shall confine myself to a few brief comments on these strategies and refer interested readers to Wildavsky's chapter on budgetary strategies for a more complete discussion.[17]

Polarizing strategies, used commonly for new programs, are not ordinarily employed for established programs, because they are incompatible with coalition leaders' objective of enlarging their supporting coalitions. Even if a polarizing strategy had been used to build a program's initial coalition, it is unlikely to be retained in subsequent years, because it has the undesirable side effect of sustaining opposing coalitions along with supporting ones. Leaders are more likely to pursue strategies that deemphasize party and ideological cleavages and thus reduce the intensity of opposition. Of course, opposition will not disappear overnight just because a polarizing strategy has been abandoned, but the chances of it diminishing are greater, in the long run, if opponents are not constantly reminded of the conflicts that led to their initial opposition. More important, the abandonment of a polarizing strategy means that new members of Congress are not "forced" into an opposing coalition, but rather are allowed to remain uncommitted and, therefore, open to the enticements offered by allocational strategies.

Bureaucrats steer clear of ideological and partisan conflicts as best they can by avoiding polarizing strategies. But other types of conflict can also threaten supporting coalitions, for example, conflict related to the competence of a program's administrators. Supporting coalitions can melt away in the wake of well-publicized scandals involving either dishonesty or extraordinarily poor judgment. Consequently, bureaucrats have an incentive to perform their assigned functions competently, or at least to create the impression of competence. Assessing administrative competence is no easy matter in government, for nothing comparable to the businessman's bottom line exists; however, identifying gross incompetence is a bit easier. When planes cannot fly, or dams fail to hold, or programs have absolutely nothing to show after the investment of billions, former supporters frequently find greater rewards as champions of economy than as advocates of further investment.

17. Aaron Wildavsky, *The Politics of the Budgetary Process* (Boston: Little, Brown, 1964), pp. 63–126.

Support-Trading Strategies

Support-trading strategies are infrequently employed for established programs, because bureaucrats, the principal coalition leaders, control nothing of value with which they might trade (excepting, of course, local benefits, which are subsumed under allocational strategies). The only types of support trading which do occasionally occur are exchanges *among* congressmen rather than exchanges between congressmen and external political actors. Policy trades between blocs of congressmen sometimes take place, especially if such trades were used to form a program's initial coalition. A second type of trade associated with established programs is the exchange between policy specialists, particularly those on the House Appropriations Committee. Members of one subcommittee expect that members of the full committee will support their decisions, in return for which they support decisions of other subcommittees.[18] Reciprocal relationships such as these, though never formally negotiated, can add crucial members to a coalition, members who otherwise would have no incentives for supporting a program.

18. Fenno, *Power of the Purse*, pp. 162–63.

4: ALLOCATING BENEFITS

What allocational strategies should bureaucrats adopt in order to maximize the size of supporting coalitions for the programs they administer? The answer is long and complex, for optimal strategies vary not only from program to program but also from year to year as the strategic situation in Congress changes. The discussion of allocational strategies will be limited to situations in which the demand for benefits exceeds the supply of benefits. (The case in which demand is less than or equal to supply is neither very interesting nor, I suspect, very common.) *Demand* refers to the number of local communities that are eligible for a share of benefits and express an interest in acquiring such a share. *Supply* refers both to the number and to the total value of shares that program administrators have available for allocation in a particular period, usually a year.

Allocational strategies are actions designed to induce positive local-benefit evaluations on the part of congressmen. Three types of actions are encompassed by allocational strategies: actions that affect the supply of benefits, actions that affect the demand for benefits, and decisions about which of the many competing localities should receive a share of benefits. Most of this chapter is concerned with the third type of action.

Bureaucrats can allocate a given supply of benefits in an almost limitless number of ways. Not only can they decide *where* funds will be spent, they can also determine *how much* will be spent in each locality. Control of these two allocational decisions gives bureaucrats the ability to regulate the flow of funds to individual congressional districts and thus, whenever it serves their purposes, to reward or punish individual congressmen by granting or withholding benefits. This chapter examines the conditions under which it is rational for bureaucrats to favor certain congressmen and attempts to determine what allocational criteria bureaucrats should adopt in specific situations to maximize their supporting coalitions.

If bureaucrats do choose to reward disproportionally certain congressmen, they are likely to employ allocational criteria related either to congressmen's general-benefit preferences or to their committee assignments. General-benefit preferences are an important criterion, because they allow bureaucrats to coordinate their allocational and general-benefit strategies in such a way that the former compensates for the weaknesses of the latter. Committee assignments are important because they suggest which congressmen are in the best position to affect bureaucrats' fortunes.

The argument will be advanced that under certain specified conditions, bureaucrats exchange benefits for congressional support of their budgets. A complication in both an exposition of the theory and its subsequent analysis is that both the budgetary process in Congress and allocational processes in agencies are continuous, overlapping processes. Bureaucrats allocate benefits under one budget at the same time that Congress is considering their budgetary requests for the following year. Consequently, allocational decisions during any given year may represent a combination of strategies, each with a different time perspective. Benefits may be allocated partly as rewards for past support, partly as payments for support during the current year, and partly to create a favorable climate for future years. Most problems associated with these differing time perspectives can be ignored while discussing theory. Whenever appropriate, however, they will be considered in the empirical chapters.

ALLOCATION ACCORDING TO GENERAL-BENEFIT PREFERENCES

General-benefit preferences, it will be recalled, have two basic attributes: direction (for or against) and intensity (ranging from very weak to very strong). A congressman's general-benefit preference can, therefore, be represented as a point along the following dimension, which has neutrality as its midpoint, intense opposition as one endpoint, and intense support as the other (figure 4.1). Similarly, his local-benefit preference can be represented along a dimension with the same range, as can his "true" preference, which is a function of his general-benefit and local-benefit preferences. If a congressman's district receives a share of a program's benefits, the congressman will have a positive local-

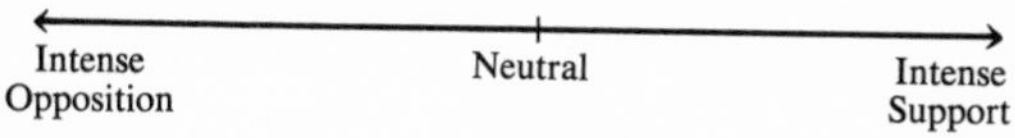

Figure 4.1. Range of General-Benefit Preferences

benefit evaluation of that program. This has the effect of shifting his true preference to the right of his general-benefit preference. If, in the beginning, he were intensely opposed, local benefits might result in a shift to moderate or even weak opposition; if, originally, he were weakly opposed or neutral, local benefits might nudge him over the line to weak support; or if he began as a weak supporter, his resulting preference would be intense support.

All of these shifts in opinion are desirable from bureaucrats' point of view. In other words, if the supply of benefits were unlimited, it would serve their purposes to allocate a share of benefits to each congressman, regardless of his general-benefit preference. Allocating benefits to those most intensely opposed to particular programs serves bureaucrats' purposes by reducing the intensity of opposition, thus eliminating one of the principal reasons why congressmen invest their time and resources in organizing coalitions against expenditure programs. The objective here is not so much to convert opponents into proponents, but rather to discourage opponents from working to increase their following. The strategy of "buying off" [1] opposition leaders so that they will not organize opposing coalitions is not peculiar to congressional-bureaucratic relations. Students of urban politics have noted that leaders of minority parties are frequently given a share of patronage in exchange for their agreement not to oppose certain actions of the dominant party. This has been observed in both machine (Chicago) and nonmachine (New York) cities. [2]

---

1. Throughout this chapter such terms as *buy off*, *pay off*, and a congressman's *price* are used. Some readers may find these terms offensive, though they are not intended to be. They are borrowed from game theory and economics and are used for descriptive purposes only; they are not meant to imply any unethical behavior on the part of either congressmen or bureaucrats.

2. See Harold F. Gosnell, *Machine Politics: Chicago Model* (Chicago: University of Chicago Press, 1937), p. 44; and Wallace S. Sayre and Herbert Kaufman, *Governing New York City: Politics in the Metropolis* (New York: Russell Sage, 1960), pp. 178–80.

Bureaucrats allocate benefits to those who are neutral or weakly opposed because they hope to convert them into proponents. Converting neutrals is relatively easy, for only a modest allocation is necessary to tip the balance. Somewhat larger allocations may be required for those weakly or moderately opposed. Each congressman, however, is assumed to have his price; if a sufficiently large allocation of local benefits is offered, conversion is assured.

Allocating benefits to those who already support a program may appear a waste of resources. It is not. Local benefits give supporters a greater stake in a program and provide an incentive to work for its continuance. More important, failure to allocate benefits to those who support a program while giving them freely to opponents could convert friends into foes. Supporters may not expect extra allocations, but they do expect to be treated fairly, a term that on Capitol Hill means "as well as everyone else." Finally, game theorists would point out that if benefits were systematically denied to supporters because their votes were taken for granted, they would begin to misrepresent their actual positions in order to obtain what genuine opponents received automatically.[3]

Although there are good reasons why bureaucrats should want to allocate benefits to congressmen from across the entire range of general-benefit preferences, they rarely have enough benefits to give each congressman a share large enough to produce the desired shifts in opinion. Their resources are scarce, and consequently they must decide what geographic pattern of allocations will do their cause the most good in the short run and the least harm in the long run. The allocational priorities they set depend, in part, on the peculiarities of particular programs and on programs' legislative and budgetary histories. But certain regularities also exist in the way priorities are set.

One method bureaucrats have for minimizing the expenditure of a program's scarce resources is to identify which of the many opponents are most likely to become leaders of opposing coalitions and which of the many proponents are most likely to lead supporting coalitions, and

3. There is evidence that some congressmen intentionally misrepresent their positions in an attempt to obtain favors from party or administration leaders. See Randall B. Ripley, *Party Leaders in the House of Representatives* (Washington, D.C.: Brookings, 1967), p. 68.

then to concentrate resources on these two groups of potential leaders. Many proponents and many opponents choose to invest their energies in areas unrelated to the program under consideration and would be uninterested in assuming leadership roles; allocating extra resources either to persuade the former or dissuade the latter from becoming leaders might alter their opinions concerning the program, but it would not affect the probabilities that they would assume leadership positions. A later section will discuss how bureaucrats attempt to identify potential coalition leaders for both supporting and opposing coalitions.

Bureaucrats' allocational priorities also depend on the distribution of general-benefit preferences among congressmen. Since the number of congressmen competing for benefits exceeds the number of shares to be allocated, the probability of an individual congressman being singled out and given a generous share of benefits depends not only on his own general-benefit preference but also on the preferences of those competing with him. Congressmen's relative positions on policy dimensions are more relevant than their absolute positions.

The number of distributions of general-benefit preferences that one can imagine bureaucrats facing is quite large. Most, however, differ in only minor details. Here the focus is on three qualitatively different distributions, each of which implies a different allocational strategy.

Consensus

First to be examined are those distributions in which there is substantial consensus concerning the merits of a program, with most congressmen either moderate or intense supporters. Typical of these distributions is the one displayed in figure 4.2, with both direction and

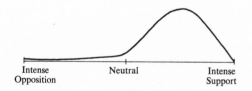

Figure 4.2. Consensus Distribution

intensity represented on the abscissa and frequency on the ordinate. Such distributions arise because congressmen value highly the collective benefits derived from programs. Examples of programs for which substantial consensus has developed are national defense, medical research, and the national park system.

Bureaucrats administering such programs have almost complete freedom in geographic allocation. They may, with two exceptions, allocate benefits as they please without worrying about the effect of each allocation on their supporting coalitions. One exception is that extra allocations to coalition leaders are still advisable to insure that they continue to perform their functions, as are allocations to potential leaders of opposing coalitions to discourage them from organizational activities. Second, it is important that bureaucrats not openly discriminate against particular localities when benefits are allocated, for such discrimination can embitter supporters and turn them into opponents. For example, during the 1960s congressmen from the Midwest were concerned that their region was being denied its fair share of research and development funds under various government programs. They formed subcommittees, held hearings, introduced amendments, and, on occasion, even passed amendments that prohibited the construction of particular research facilities in areas already saturated with them. At least one observer believes that their activities influenced bureaucrats' decisions to build the world's largest proton accelerator in Weston, Illinois rather than in Berkeley or Brookhaven, and to locate certain Environmental Health Research Centers in Ohio, West Virginia, and North Carolina rather than in the Washington area, the location preferred by the Department of Health, Education, and Welfare.[4]

Indifference

Second are distributions characterized largely by indifference or weak preferences, with few congressmen having strong preferences one way or the other. Figure 4.3 displays a typical distribution, though the midpoint need not coincide with the point of indifference, and some distributions may be flatter than others. Such distributions are com-

4. See Thomas P. Murphy, *Science, Geopolitics, and Federal Spending* (Lexington, Mass.: Heath Lexington Books, 1971), pp. 18–57, 265–326.

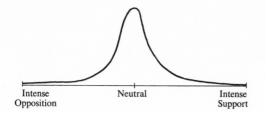

| Intense | Neutral | Intense |
| Opposition | | Support |

Figure 4.3. Indifference

monly associated with public works programs or grants of general assistance to state and local governments, programs that provide immense benefits at the point where funds are actually expended but few benefits that spill over into neighboring congressional districts and virtually no benefits for distant districts. Congressmen are unlikely to have strong general-benefit preferences, because there are few general benefits for them to evaluate.

Coalitions for such programs are almost always built on a foundation of local benefits. Bureaucrats must arrange for at least a majority of congressional districts to receive shares of benefits, because only those congressmen who do receive shares will have any incentives to support the program, while others are more likely to withhold their support. At a minimum this requires that a program's *geographic scope* be quite large so that many localities will be eligible for benefits. Programs with beneficiaries concentrated in only a few districts and which have general-benefit distributions of this type simply cannot survive (unless, of course, support trading occurs with the beneficiaries of other programs). Whenever a program's geographic scope encompasses less than a majority of districts, bureaucrats have no choice but to work to enlarge it either by altering administrative regulations or, if necessary, by seeking legislative changes. But geographic scope is only one factor that affects a program's demand schedule. The other is the *geographic pattern of applications*. Bureaucrats can define an urban program in such a way that even the smallest cities are eligible, but this will not help them attract rural congressmen unless small cities located in their districts actually apply. Occasionally bureaucrats must "advertise" their programs in order to encourage potential beneficiaries to apply. All these actions are designed to increase a program's demand so that a sufficient number of congressmen will be in a position to receive benefits. Bureaucrats may also have to enlarge a program's supply of benefits, either by increasing the number of shares to be allocated or by requesting a larger budget so that each share will be worth more to congressmen.

If bureaucrats are able to fashion a program that has broad geographic scope, attracts applications from the entire range of congressional districts, and has sufficient shares of benefits to reward a majority of congressmen regularly (if not annually), their battle is almost won. Ordinarily, the process of selecting applicants for awards is not difficult. Although it is important for benefits to be distributed among many districts, it is not clear that any class of congressmen (other than coalition leaders) deserves special attention. All congressmen have similar general-benefit preferences; therefore, there are only slight differences in the costs required to bring different congressmen into a supporting coalition. Some form of discrimination may be advisable for a closely fought battle in which the supply of benefits is severely limited and for which it is possible to attract some congressmen (e.g., neutrals) with slightly fewer benefits than others (e.g., weak opponents). Similarly, bureaucrats may want to withhold benefits from congressmen who, in a previous year, failed to support a program after receiving generous shares of benefits, for such actions remind congressmen of the connection between benefits and support. Ordinarily, however, discrimination serves no useful purpose. If both supply and demand are sufficient, bureaucrats can give at least small shares to every congressman and thus maximize a program's supporting coalition.

Polarized Distributions

Third are polarized distributions, those consisting of many moderate and intense supporters, a nearly equal number of moderate and intense opponents, but few neutrals, weak supporters, or weak opponents. A typical distribution is displayed in figure 4.4. Such distributions arise for programs that when first passed were the subject of intense ideological or partisan conflict. Model cities and the poverty programs are prime examples.

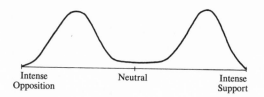

Intense
Opposition   Neutral   Intense
                                                                          Support

Figure 4.4. Polarized Distribution

Polarized distributions confront bureaucrats with more difficult problems than any others. Even when proponents outnumber opponents, victory is uncertain, for the congressional process offers minorities, particularly intense minorities, frequent opportunities to thwart majorities. Furthermore, changes in the composition of Congress (of a magnitude no greater than the norm for midterm elections) can easily transform a program's supporting coalition into a losing one. In sum, the long-term prospects for a program's survival are not good if nothing is done to reduce the size and intensity of opposition.

Allocational strategies alone can do little to reduce the size of opposition. Although all opponents are assumed to have their price, the strength of that opposition suggests that these prices will be high indeed. Few programs could possibly have enough benefits to convert more than a handful of opponents into proponents. Allocational strategies are probably best employed to produce the margins of victory necessary to keep a program alive in the short term, while general-benefit strategies that deemphasize partisan and ideological cleavages are used to build foundations for larger and more stable coalitions in the long term.

Bureaucrats' first allocational priority must be coalition leaders, both those who support and those who oppose a program. It is particularly important to reward opposition leaders, because their actions determine how stable an opposing coalition will be. If they decide to remain coalition leaders, opponents will be reminded constantly of the reasons that gave rise to their initial opposition. On the other hand, if they can be induced to cease their leadership activities, opponents are more likely to be receptive to bureaucrats' new general-benefit strategies. In fact, if rewards to opposition leaders actually convert them into supporters rather than just reducing the intensity of their opposition, other opponents may, out of habit, follow their cue and become supporters themselves, even though their districts do not receive benefits. It may, at first, seem implausible that opposition leaders—initially a program's strongest opponents—would become proponents simply because they received a generous allocation of benefits. Such conversions are not so surprising if one considers that these allocations generate sizable groups of beneficiaries who have a vested interest in a program's continuance and who expect their congressmen to support it. It is far easier to oppose a proposed program that *might* provide benefits for one's constituents than it is to oppose one that already benefits large groups of well-organized voters.

A second priority must be to allocate benefits to those who, as evidenced by their previous public positions on a program, are predisposed to support its budget. It is easy to take for granted the support of such congressmen and assume that it will be forthcoming regardless of allocational decisions. In fact, it is far from certain. In most cases, these congressmen became strong supporters as a result of polarizing strategies used when a program was first passed. But when bureaucrats abandon these strategies in an effort to reduce the intensity of opposition, nothing remains to reinforce the strong preferences of proponents. Without benefits to allocate, bureaucrats would have a rather difficult time in trying to eliminate the strong preferences of one group while preserving the strong preferences of another.

Third, bureaucrats can, when necessary, use benefits to convince a few opponents to become supporters and thus transform a losing coalition into a winning one. Rational bureaucrats will not select these congressmen haphazardly, but rather will concentrate their benefits on the weakest opponents, since smaller shares are required to persuade them to switch their positions.

Allocational strategies such as these do not build large, stable coalitions, but they do allow programs to survive while bureaucrats devise and implement general-benefit strategies that can reduce the intensity of conflict. If these strategies eventually succeed, the distribution of preferences should lose its depressed middle range and begin to resemble one of the other distributions already discussed; bureaucrats may then adopt the appropriate allocational strategies.

ALLOCATION ACCORDING TO COMMITTEE ASSIGNMENTS

Under certain conditions bureaucrats allocate extra benefits to members of those committees with jurisdiction over their programs. For each program two House committees are potentially important: a legislative committee, which authorizes all funds and sets conditions for their expenditure, and the subcommittee of the Appropriations Committee that reviews a program's past expenditures and recommends how much should be appropriated for the following year. (The full Appropriations Committee is less important, because it usually accepts, without question, the recommendations of its subcommittees.)

The principal reason members of these two committees receive special attention is that they make more decisions with a direct impact on bureaucrats' fortunes than nonmembers. First, committee members set the agenda for all legislative activity concerning a program, particularly its authorization and appropriations ceilings. Most congressmen only have an opportunity to vote on bills and amendments; committee members shape them from the beginning. Usually this initial involvement gives them greater influence over final outcomes than nonmembers.

Second, committee members have nonstatutory techniques for influencing bureaucratic behavior, techniques unavailable to nonmembers. The committee report is the most important of these. Committee reports frequently contain detailed instructions as to what bureaucrats can and cannot do, how funds should be spent, and sometimes even *where* funds are to be spent. Bureaucrats treat the provisions in such reports just as seriously as they do statutory provisions; the major difference is that the former are completely written in committees, whereas the latter are drafted in committees and then reviewed and occasionally revised on the floor.[5] In addition, committee members are more likely to know and have frequent contacts with program administrators, both formally during hearings and informally throughout the year. These contacts give them better opportunities to criticize past bureaucratic actions and make suggestions about future actions. Com-

5. See Michael W. Kirst, *Government without Passing Laws* (Chapel Hill: University of North Carolina Press, 1969) for a discussion of nonstatutory techniques for controlling bureaucratic behavior.

mittee members can also affect the public's image of both bureaucrats and the programs they administer just by the way in which they conduct congressional hearings and investigations. Bureaucrats sensitive about such images (and few can afford not to be) find that friendly relations with committee members are valuable.

If these various statutory and nonstatutory techniques for affecting bureaucratic behavior prove inadequate, Congress has one final, quite effective method: the legislative veto. But, once again, committee members are in the best position to use it. The legislative veto is a statutory provision that gives Congress the right to overrule specific bureaucratic decisions after they have been promulgated. Sometimes a committee is given the right to overrule bureaucratic decisions; but even if the whole House reserves this right for itself, committee members are, by virtue of their greater interest, information, and expertise, likely to control the situation. The legislative veto has been used most frequently to influence bureaucratic decisions on matters relating to geographic allocation—for example, real estate transactions by the Defense Department, disposal of surplus federal land or obsolete facilities, and the award of specific grants and contracts by the Interior Department.[6]

The second reason why bureaucrats sometimes choose to allocate extra benefits to committee members is that most of them are potential coalition leaders, either for supporting or opposing coalitions. Allocating generous shares to those favorably disposed may persuade them to lead supporting coalitions, while similar allocations to those negatively inclined may dissuade them from leading opposing coalitions. Of course, all potential coalition leaders will not sit on the committees that oversee a particular program, but many will. Committee membership thus serves as a guide to bureaucrats interested in identifying potential leaders.

Committee members perform as coalition leaders whenever they intentionally affect other congressmen's evaluations of programs. At the very least leaders attempt to convince others of a program's worthiness on general-benefit grounds. In addition, if they have sufficiently intense preferences or if they are due to receive large shares of local benefits and fear a program's budget may not pass, they may offer trades of support or

6. For discussions of the legislative veto, see Joseph P. Harris, *Congressional Control of Administration* (Washington, D.C.: Brookings, 1964), pp. 204–48; and John S. Saloma III, *Congress and the New Politics* (Boston: Little, Brown, 1969), pp. 139–42.

call in past obligations in an effort to attract enough congressmen to their side.

For all these reasons, committee members are potentially more important to bureaucrats' fortunes than nonmembers. The important thing, however, is not the *availability* of committee members' sanctions, but rather the *probability* that they will be used (or more precisely, bureaucrats' estimates of that probability). These probabilities vary from committee to committee and from program to program.

They vary, first of all, because some committees engage in frequent oversight activities while others review programs only occasionally. A committee that annually passes judgment on a program's budget, such as the relevant appropriations subcommittee, is much more likely to affect bureaucrats' fortunes than one that passes huge multiyear authorizations and then pays little attention to the program's administration. All appropriations subcommittees perform annual reviews, but only some legislative committees do. The House Armed Services Committee is an example of a legislative committee that, during the 1960s, switched from general, continuing authorizations to specific, annual authorizations. According to one author, the committee gained greater influence over defense programs as a result of this change.[7]

Second, some committees set budgetary ceilings far below program administrators' requests, while others are so filled with program enthusiasts that they are willing to approve almost anything requested. The former are a genuine threat to bureaucrats' goals, and consequently, bureaucrats find it useful to allocate extra benefits to their members in an effort to persuade them of a program's value. The latter present no threat at all. No special allocations are required for committee members in this case, just as no special allocations are necessary when the House is filled with intense supporters on general-benefit grounds. Legislative committees are more likely to be overrun with program enthusiasts than appropriations subcommittees, but there are exceptions on each side. Some legislative committees authorize much less than bureaucrats request; others give bureaucrats almost everything they want.

Third, committees differ with respect to the types of congressmen

7. Herbert W. Stephens, "The Role of the Legislative Committee in the Appropriations Process: A Study Focused on the Armed Services Committees," *Western Political Quarterly* 24 (1971): 160.

they attract. Committees filled with congressmen whose primary goal is constituency service[8] make it easy for bureaucrats to build large coalitions, assuming, of course, that there are enough benefits to give each member a small share. Committees that attract congressmen who have a greater interest in national policy issues than in constituency service make bureaucrats' task more difficult, particularly when a committee is evenly divided over the merits of a particular program (Education and Labor is an obvious example).[9] Members of these committees are less susceptible to the enticements of local benefits than those whose primary goal is constituency services.

PARTY AND SENIORITY

The theory developed here includes no references to a congressman's party or seniority. Since this runs contrary to what others have hypothesized about the politics of geographic allocation, it is important to show why.[10]

Party could be an important consideration under two circumstances. If the president made allocational decisions himself or had substantial control over those who did *and* if he took his role as party leader so seriously that he diligently sought ways of helping his party at the polls, party would surely be an important part of any allocational theory. But presidents usually have little influence over the many thousands of allocational decisions bureaucrats make annually; and even when they can influence a few of them, they usually choose to use this influence to advance their legislative programs or other personal projects rather than their party's electoral fortunes.[11] Party could also be important if con-

8. Constituency service is one of the three basic goals that Fenno uses to analyze differences in committee operations. Richard F. Fenno, Jr., *Congressmen in Committees* (Boston: Little, Brown, 1973), p. 5.

9. Ibid., pp. 227–42.

10. See, for example, Carol F. Goss, "Military Committee Membership and Defense-Related Benefits in the House of Representatives," *Western Political Quarterly* 25 (1972): 215–33; Barry S. Rundquist, "The House Seniority System and the Distribution of Prime Military Contracts," paper presented at the American Political Science Association Meeting, 1971.

11. The one documented exception to this is Roosevelt, who, according to the evidence, allocated various types of benefits in an effort to insure his reelection in 1936. Roosevelt had the advantage of dealing with completely new agencies rather than old,

gressional parties were well organized and cohesive, with the members of one party voting together and then, in the fashion of Riker's or Buchanan and Tullock's legislators, reserving benefits for themselves. In reality, however, no expenditure programs are supported exclusively by one-party coalitions. Bureaucrats do not discriminate on the basis of party, because they are interested in building and maintaining large coalitions, which necessarily must include members of the minority party.

A slightly better case can be made for bureaucrats discriminating among committee members on the basis of party or seniority. The argument is sometimes advanced that such discrimination is rational, because majority-party members are in a better position to impose sanctions than minority-party members, and because senior committee members are in a better position than junior members. The argument is correct, but incomplete. One could also argue that the most junior members really deserve special allocations, for they have had less experience with a program, have taken fewer public positions on it, and quite possibly have established no voting histories at all on the issues. In short, they are likely to be uncommitted and, therefore, are more susceptible to the enticements of local benefits than their more senior colleagues who have repeatedly taken positions on a program. Probably the best allocational strategy is for bureaucrats not to discriminate at all on the basis of party and seniority, but rather, as long as the supply of benefits lasts, to allocate generous shares to *all* committee members. Such a strategy increases the chances of a united committee, and as previous research has shown, a united committee is less likely to be reversed on the floor than a divided one.[12]

DURATION OF ALLOCATIONS

Throughout this chapter I have been referring (at least implicitly) to what might be called *limited-duration* benefits. These are benefits allo-

established agencies, which tend to be more independent of presidential authority. See Gavin Wright, "The Political Economy of New Deal Spending: An Econometric Analysis," *The Review of Economics and Statistics* 56 (1974): 30–38.

12. Richard F. Fenno, Jr., *The Power of the Purse* (Boston: Little, Brown, 1966), pp. 460–69; John W. Kingdon, *Congressmen's Voting Decisions* (New York: Harper and Row, 1973), pp. 243–45.

cated for specific projects to be completed in relatively short periods of time—a few years at most. Grants to state and local governments for public works projects are an example. When bureaucrats allocate shares of these benefits, the recipients do not acquire preferential rights to additional benefits in subsequent years. These can be contrasted with *semipermanent* benefits for which recipients *do* expect the flow of benefits to continue for many years. The most obvious examples are federal facilities such as military installations, veterans hospitals, government offices, and laboratories. Once federal facilities have been constructed, everyone expects that annual allocations will be made to keep them open. Other examples are grants designed to help local governments meet operating expenses—for example, educational assistance to "federally impacted school districts."

Bureaucrats who administer programs with semipermanent benefits face a very different strategic situation from that associated with limited-duration benefits. In the first place, during any given year (except the first) they can make only marginal changes in the geographic distribution of benefits. Conversely, limited-duration benefits can be turned on and off at will and used selectively to reward or punish individual congressmen. Since bureaucrats cannot quickly shift the distribution of semipermanent benefits, they are unable to respond quickly to important changes in Congress. They cannot, for example, move military installations from the districts of those who no longer serve on the House Armed Services Committee to the districts of those who have just joined. Of course, in the long run they can, if they wish, make appropriate adjustments. During periods of retrenchment they can close installations that no longer serve their political purposes, and during periods of expansion they can select sites according to whatever political criteria seem appropriate.

The situation is also different from the congressman's point of view. Beneficiaries of programs that dispense semipermanent benefits quickly become accustomed to a continuous flow of funds and would regard discontinuance as a punishment. Consequently, whenever a congressman's district receives a significant share of such benefits, he is almost forced to become a supporter of the program, because the beneficiaries might interpret any opposition as a threat either to the program as a whole or to their share of benefits. A congressman must support a program not because he receives rewards for its continuance but rather because he fears the effects of its discontinuance. This can be contrasted with programs that dispense limited-duration benefits. Since beneficiaries of these programs ordinarily do not develop firm expectations about future allocations, program termination is more a disappointment than a punishment. Congressmen are consequently in a better position, because they are rewarded for procuring shares of benefits but not necessarily penalized for failing to obtain shares.

5: MEASURING INFLUENCE

The exchange relationships discussed in the previous chapters are composed of two reciprocal influence relations. On the one hand, congressmen are said to influence bureaucrats' decisions on matters of geographic allocation, while on the other, bureaucrats are said to influence congressmen's decisions on how to vote, on whether or not to become coalition leaders, and on how to behave as committee members. The first of these influence relations is the principal subject of this book and, from this point on, is my exclusive concern.

DEFINING INFLUENCE

Few concepts in political science are more fundamentally important than the concept of influence (or power),[1] and few have provoked greater debate as to how they should be defined. The problem with the concept of influence is that various definitions are commonly used, which hinders communication among those who, because they use identical vocabulary, sometimes believe that they are referring to the same phenomenon.

Here I adopt Nagel's definition of influence, which, in my opinion, will eventually prove superior to previous definitions both for the development of theory and for empirical applications. As Nagel has demonstrated, most recent writers define influence as a causal relation between individuals in which both cause and effect must be the *behavior* of these individuals.[2] Dahl's definition is a well-known example: "A

1. In this work *power* and *influence* are considered to be synonymous. I prefer the word *influence* because it has a convenient verb form.

2. Jack H. Nagel, *The Descriptive Analysis of Power* (New Haven: Yale University Press, 1975), pp. 9–22.

influences B to the extent that he gets B to do something that B would not otherwise do."[3] But definitions of this type exclude causal relations based on anticipated reactions. They consider an occurrence such as B shaping his behavior to conform with what he believes are A's preferences (without A making any conscious effort to affect B's behavior) to be a phenomenon distinctly different from influence. Nagel argues convincingly that there is no fundamental difference between the traditional concept of influence and the rule of anticipated reactions and offers a new definition that incorporates the two. Influence is defined as "a causal relation between the *preferences* of an actor regarding an outcome and the outcome itself."[4] In his definition, *actor* refers to an individual, group, or organization, while *outcome* must be a "variable indicating the state of another social entity—the behavior, beliefs, attitudes, or policies of a second actor."[5]

According to this definition, a congressman is regarded as influential whenever bureaucrats' allocational decisions reflect in some way the congressman's preferences regarding allocation. Two possible causal links connect congressmen's preferences and bureaucrats' decisions. First is the link implied by the traditional definition of influence: congressman A's preferences regarding allocation initially affect his own behavior (e.g., he issues conditional threats or promises), and his behavior in turn affects bureaucrat B's allocational decisions. Second is the link implied by the rule of anticipated reactions: congressman A's preferences regarding allocation affect bureaucrat B's expectation about how A might react to various alternative allocational decisions, and this expectation in turn affects B's actual decisions. In this work I do not attempt to differentiate between the two causal links—i.e., between influence resulting from a congressman's actual behavior and influence resulting from anticipation of his possible future behavior. My goal, in other words, is to identify and measure influence relations rather than to distinguish among various possible types of relations.

3. Robert A. Dahl, *Modern Political Analysis* (Englewood Cliffs, N.J.: Prentice-Hall, 1963), p. 40. Note, however, that Dahl has recently abandoned this definition for one very similar to Nagel's. See his 3d edition, 1976, pp. 29–32.
4. Nagel, *The Descriptive Analysis of Power*, p. 29.
5. Ibid.

MEASURING INFLUENCE

If influence is defined as a causal relation between congressmen's preferences and bureaucrats' decisions, then measuring influence requires information about congressmen's preferences regarding allocational decisions, information about what allocational decisions are actually made, and a method for estimating the effects of the former on the latter.

In this work I have substituted an *assumption* about congressmen's allocational preferences for direct evidence about each congressman's complete preference ordering regarding all available allocational alternatives. The assumption, developed and defended in chapter 2, is that each congressman prefers that more benefits be allocated to his district. In addition, at least during the final stage of the allocational process (though not during the agenda-setting stage), I have assumed that the intensities of these preferences are approximately equal for all congressmen with respect to a particular type of benefit. There are, of course, occasions in which some congressmen are *not* eager to acquire particular types of benefits,[6] and there are occasions in which the intensities of congressmen's preferences are unequal. However, such occasions occur infrequently and usually involve a small fraction of all congressmen. Nevertheless, whenever exceptions such as these do arise, my estimates of congressional influence will be slightly biased.[7]

Two types of information are necessary for a careful assessment of congressional influence in the process of bureaucratic choice. First, one needs precise information about the agenda of alternatives from which bureaucrats select localities for funding. An agenda represents the total range of alternative allocational schemes available to bureaucrats; localities not included on the agenda can neither be rewarded nor punished by subsequent bureaucratic action. Second, one needs to know the outcome of the decision-making process: information about which of the alternatives were selected for funding and which were rejected or deferred.

6. For specific instances, see John A. Ferejohn, *Pork Barrel Politics* (Stanford: Stanford University Press, 1974), pp. 19–20, 51.
7. My reasons for analyzing congressional influence by focusing on allocational decisions rather than on some other bureaucratic decisions should now be clear. For no other decisions could one make such detailed assumptions about congressmen's preferences.

A congressman should be regarded as influential if the alternatives he most prefers (allocations to his own district) prevail in competition against those he least prefers *and* if these favorable allocational decisions are unexplainable in terms of either objective criteria or other simple bureaucratic decision rules. Unfortunately, it is nearly impossible to assess the influence of individual congressmen over specific allocational decisions, for such a task would require one to know precisely which decisions bureaucrats would make in the absence of any congressional influence. In other words, one would have to know which objective criteria bureaucrats employed to evaluate alternatives, how they ranked each alternative according to these criteria, and what decision rule they used to combine these rank orderings into a single preference ordering. Although it is virtually impossible to assess the influence of individual congressmen, it is possible to make judgments about whether certain broad classes of congressmen (e.g., members of particular committees or program supporters) were more influential than other classes of congressmen (e.g., members of other committees or opponents). Such judgments merely require a few reasonable assumptions about the way in which various objective conditions are distributed among alternatives.

SIMPLE MODEL

For the following discussion, the term *objective criteria* refers to the standards a bureaucrat would employ if he were motivated solely by a desire to further his own conception of the public interest rather than by goals of budgetary security or budgetary growth. Such standards might include criteria of efficiency, need, or equality. The term *political criteria* refers to the standards he would employ if budgetary security and growth were his only goals. These criteria include congressmen's committee assignments and general-benefit preferences.

The simplest assumption one can make in order to assess congressional influence is that all these objective criteria are distributed independently of political criteria. Such an assumption allows one to ignore the effects of objective criteria and concentrate on the effects of political factors, for whenever two sets of variables are uncorrelated, one can make unbiased estimates of the effects of each variable in the first set without even considering the effects of the second set. Of course, one can never be certain that objective criteria are uncorrelated with political criteria without actually collecting the appropriate data and calculating the correlation matrix. But there are occasions when one has no reason to suspect any correlation between the two sets of variables.

Whenever it does seem reasonable to assume that the two sets of criteria are uncorrelated, assessing congressional influence is relatively straightforward. If, for example, one wishes to test the hypothesis that members of a particular committee are more influential than nonmembers, one merely compares the frequency with which bureaucrats acted favorably on applications from committee members' districts with the frequency with which they acted favorably on applications from other congressmen's districts. If the two are equal, there is no support for the hypothesis; but if the former is greater than the latter, there may be some support for it. Furthermore, the difference between the two frequencies can be used as a measure of the magnitude of committee members' influence.

However appealing this method for assessing influence may seem, it can be used to study the effects of only one or two variables at a time (unless the number of cases is very large indeed). Although one can study as many variables as one wants by examining one or two at a time, the resulting estimates of influence will be biased whenever the political variables are themselves intercorrelated (as they commonly are). Clearly, both a multivariate model and a means for estimating it are required to handle this situation and the situation in which objective and political criteria are intercorrelated.

MULTIVARIATE MODEL

I shall suppose that bureaucrats select applications for funding in three steps: they evaluate each competing application according to a set of political and objective criteria; on the basis of these evaluations they rank order all applications on some scale of attractiveness; and they select applications for funding, beginning with the most attractive applications and moving down the scale until they have committed their entire budgets. According to this scheme, no single variable is determinative. Instead, each merely affects the *probability* of an application being accepted by first affecting its rank on the scale of attractiveness. Theory suggests how each political variable should affect the probability of acceptance (positively, negatively, or not at all), and subsequent discussions in the empirical chapters will suggest how each objective variable should affect this probability. But theory does not suggest how bureaucrats might *weight* these various political and objective criteria when evaluating applications. This question is better answered with empirical evidence.

When bureaucrats consider applications for a particular type of benefit they are assumed to evaluate all applications according to the same criteria and with the same weighting scheme.[8] The probability of an application being selected is considered to be a linear function of certain political variables, certain objective variables, and a normally distributed disturbance term. Let P_i represent the probability that the ith application will be selected, X_{ij} represent the value of the jth variable for the ith application, B_j represent the weight of the jth variable, and u_i represent the disturbance term for the ith application. Then, by assumption,

$$P_i = B_0 + \sum_j B_j X_{ij} + u_i, \text{ for all i,}$$

where u_i is distributed normally and has a mean of zero, a constant variance across all observations, and a covariance of zero for any pair of observations.

Estimating the coefficients (B's) associated with each political variable in the model allows one to test various hypotheses about congressional influence. In addition, these coefficients can serve as measures of the *magnitude* of congressmen's influence over bureaucrats' decisions. Estimating coefficients for a model of this type is somewhat more difficult than estimating coefficients for a standard linear model. For various reasons, multiple regression is an inappropriate method. First, multiple regression permits no restrictions on the range of the dependent variable, whereas the dependent variable in this model (a probability) is inherently limited to the closed interval from zero to one. Second, although the underlying dependent variable is appropriately conceptualized at the interval level, it is observed only as a dichotomous

---

8. Other bureaucrats administering other programs may, of course, adopt completely different criteria and weighting schemes.

variable.[9] The only information available for estimating the model is whether or not an application was eventually selected or rejected.

PROBIT ANALYSIS

Probit analysis is an appropriate method for estimating the model. The method was originally developed in biology to estimate the potency of drugs (and poisons) by observing whether small animals to which they had been administered either lived or died. The observed variable was dichotomous, but the underlying variable clearly was not.[10] Econometricians have since extended the probit model to handle multivariate analysis; it has been used, for example, to estimate certain types of consumer behavior (e.g., the decision to buy or not to buy a car).[11] Recently a few political scientists have employed it to estimate multivariate models of political behavior—for example, the committee assignment process in Congress and American voting behavior.[12]

Although it is not necessary for the reader to understand precisely how probit coefficients are estimated[13] (any more than one must be skilled in matrix algebra to interpret regression coefficients), a familiarity with the theoretical foundation of the probit model is important. The probit model assumes that the relationship between a set of independent

9. Using regression methods to estimate a model such as this can yield misleading results because the classical assumption of homoscedasticity (the assumption of a constant variance for the disturbance terms of all observations) is necessarily violated whenever the dependent variable is dichotomous. See Arthur S. Goldberger, *Econometric Theory* (New York: Wiley, 1964), p. 249.

10. See D. J. Finney, *Probit Analysis*, 3rd ed. (Cambridge: Cambridge University Press, 1971).

11. See James Tobin, "The Application of Multivariate Probit Analysis to Economic Survey Data," Cowles Foundation Discussion Paper, number 1 (1955), also reprinted in James Tobin, *Essays in Economics*, vol. 2 (Amsterdam: North-Holland Publishing, 1975), pp. 447–66.

12. For examples, see Christopher H. Achen and John S. Stolarek, "The Resolution of Congressional Committee Assignment Contests," paper delivered at the 1974 Annual Meeting of the American Political Science Association; Gerald H. Kramer, "The Effects of Precinct-Level Canvassing on Voter Behavior," *Public Opinion Quarterly* 34 (1970): 560–72; and Orley Ashenfelter and Stanley Kelley, Jr., "Determinants of Participation in Presidential Elections," *Journal of Law and Economics* 18 (December 1975): 695–733.

13. Two discussions of how they are estimated using maximum liklihood methods are James Tobin, "The Application of Multivariate Probit Analysis . . . " and Arthur S. Goldberger, *Econometric Theory*, pp. 248–55.

variables and the probability of an event occurring (the dependent variable) can best be represented by a nonlinear S-shaped function rather than by a linear function, as is common for the regression model. The particular S-shaped function used is the cumulative standard normal distribution. (This does not reflect a conscious choice, but rather follows logically from an assumption made about the distribution of certain attributes among observations.)[14] Two important properties of this distribution can be illustrated with a graph of the relationship between a single independent variable and the probability of an event occurring (figure 5.1). First, the probability of any event taking place is, as it should be, constrained to the interval from zero to one, no matter what value the independent variable might take. Second, the distribution is flatter at the tails than in the middle, which reflects that it is considerably more difficult to increase the probability of an event's occurrence from .91 to .99 than it is to increase it from .51 to .59.

Hypothesis testing is possible with probit analysis because, like its cousin, regression analysis, it allows one to estimate both a variable's coefficient and its standard error. For many readers a discussion of the proper role of significance tests in social science research is unnecessary. Some comment, however, does seem appropriate, particularly because of the position taken by some authors who have attempted to test hypotheses about geographic allocation. Three authors (Ferejohn, Strom, and Ritt) have argued that significance tests are unnecessary when one examines an entire statistical universe rather than a sample from a larger population.[15] In fact, most analyses of geographic allocation have been conducted without significance tests.[16] Their position is totally without foundation. The value of significance tests is unrelated to how much of the available evidence one chooses to examine. The principal function of significance tests is to inform one of the likelihood

14. See S. M. Goldfeld and R. E. Quandt, *Nonlinear Methods in Econometrics* (Amsterdam: North-Holland Publishing, 1972), pp. 128–29.

15. John A. Ferejohn, *Pork Barrel Politics* (Stanford: Stanford University Press, 1974), p. 139; Gerald S. Strom, "Congressional Policy Making: A Test of a Theory," *Journal of Politics* 37 (1975): 723; and Leonard G. Ritt, "Committee Position, Seniority, and the Distribution of Government Expenditures," *Public Policy* 24 (1976): 469.

16. In addition to Ferejohn and Strom, see Carol F. Goss, "Military Committee Membership and Defense-Related Benefits in the House of Representatives," *Western Political Quarterly* 25 (1972): 215–33, and Charles R. Plott, "Some Organizational Influences on Urban Renewal Decisions," *American Economic Review* 58 (1968): 306–21.

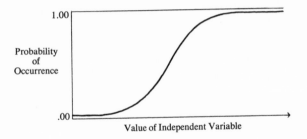

Figure 5.1. Sample Probit Function

that a particular relationship might have arisen purely by chance rather than according to the hypothesized causal mechanism. Sampling error is merely *one* of the ways in which a relationship might have arisen because of chance; there are many more. Such a relationship could be the result of measurement error; it could be a consequence of the exclusion from the model of relevant variables; or it could reflect some truly random phenomenon.[17] Given this, it is difficult to imagine why one would want to protect oneself from sampling error but not from these other, equally serious sources of error.

Although tests of statistical significance are enormously valuable for the proper interpretation of evidence, it is equally important that their function not be elevated to a position in which some arbitrary significance level separates confirmed hypotheses from unconfirmed hypotheses. There is nothing sacred about the .05 level or the .01 level, and there is certainly no reason to toss aside an hypothesis merely because it fails by a small margin to be confirmed at one of these levels.[18]

ALTERNATIVE APPROACHES

This chapter could have been terminated at this point, for I have finished developing the basic methodology necessary for testing the

17. See J. Johnston, *Econometric Methods*, 2d ed. (New York: McGraw-Hill, 1972), pp. 8–13.
18. For an excellent discussion of significance testing, see Edward R. Tufte, "Improving Data Analysis in Political Science," *World Politics* 21 (1969): 641–54.

theory's validity. Instead, I have chosen to append a critical analysis of the approach others have used to measure congressional influence over allocational decisions, an approach very different from my own. Considerable space is devoted to this analysis because I believe that the methods used are completely inadequate either for the task of testing hypotheses about congressional influence or for the more difficult task of measuring influence.

Seven studies have attempted to test various hypotheses about committee members' influence in the geographic allocation of expenditures. There are studies by Ferejohn on rivers and harbors projects,[19] Goss on military employment,[20] Rundquist on military contracts,[21] Strom on waste treatment plants,[22] Plott on urban renewal projects,[23] Ray on expenditures by seven major government departments,[24] and Ritt on expenditures by six major departments.[25] For illustrative purposes, I focus attention on two of these studies (Ferejohn and Goss), though most of the same methodological criticisms are equally appropriate for the others. In appendix A I discuss briefly the other studies.

Ferejohn's book analyzes the politics of rivers and harbors legislation from 1947 to 1968. The chapters of interest here are chapters 8 through 10, which test various hypotheses about the effects of committee mem-

19. John A. Ferejohn, *Pork Barrel Politics* (Stanford: Stanford University Press, 1974).

20. Carol F. Goss, "Congress and Defense Policy: Strategies and Patterns of Committee Influence" (Ph.D. dissertation, University of Arizona, 1971), with portions of the dissertation published as "Military Committee Membership and Defense Related Benefits in the House of Representatives," *Western Political Quarterly* 25 (1972): 215–33.

21. Barry S. Rundquist, "Congressional Influence on the Distribution of Prime Military Contracts" (Ph.D. dissertation, Stanford University, 1973).

22. Gerald S. Strom, "Congressional Policy-Making and the Federal Waste Treatment Construction Grant Program" (Ph.D. dissertation, University of Illinois, 1973), with excerpts published as "Congressional Policy Making: A Test of a Theory," *Journal of Politics* 37 (1975): 711–35.

23. Charles R. Plott, "Influences of Decision Processes on Urban Renewal" (Ph.D. dissertation, University of Virginia, 1966), with portions published as "Some Organizational Influences on Urban Renewal Decisions," *American Economic Review* 58 (May 1968): pp. 306–21.

24. Bruce A. Ray, "Congressional Committees and the Geographic Distribution of Federal Spending," paper delivered at the 1976 Annual Meeting of the Midwest Political Science Association, and "Investigating the Myth of Congressional Influence: The Geographic Distribution of Federal Spending," paper delivered at the 1976 Annual Meeting of the American Political Science Association.

25. Leonard G. Ritt, "Committee Position, Seniority, and the Distribution of Government Expenditures," *Public Policy* 24 (1976): 463–89.

bership and such intracommittee institutions as seniority, party, and subcommittee membership on the distribution of new rivers and harbors projects. Ferejohn attempts to explain the geographic distribution of two dependent variables in 1967: the number of new projects recommended for funding by the Bureau of the Budget (about fifty-two in 1967, by my count) and the number of new projects added to the budget by the House (sixty-three, by his count).[26] He uses the state as his basic analytic unit and asks whether states that enjoyed representation on certain committees received more budgeted new starts or House-initiated new starts than states without such representation.

Actually, Ferejohn is interested in testing for the effects of an immense number of variables (twenty independent variables and one control variable, by my count). He asks, for example, whether states represented on the House Public Works Committee by high-seniority Democrats do better than states represented on the same committee by high-seniority Republicans. (He finds the reverse to be true.)[27] He employs multiple regression analysis to assess the effects of each of twenty variables, but uses the peculiar technique of estimating equations by including only two or three variables at a time, a technique that requires that no less than twenty-one equations be estimated for the two dependent variables. In general, Ferejohn finds support for his hypotheses about the importance of membership on the House Public Works and House Appropriations Committees. He also finds some support for his hypotheses about seniority, party, and subcommittee membership, but is surprised to find instances in which (according to his tests) the relationships are just the opposite of what he had predicted.[28]

Goss's study examines whether members of various House military committees are better able to obtain military employment for their districts than nonmembers. Although her suppositions are not always expressed in hypothesis form, it is clear that she is testing hypotheses about committee influence, hypotheses very similar to those examined by Ferejohn.[29] Goss is interested in three dependent variables: military personnel, civilians employed at Defense Department installations, and

26. Ferejohn, *Pork Barrel Politics*, p. 133.
27. Ibid., p. 141.
28. Ibid., pp. 139, 145, 177.
29. Goss, "Congress and Defense Policy," pp. xi, 22; and Goss, "Military Committee Membership," pp. 216, 231–32.

civilians engaged in defense work in the private sector. Her independent variables are representation on the House Armed Services Committee, representation on one of the two military subcommittees of the House Appropriations Committee, party, and committee seniority. She uses the congressional district as her basic unit of analysis and tests hypotheses by comparing the mean military employment in districts of one type (e.g., committee members) with the mean military employment in all districts in 1968.

Goss uncovered important relationships involving both military personnel and civilian employment at Defense Department installations but no interesting relationships involving defense work in private plants. She discovered, for example, that members of the House Armed Services Committee had an average of 14,030 jobs at military installations in their districts as compared with the House average of 6,041, and thus concluded that committee members were more influential than nonmembers.[30] Her hypotheses about the advantages of majority-party representation were generally supported, while her seniority hypothesis was refuted, with junior committee members enjoying *higher* military employment than more senior members.[31]

UNIT OF ANALYSIS

The principal problem with these two studies (as well as the five discussed in the appendix) is that the basic unit of analysis is the constituency rather than the decision. Now there is nothing inherently wrong with constituency as an analytic unit. It does, however, have serious limitations. Its main disadvantage when compared with the decision as an analytic unit is that one must make all the assumptions discussed earlier in the chapter *plus* some additional ones. Frequently these additional assumptions are untenable.

Ferejohn's study provides a good place to begin, for his problems stem not only from his decision to employ constituency as an analytic unit but also from his selection of state rather than congressional district as the proper constituency for analysis. It appears that Ferejohn himself

30. Goss, "Military Committee Membership," p. 219.
31. Ibid., p. 224.

was unsure as to whether state or district was the better selection, for he reveals that he also estimated his model for district-level data. However, as he puts it, "all of the relationships were of inconsequential size and frequently went in the 'wrong' direction."[32] One might wonder why data at the state level provide such strong support for the hypotheses while data from the district level provide absolutely no support for them. Ferejohn replies that these differences "suggest the importance of the state delegation as an institution for mediating exchange among certain policy areas."[33] In other words, congressmen from the same state work together to acquire benefits for each other with, for example, a state's representative on the Public Works Committee looking after the interests of every district in the state rather than just his own district's interest. Of course, Ferejohn may be correct, and the remarkable differences between his state-level and district-level analyses may merely reflect the importance of state delegation. However, the question cannot be answered simply by juggling the analytic unit.[34] One tests hypotheses about the importance of state delegation by introducing an appropriate set of variables into a district-level model, variables such as whether or not a district was represented on particular committees by a member of its own state delegation. In fact, a district-level model with two sets of variables (one for a district's direct representation on various committees and the other for its indirect representation by members of its state delegation) would allow one not only to test the state delegation hypothesis but also to determine if committee members work as hard for the interests of their state delegation as they do for their own districts.

Selecting states as analytic units has, at a minimum, resulted in biased estimates of congressional influence; conceivably it could have created the illusion of disproportionate influence where none exists. States differ enormously in population, and quite apart from any theories of congressional influence, one expects populous states to receive more shares of benefits than less populous states (unless, for some reason, a program's intended beneficiaries are concentrated in small

32. Ferejohn, *Pork Barrel Politics*, p. 68.
33. Ibid., p. 68.
34. Any more than one tests the adequacy of psychological and sociological theories of voting behavior by testing the former with data on individuals and the latter with data on groups. One tests alternative hypotheses by introducing new independent variables, not by altering the analytic unit.

states—e.g., Indians). It is clear that Ferejohn's two dependent variables are highly correlated with state population. To illustrate, in 1967 twenty-two states with a mean population of 1,687,000 received no House-initiated new starts, while each of sixteen states with a mean population of 3,595,000 received a single new start, six states with a mean population of 5,641,000 received two new starts, and six states with a mean population of 12,329,000 received between three and seven new starts each. Eight of the ten largest states (80 percent) received two or more such starts, whereas only *four* of the remaining forty states (10 percent) received that many.[35] In addition, almost all of Ferejohn's independent variables are highly correlated with state population. Populous states are more likely than small states to have at least one congressman on any given committee, and the same holds true for representation on a committee by a senior member, by a majority-party member, or by a member from almost any other class of congressmen. That both independent and dependent variables are correlated with state population means that one's estimates of the effects of the former on the latter will be biased unless a control is instituted for state population. It is conceivable that Ferejohn's estimates of congressional influence reflect nothing more than the effects of state population on both sets of variables.

The case has been made for using the district rather than the state as an analytic unit when testing hypotheses about congressional influence. An even stronger case can be made for using the decision as an analytic unit, for it avoids many of the problems inherent in any constituency-oriented approach.

CAUSAL DIRECTION

A constituency-oriented approach allows one to determine whether committee membership is associated with constituency benefits; unfor-

35. Actually my evidence does not correspond exactly to that used by Ferejohn. He found sixty-three House-initiated new starts, while I found only fifty-three in the documents I examined. However, the relationship between population and new starts would hold no matter how the remaining ten projects happened to be distributed among states. The relationship between population and budgeted new starts is as strong as the one reported in the text for House-initiated starts.

tunately, it does not allow one to determine which is the cause and which the effect. Such an association between committee membership and benefits could arise as a consequence of three alternative (though not mutually exclusive) causal mechanisms. First, it may reflect differences in the attractiveness of committees. Congressmen generally seek membership on those committees that handle programs of direct interest to their constituencies. Second, it may reflect aspects of the committee assignment process. Those who decide which congressmen should sit on which committees may prefer to assign congressmen to committees handling programs related to their districts' needs because such assignments are thought to be electorally useful. Third, it may be a consequence of congressional influence over the allocation of benefits.

As long as one employs constituency as an analytic unit, it is impossible to test individually the three hypotheses or to disentangle their effects. This is most obvious in Goss's study of military employment. That *districts* represented on House Armed Services enjoyed above-average levels of military employment says nothing about congressmen's *decisions* to seek seats on the committee; it says nothing about the committee on committees' *decisions* about who should receive these seats; and it says nothing about bureaucrats' allocational *decisions*. Her evidence most certainly supports at least one of the three hypotheses, but which one is unclear. Since geographic allocations of military employment tend to be relatively stable from year to year (because of large investment costs), a district's present level of employment is usually a function of both recent bureaucratic decisions, which the incumbent congressman could have affected, and past decisions for which he could not possibly be responsible.

The same problem is inherent in Ferejohn's research design, though less obvious. An alternative explanation for his finding that constituencies represented on the House Public Works Committee receive a disproportionate number of rivers and harbors projects rests on the assumption that constituencies differ in terms of their demand for projects. As a consequence, congressmen from districts with a high demand may be more likely than others to seek and gain membership on the committee.[36] A second consequence is that local groups from these constituen-

36. This inference is supported by James T. Murphy's article on the Public Works Committee. See "Political Parties and the Porkbarrel: Party Conflict and Cooperation in House Public Works Committee Decision Making," *American Political Science Review* 68 (1974): 171–72.

cies may apply for more projects and push harder for their funding. If all this is true, the association between benefits and committee member- ship would reflect the committee recruitment process rather than an allocational system in which some congressmen had disproportionate influence.

The solution to these problems is to model more carefully the actual processes of committee recruitment, committee assignment, and bene- fit allocation, and then to collect and analyze the appropriate data. The attractiveness hypothesis can easily be tested if one knows precisely which committee assignments individual congressmen request; one can then determine if congressmen tend to request seats on committees with jurisdiction over programs that directly benefit their districts. A recent study that used such evidence found strong support for the hypothesis, at least for Democratic assignments to Agriculture, Armed Services, Banking and Currency, Education and Labor, and Interior.[37] The committee-assignment hypothesis can be tested by examining whether the probability of a congressman receiving his requested committee depends in any way on his district's potential or actual demand for benefits. Such a test requires evidence about which assignments con- gressmen request and which they actually receive. A recent study by Achen and Stolarek using evidence of this type concludes that the Democratic committee on committees does, at least for some commit- tees, favor congressmen coming from districts with above-average de- mand for the benefits handled by those committees.[38] Finally, as dis- cussed earlier in this chapter, the allocational hypothesis can be tested by examining actual decisions about which of the competing requests for benefits have been granted. In sum, one avoids the causal direction problem by modeling carefully the three decision-making processes, which inevitably leads to the decision as the basic unit of analysis.

AGENDA SETTING AND CHOICE

Even if there were no political influence in the allocational process, one would not expect most benefits to be distributed equally among

37. David W. Rohde and Kenneth A. Shepsle, "Democratic Committee Assignments in the House of Representatives," *American Political Science Review* 67 (1973): 889–905.

38. Christopher H. Achen and John S. Stolarek, "The Resolution of Congressional Committee Assignment Contests," paper delivered at the 1974 Annual Meeting of the American Political Science Association.

constituencies. Areas differ in their demand for benefits, in their pro-
pensities for turning to the federal government for assistance, and in the
quality of the applications they submit. Previous studies have either
ignored such factors or introduced a single control variable to represent
the amount a constituency might receive in the absence of political
influence. Ferejohn, for example, selects as a measure of a state's *demand* for benefits the *actual* amount spent for rivers and harbors projects during the previous year.[39] The control variables used in these
studies have not, in my opinion, been very successful, for they are only
tenuously connected to the factors that need to be controlled. The
solution is not to create better control variables, but rather to recognize
that two separate processes need to be modeled: agenda setting and
choice. Previous studies have treated the two processes as one, which of
course is unavoidable as long as one retains constituency as the basic
analytic unit.

Agenda setting is ordinarily outside the range of congressmen's interests or influence. Most agenda are set by local initiative when either
governmental or nongovernmental organizations submit applications
for benefits. As such, agenda reflect not only the underlying demand for
benefits but also the propensity of organizations to request federal assistance. Some congressmen may, in their entrepreneurial role, affect
agenda by encouraging local groups to apply for benefits; but such
influence over constituents' behavior is unrelated to the question of
congressional influence over allocational decisions.

Choice is the stage at which one expects some congressmen might
have disproportionate influence over decisions. One should model the
process of choice as it actually occurs, with decision makers facing an
agenda of alternatives from which they select applications for funding
according to various objective and political criteria. Since one begins
with an agenda of alternatives, one can study the choice process exclusively, while demand and the propensity to request benefits are, in
effect, held constant, for such factors are important only at the agenda-
setting stage. By separating the two processes for study, one can insure
that whatever relationships emerge between committee membership

39. It is a curious choice. At one point Ferejohn argues that rivers and harbors expenditures are inappropriate for use as a dependent variable because they fluctuate widely
from year to year (p. 132). But the same fluctuations should make expenditures equally
inappropriate for use as a control variable.

and allocational decisions reflect committee members' influence rather than differences in constituency demand. Moreover, with a decision-making approach, one can introduce variables to represent applications' merit; such variables cannot be included with the constituency-benefits approach, because merit is an attribute of applications not constituencies.[40]

The differentiation between agenda setting and choice is equally important for those programs that do not require local applications. Military employment is an obvious example. Pentagon officials who allocate such employment do not begin each year with a clean slate. Instead, they begin with an existing distribution of employment (in effect, their agenda of alternatives); in any given year they can make only marginal changes in this distribution either by closing existing installations, reallocating employment among installations, or building new ones.[41] Once again, by separating the agenda-setting and choice processes, one can measure influence over allocational decisions without the confounding effects of differing initial distributions of employment.

EVIDENCE AND METHODS

Regardless of whether one constructs a model with constituency or decision as the basic analytic unit, good multivariate methods are required to estimate it. Bivariate methods are justifiable only if the hypothesized independent variables are uncorrelated with each other. Most of the previous studies either fail to employ multivariate methods or use them incorrectly. I have already commented on the absence of significance tests in most of these studies; in fact, the methodological problems go much deeper.

Ferejohn's methods are particularly interesting. He uses multiple regression to assess the independent effects of no less than twenty var-

40. Ferejohn writes that both the cost-benefit ratio and the type of project (flood control, navigation, etc.) are important determinants of selection (pp. 145–46). However, he is unable to include such variables in his constituency-oriented model.
41. Actually, the initial distribution of employment constitutes an agenda only for closing and reallocation decisions but not for opening decisions. Such distinctions are discussed in chapter 6.

iables on his two dependent variables. However, instead of estimating two equations with twenty variables each, he estimates twenty-one separate equations, each with only two or three independent variables. The approach would be justifiable if the independent variables were uncorrelated; but as I have demonstrated previously, all tend to be highly intercorrelated with state population and therefore with each other. In fact, Ferejohn's correlations are so amazingly high that they must, in large part, be a reflection of state population. For example, he finds that a *single* variable (the number of members a state had on the House Appropriations Committee in 1966) explains 57 percent of the variance in House-initiated new starts in 1967.[42] It is difficult to think of *any* single-variable explanations in all of social science which are as successful! Furthermore, no matter which variables Ferejohn happens to throw into his equations, he explains about the same proportion of variance (between 57 and 72 percent for House-initiated new starts and between 23 and 36 percent for budgeted new starts). This is further evidence that his various independent variables are measuring essentially the same thing.

The *only* way to assess the independent effects of twenty variables is to include all in the same equation (with, of course, a control for state population). Unfortunately, Ferejohn has insufficient evidence to estimate an equation this large. Not only is his "sample" very small (n=50), but his dependent variables lack much variation to explain (e.g., sixty-three House-initiated new starts are distributed among fifty states as follows: twenty-two states had none, sixteen had one, six had two, and six had between three and seven). In short, he has more interesting questions than he has evidence with which to answer them.

This is a general problem in these studies. The capacity of the authors to generate interesting questions far exceeds their capacity to collect sufficient evidence to answer them. However interesting it might be to determine the relative influence of every imaginable small group of congressmen (e.g., senior Republicans on a small subcommittee), the task is virtually impossible given the quantity of evidence available. Strom's study provides an extreme but illustrative example. At one point he attempts to determine if senior Republicans on the Public Works Committee during the Eighty-ninth Congress are more influential than

42. Ferejohn, *Pork Barrel Politics*, p. 170.

junior Republicans; unfortunately, his comparison involves only *three* committee members—one senior Republican and two junior Republicans![43] Significance tests would help. The lesson is this: no matter how powerful one's statistical methods, only limited information can be extracted from small quantities of data.

43. Strom, "Congressional Policy Making: A Test of a Theory," p. 730.

PART TWO
THE THEORY APPLIED

6: MILITARY EMPLOYMENT

The conventional wisdom about Congress, at least as expressed by political journalists, is that some congressmen have used their positions in Congress to acquire substantial shares of military benefits for their constituencies.[1] The late Mendel Rivers (D., S.C.), former chairman of the House Armed Services Committee, is everyone's favorite example. Congressmen used to joke that if Rivers placed any more military installations in his district the whole thing would sink. Surprisingly, there has never been a serious attempt to determine just how influential Rivers was over allocational decisions.[2] More important, there are no studies designed to determine whether his supposed influence was the exception or the rule for congressmen in similar positions. In this chapter I attempt to determine if, in fact, certain classes of congressmen have disproportionate influence over bureaucrats' decisions about the geographic allocation of military employment. At the end of the chapter I examine the case of Mendel Rivers's district.

The principal military benefit sought by congressmen is assumed to be military employment. Such employment, even at a small installation, can pump millions of federal dollars into a local economy every year. For the most part, decisions about the geographic allocation of military employment are bureaucratic decisions. Subject to the availability of adequate facilities, Pentagon officials are free to transfer military employees from installation to installation, and even to close installations by withdrawing all employees. But facilities are not always

1. See, for example, Seymour Hersh, "The Military Committees," *Washington Monthly* 1 (1969): 84–92; and Michael Barone, Grant Ujifusa, and Douglas Matthews, *The Almanac of American Politics* (Boston: Gambit, 1972), pp. 161, 167, 423, 738, 801, 815.

2. There are studies that have catalogued the vast military spending in Rivers's district. The implication is that Rivers was responsible for it all. See, for example, Drew Pearson and Jack Anderson, *The Case Against Congress* (New York: Simon and Schuster, 1968), pp. 264–73.

adequate to accommodate military needs. Changing missions may require the construction of new installations or the expansion of existing ones. Although Pentagon officials also control much of the decision making associated with military construction, Congress also plays a role (chapter 1). The congressional role, however, is largely one of reviewing bureaucratic decisions and either accepting or rejecting them. Thus, decisions about the allocation of military employment are principally bureaucratic decisions, whether they involve employment directly or concern the location of installations.

ALLOCATIONAL STRATEGIES

What allocational strategies should bureaucrats adopt for the case of military employment? The strategies bureaucrats choose, it will be recalled, depend in part on the distribution of general-benefit preferences among congressmen. For defense spending this distribution has been one of consensus throughout the period 1952 to 1974. Both in Congress and in society at large there has been substantial agreement on the desirability of maintaining a large defense establishment.[3] There have, of course, been conflicts over specific defense issues, for example, Vietnam, ABM, or the B-1 bomber. But never has more than a small fraction of the population (and a similarly small fraction of congressmen) advocated deep cuts in the defense budget.[4] Even the congressmen most antagonistic towards the defense establishment during the last days of the Vietnam War were advocating cuts of less than 10 percent. In fact, although conflict over the defense budget has been relatively intense during the past decade, the *range* of conflict has always been small, increases and decreases of only a few percent. Never has there been conflict over the *existence* of a large defense establishment. Figure 6.1 displays an approximation of how the distribution of

3. The same may not be true of other periods. For example, there was substantially less consensus during the period between World War II and Korea, when many argued that defense expenditures (then less than $12 billion) were too low.

4. Public opinion data during the late 1960s and early 1970s show considerable sentiment for lower defense spending. But at least part of this probably reflects disenchantment with the Vietnam War. See Bruce M. Russett, "The Revolt of the Masses: Public Opinion and Military Expenditures," in his *Peace, War and Numbers* (Beverly Hills, Calif.: Sage Publications, 1972), pp. 299–319.

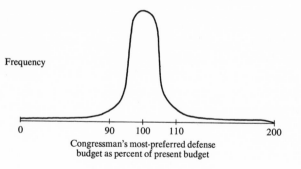

Frequency

0   90   100   110   200

Congressman's most-preferred defense
budget as percent of present budget

Figure 6.1. Attitudes Toward the Defense Budget

general-benefit preferences among congressmen might look, with each congressman's most preferred defense budget represented along the abscissa. Some readers might argue that congressmen support high levels of defense spending not because they believe such spending is desirable but rather because each fears the effects of defense cutbacks on his district's economy. This is a plausible explanation, but it ignores the fact that there is no relationship between constituency benefits and voting on defense issues. Congressmen from districts with little defense spending are no more likely to oppose the size of the defense budget than those from districts economically dependent on it.[5]

A consensus distribution such as this gives bureaucrats almost complete freedom in allocating benefits, for their supporting coalitions are built on foundations of collective benefits and not on local benefits. However much a congressman may want a share of military spending for his district, his support of the defense budget is not contingent upon it. If a base in his district is closed, he may support defense spending with less enthusiasm than he would otherwise; but as long as he values the collective benefit such spending produces (national defense), he will support it. Rank-and-file congressmen are in a weak bargaining situation. All they have to offer in trade for shares of military benefits are their votes; yet both congressmen and bureaucrats know that any threats

5. See Wayne Moyer, "House Voting on Defense: An Ideological Explanation," in Bruce M. Russett and Alfred Stepan (eds.), *Military Force and American Society* (New York: Harper and Row, 1973), pp. 106–41.

to vote against defense spending on local-benefit grounds would not be credible.

Members of military committees (the Armed Services Committee and the Defense and Military Construction Subcommittees of the Appropriations Committee) are in a far better bargaining situation, for they control a wide range of services needed by Pentagon officials. These are discretionary services, which committee members may provide or withhold as they please, as contrasted with roll-call votes, which resemble obligatory activities in that congressmen dare not miss important ones. It follows that committee members will perform such discretionary activities only if sufficient incentives are provided to justify the investment of their scarce resources, particularly time. Conversely, there are other activities from which bureaucrats prefer that committee members completely refrain; once again, members' decisions on these matters depend on the incentives provided. Bureaucrats can employ local benefits both as carrot and stick when dealing with committee members, both to encourage their performance of certain activities and to discourage their performance of others.

One of the most important services that committee members provide for Pentagon officials is to lead coalitions for whatever causes they seek to advance in Congress, whether budgets, weapons systems, pay, or benefits. Although bureaucrats themselves can perform some leadership functions, they also need the services of congressmen to fight their battles in Congress, arrange necessary compromises, and provide cues for fellow congressmen. Committee members are logical candidates for these tasks because they enjoy an information advantage over their colleagues. Particularly in a complex area such as defense policy, superior information (or the perception by others that it is superior) permits one to influence those who fear that they lack adequate information. Bureaucrats encourage committee members to act as coalition leaders by favoring the members' constituencies when they make allocational decisions, for such decisions then give congressmen publicity, a healthy local economy, and the opportunity for credit claiming. Conversely, when they make unfavorable decisions, for example closing a large base in a member's district, they remove any such incentives. Placing and keeping military bases in a member's district has another important effect. It means that a large proportion of his constituents will be military employees and, thus, directly interested in certain defense issues. Congressmen from such constituencies gain rewards from publicly leading coalitions for increased military pay and benefits, just as those from constituencies with substantial Air Force employment are obvious candidates to lead coalitions for the development of new military aircraft.

Local benefits also help restrain military committee members from leading coalitions *against* projects advocated by Pentagon officials. Leading such coalitions is particularly risky for those committee members who already have large military installations in their districts, both because it might tempt bureaucrats in turn to close the installations and because publicly leading antimilitary coalitions increases the probability that members' constituents might blame them for such closures. Would Les Aspin (D., Wisc.), member of the Armed Services Committee and persistent critic of military policies, have dared to adopt the role of opposition leader if his district were filled with large military installations? Probably not. In fact, only a few members of the dovish minority on that committee have represented districts containing large military installations. The "fearless five," as the faction was originally known, did not really have much to fear.

The same argument about local benefits holds for all the other activities that committee members perform. Bureaucrats want congressional hearings to be friendly and to avoid topics likely to tarnish their public image. They want their budget requests to be examined sympathetically, with any doubts resolved in their favor. They want new weapons systems authorized quickly and adequate funds authorized for their development. They want help resisting and sometimes reversing unfavorable directives from their executive branch superiors: the service secretaries, the secretary of defense, or the president. For all of these, committee members are more likely to act appropriately if bureaucrats have taken into account their preferences when making allocational decisions.

Members of the military committees present real, not just hypothetical, threats to bureaucrats' goals. Bureaucrats cannot safely assume committee support will be forthcoming without any effort on their part. Both the Defense and the Military Construction Subcommittees of the House Appropriations Committee are noted for conducting careful budgetary reviews and for reducing appropriations requests, as contrasted with the Subcommittee on Labor, Health, Education, and Welfare, which once had a reputation for approving more than some agencies had requested.[6] Similarly, the Armed Services Committee has carefully developed means for controlling defense spending, principally a requirement that most expenditures have specific, annual authorizations rather than general, continuous ones.[7] Thus, the defense budget has two committee hurdles to clear annually, neither of them a sure thing.

Finally, when committee members do not like bureaucrats' allocational decisions, they are in a better position to do something than are rank-and-file congressmen. After McNamara announced in early 1961 the closing of seventy-three military installations, the Armed Services Committee held extensive hearings. The hearings dealt with only six of the seventy-three decisions and focused, quite predictably, on the only one that affected a committee member's district.[8] The decision was not reversed, but the message to Pentagon officials was clear: "Look out for our interests." The committee also has more direct methods of control. In 1951, Congress added an amendment to the military construction bill which required the Defense Department to "come into agreement" with the Armed Services Committees on any real estate transaction over $25,000 (whether purchase, sale, or transfer). The requirement was altered in 1960 so that such property transactions need only be "reported" to the committees within thirty days; however, the intention (and probably the effect) of the clause was no different.[9] In 1965, Congress reacted to a sharp increase in base closings by adding a requirement that the secretary of defense give Congress at least thirty days to review proposed closures.[10] Each of these oversight mechanisms communicates congressional concerns about allocational decisions to Pentagon officials; but it is the concerns of committee members which are transmitted most effectively.

6. Richard F. Fenno, Jr., *The Power of the Purse* (Boston: Little, Brown, 1966), pp. 232–35.

7. Herbert W. Stephens, "The Role of the Legislative Committee in the Appropriations Process: A Study Focused on the Armed Services Committee," *Western Political Quarterly* 24 (1971): 146–62.

8. U.S., House Committee on Armed Services, *Military Base Closures: Hearings before the Subcommittee for Special Investigations*, 87th Cong. 1st sess. 1961.

9. Raymond H. Dawson, "Congressional Innovation and Intervention in Defense Policy," *American Political Science Review* 56 (1962): 46–47.

10. Congressional Quarterly, *Congress and the Nation*, vol. 2 (Washington, D.C.: Congressional Quarterly, 1969), p. 837.

Bureaucrats who allocate military employment actually make three types of decisions: where to build new military installations during times of expansion, which existing installations should be closed during times of retrenchment, and how to reallocate military employment among existing installations either to reflect changing military priorities or to compensate for the closing of other installations. There are good reasons to expect that the extent of committee members' influence will not be the same for the three types of allocational decisions, because both the structure of congressional incentives and the allocational processes themselves differ for each. In general, congressmen are more interested and involved in retaining the installations and military employment that their districts already enjoy than they are in acquiring new installations or increasing employment at existing ones.

Congressmen have little choice but to work to protect the military installations in their districts, because local beneficiaries see such installations as semipermanent benefits. Soon after communities acquire military installations, they grow accustomed to receiving continuous flows of federal funds. Community leaders come to believe that the health of their local economies depends on these infusions; consequently, they regard discontinuance as a punishment, not merely a disappointment. Congressmen work to protect such installations not so much because they receive formal requests to do so but rather because they fear their constituents might hold them responsible for both the loss of benefits and the resulting poor performance of the economy. Risks associated with closure are even greater for military committee members; since they sit on what are popularly thought to be influential committees, adverse decisions may suggest incompetence or lack of interest to their constituents.

Congressmen need not become involved in bureaucratic decisions about where new installations should be built or which existing installations should receive additional shares of employment unless they choose to do so. Some congressmen do adopt the entrepreneurial role and attempt to acquire new shares of employment; but they are free to adopt or reject the role as they please. There are no pressures forcing it upon them, because most communities do not even know when they are competing for new installations or for additional shares of employment. There is no public competition for which localities must apply; instead, bureaucrats first generate an agenda of alternatives and then select the lucky communities from this list. Congressmen who do adopt an entrepreneurial role can affect allocational decisions either by encouraging bureaucrats to include certain alternatives on their agenda or by influencing their final choice.

DATA BASE

For both theoretical and methodological reasons, separate analyses are required for measuring the influence of military committee members over opening, closing, and reallocational decisions. First, theory suggests that the extent of committee members' influence varies for these decisions; combining the three would preclude testing for these differences. Second, the process of decision making differs for each; one could analyze them together only if one believed process had no effect on policy. For each test, the basic analytic unit is the military installation, not the congressional district. Congressional districts may shape some of the forces that affect decisions, but it is important to remember that bureaucrats make decisions about military installations: where to build them, which ones to close, and how to reallocate employment among them.

The data base used throughout this chapter consists of histories of all major Defense Department installations over a twenty-two-year period from 1952 to 1974. For each installation I have compiled information about the year it was opened (if this occurred after 1952), the year a decision was made to close it (if this occurred before 1974), the number of military and civilian personnel it employed (observed at two-year intervals), and the military functions it performed. In addition, I have ascertained the congressional district in which each installation was located, who its congressman was during each two-year period, and what his party, seniority, and committee assignments were.

Although I have collected information for Army, Air Force, and Navy installations, I have analyzed only the Army and Air Force data. I have chosen not to analyze the Navy data principally because it would require nearly two months to organize all the necessary information. The returns from such an effort would probably be minimal, particularly since my separate analyses of the Army and Air Force data uncovered no important differences between the two services. Furthermore, the Navy has a much larger proportion of its installations located in large cities, which introduces a whole series of theoretical and methodological problems (discussed in previous chapters).

The total number of military installations in the United States is quite large; one author counted nearly 4,500 a few years ago.[11] Most, however, are small (e.g., radar installations) and thus of little political importance. For purposes of this chapter I have defined a major military installation as one that employed a minimum of one thousand civilian and military personnel during at least one year between 1952 and 1974. Any installation that met this criterion was included in the analysis even for those years in which its employment dipped below this threshold; all others were deleted from the file. Other installations excluded from the analysis were military hospitals, the service academies, facilities operated by the Army Corps of Engineers, and those located in Alaska, Hawaii, the Washington metropolitan area, or in multimember districts. This final category includes all facilities in North Dakota until 1962 and all facilities in New Mexico until 1968, for both states elected their congressmen at large.

The data used in this chapter were assembled from unpublished reports and documents in the Pentagon to which I gained access during a month of research there. The data come from a variety of sources, including employment records, military maps, internal memoranda, and press releases.[12] In addition, I used the standard congressional reference works[13] (in conjunction with military maps) to ascertain who represented an installation in the House during each of the eleven Congresses, as well as what each congressman's party, seniority, and committee assignments were.

11. Thomas P. Murphy, *Science, Geopolitics, and Federal Spending* (Lexington, Mass.: Heath Lexington Books, 1974), p. 405.

12. None of the sources were secret or classified. Nevertheless, each Pentagon official who gave me access to files under his control asked for (and received) assurances that I would not reveal the precise location of the files. I am very much indebted to these officials, for they went well beyond the call of duty in helping me locate and interpret the proper information. One official even allowed me to camp out in his private office for an entire week while I searched his filing cabinets and copied the appropriate data.

13. For example, *Congressional Directory* (Washington, D.C.: Government Printing Office) and *Congressional District Atlas* (Washington, D.C.: Government Printing Office).

REPRESENTATIVENESS

Before actually testing the hypotheses about committee members' influence, it is useful to examine the question of how typical are members' constituencies. This is essentially the question Goss explored in the article discussed in chapter 5. Goss, it will be recalled, discovered that districts represented on the House Armed Services Committee in 1968 had an average of 14,030 military employees as compared with the House average of 6,041.[14] According to her evidence, the committee was not very representative of the House in terms of constituency benefits. Although this was certainly true in 1968, it has not been the case throughout the entire period 1952 to 1974. As figure 6.2 demonstrates, the mean military employment of districts represented on the committee has fluctuated widely. Although it has always exceeded the mean for all districts, the difference has sometimes been small (e.g., only one thousand employees in the Eighty-sixth and Eighty-seventh Congresses).[15] In fact, it was not until the Eighty-ninth Congress that a large difference appeared.

Means are not very good measures of representativeness. Just as a community's mean income is distorted by the arrival of a Rockefeller, so too is a committee's mean military employment distorted by the arrival or departure of a few members with extraordinarily high employment levels. (One reason for the peak in figure 6.2 during the Congress Goss examined was that freshman Jack Brinkley [D., Ga.] had just joined the committee and added more than 75,000 military employees to the total represented on the committee.) Two other measures give a better sense of the changes occurring during this period. One measure is the proportion of committee members who represented districts already receiving some military benefits. Figure 6.3, which compares the proportion of committee members who represented districts containing at least one major military installation with the same proportion for all House districts, suggests that until about 1963, the committee was practically a mirror image of the House; not until the Eighty-eighth Congress were

14. Carol F. Goss, "Military Committee Membership and Defense Related Benefits in the House of Representatives," *Western Political Quarterly* 25 (1972): 215–33.
15. The data set used to construct figure 6.2 does not include employment at naval installations, whereas the data set used by Goss does. It is unlikely that including the Navy would change the relationship significantly.

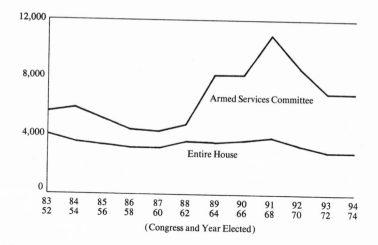

Figure 6.2. Mean Army and Air Force Employment for Districts on Armed Services Committee

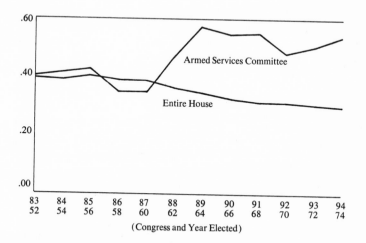

Figure 6.3. Proportion of Districts on Armed Services with at Least One Army or Air Force Installation

committee members more likely than nonmembers to represent districts containing one or more installations. A second measure is the extent to which the committee overrepresented districts with high levels of military employment. Figure 6.4 plots the proportion of committee members in the top decile (and the top quartile) of all districts rank ordered according to military employment. As the reader can see, the committee has always included a disproportionate number of districts with very high levels of military employment. Since the early 1960s the degree of overrepresentation has been increasing, with more and more committee members coming from districts that contain very large installations.

Contrary to public perceptions, the House Armed Services Committee has not always been unrepresentative of the House. During the 1950s the mean military employment of districts on the committee exceeded slightly the House average, but this reflected the above-average military employment of a few committee members' districts rather than a committee composed predominantly of congressmen from military districts. Only recently has its membership become dominated by congressmen from districts with significantly more military installations and higher military employment than nonmembers. Later in this chapter I examine possible explanations for these changes.

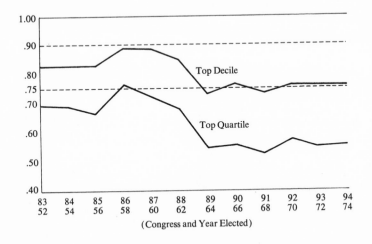

Figure 6.4. Proportion of Armed Services Members Coming from Districts in Top Decile and Top Quartile of All Districts, Ranked by Army and Air Force Employment

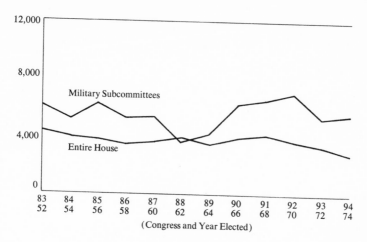

Figure 6.5. Mean Army and Air Force Employment for Districts on Military Subcommittees of Appropriations Committee

The Defense and Military Construction Subcommittees of the House Appropriations Committee have been fairly representative of the House throughout the entire period. The mean military employment of districts on these subcommittees has usually exceeded the House average (figure 6.5), but this difference has been very slight and, in fact, would vanish if just a single subcommittee member resigned.

INFLUENCE OVER CLOSING DECISIONS

Measuring committee members' influence over closing decisions would be practically impossible if one's attention were restricted to just a year or so, for only a handful of installations are closed in any given year. Even the most elementary analysis would require evidence from an extended time period. The following analysis focuses on the decisions to close 125 military installations between 1952 and 1974, representing 41 percent of the major Army and Air Force installations in operation at any time during this period.

For purposes of analysis I have assumed that once during every two-year period Pentagon officials survey all military installations and decide which should be closed and which should remain open. The assumption of a two-year decision cycle is admittedly arbitrary, but it has the virtue of making the decision process coincide with the electoral cycle and thus with the biennial changes in Congress. Furthermore, it is not an unrealistic assumption, given that a minimum of three installations were closed during every two-year period between 1952 and 1974. Pentagon officials are assumed to make a separate decision for each installation during each two-year period. If there were one hundred military installations in existence, they would make one hundred separate decisions during a single two-year period, and nearly 1,100 over a span of twenty-two years (less those installations closed in earlier periods and thus not vulnerable in later periods). Most of these decisions would be for no change in status, but a few would be decisions to close particular installations. The question of interest here is whether the probability of an installation being closed during a particular period was lower for installations represented on the military committees than it was for those without such representation.

The evidence in tables 6.1 and 6.2 provides strong support for the hypothesis that military committee members were better able to protect their installations than were rank-and-file congressmen. This holds true for both Army and Air Force installations. During any two-year period, the average Air Force installation had a 5.9 percent chance of being closed, while the average installation represented on Armed Services had only a 2.3 percent chance, and the average installation on the military subcommittees had only a 1.3 percent chance. The closing rates for Army installations were practically identical: 5.5 percent for installations with no committee representation, 2.6 percent for those on

Table 6.1. Effects of Military Committee Membership on Decisions to Close Major Air Force Installations (1952–74)

Air Force Installation Represented on	Decision to Close	Remains Open	Total Decisions	Probability of Closing
Military Subcommittees of Appropriations Committee	1	74	75	.013
House Armed Services	4	172	176	.023
Neither committee	62	991	1053	.059
Total	67	1237	1304	

Chi-Square = 6.41   Significance level = .04

Unit of analysis: major installations (n = 164) observed every two years over twenty-two-year period.

Table 6.2. Effects of Military Committee Membership on Decisions to Close Major
Army Installations (1952–74)

Army Installation Represented on	Decision to Close	Remains Open	Total Decisions	Probability of Closing
Military Subcommittees of Appropriations Committee	0	45	45	.000
House Armed Services	4	151	155	.026
Neither committee	54	921	975	.055
Total	58	1117	1175	

Chi-Square = 4.92   Significance level = .08

Unit of analysis: major installations (n = 143) observed every two years over twenty-two-year period.

Armed Services, and zero for those on the Appropriations subcommittees. Committee representation seems to reduce the probability of an installation being closed by at least one half. Significance tests, and the fact that separate analyses of Army and Air Force installations yielded identical results, give one confidence that the relationships reflect more than mere happenstance.

Although the evidence in these tables seems persuasive, the relationships could well be spurious. Alternative causal mechanisms could easily account for the association between committee membership and closing decisions. Such an association might arise if the objective criteria that bureaucrats employed in their evaluations also happened to be correlated with committee membership. The size of a military installation is an obvious candidate, for it is both a plausible criterion for decision making and a known correlate of committee membership. If bureaucrats decided to close small installations in preference to large ones, and if base size were positively associated with membership on the military committees (as it usually is), then the relationship between committee membership and base closing could reflect nothing more than the effects of base size on each. Similar arguments for other objective criteria could also explain the association.

The only way to be certain that committee members do, in fact, influence closing decisions is to develop and test a multivariate model that incorporates both the committee hypothesis and the alternative causal mechanisms. If one were interested in developing a complete explanation of closing decisions, one would incorporate every variable that one suspected might affect decisions. Here, however, since the goal is merely to obtain unbiased estimates of committee influence, one need include only those variables that might themselves be correlated with committee membership.

Three alternative explanations of bureaucrats' closing decisions merit attention. First is the one discussed previously, in which bureaucrats select installations in part according to their sizes, with small bases closed in preference to large ones. Base size is a sensible criterion for decision, both because economies of scale make larger bases more efficient and because reallocating a small base's employment is easier than reallocating employment from larger ones. Second is a cyclical explanation. The probability of a single installation being closed during a given two-year period depends in part on the total number of bases scheduled for closing, a number that varies according to whether total military employment is expanding, contracting, or stable. Third is an explanation based on changes in military function. The Air Force of the early 1960s differed considerably from the Air Force of the early 1950s; for example, the need for fighter bases surrounding and protecting major cities had lessened, while the need for bomber bases scattered throughout sparsely populated areas had grown. It follows that the probability of an installation being closed during a given period depends in part on whether the military function it performs is expanding or contracting in importance.

Although the reasons why these three objective criteria affect decision making are obvious, the reasons why they correlate with committee membership may not be apparent. Base size is so correlated principally because congressmen from districts with very large bases were more likely to seek and gain seats on military committees. The total number of bases being closed is correlated with committee membership, because, as I demonstrate at the end of this chapter, congressmen from military districts were much more likely to join the military committees during periods of retrenchment. Changes in military functions are correlated with committee membership simply because major changes in Air Force missions (around 1962) happened to coincide with changes in the composition of the military committees (as displayed in figures 6.2 through 6.5).[16]

16. Ideally, one would develop a theory of base closings that incorporated both political and nonpolitical criteria. My theory is exclusively political, because there are no

The basic structure of the multivariate model is as described in chapter 5. I assume that the probability of an installation being closed during a particular two-year period is a linear function of three variables representing objective criteria, three committee variables, and a random error term. The objective variables are base size, as measured by an installation's peak employment (in thousands) between 1952 and the year in question; base closings, as measured by the total number of major installations closed during the current two-year period; and military function, a dummy variable that takes a value of one if an installation's principal military function is declining in relative size at the national level, and a value of zero otherwise.[17] Each committee variable is a dummy variable which takes a value of one if an installation is represented on a particular committee and zero otherwise. The committees coded are the Armed Services Committee, the military subcommittees of the Appropriations Committee, and the full Appropriations Committee (excepting those on its military subcommittees). This final category is included not because members of the full committee are thought to influence bureaucrats' closing decisions but rather to facilitate comparisons in later chapters.

Probit analysis has been employed to estimate the multivariate model, first for Air Force bases and then for Army installations. The results generally support the committee hypothesis, though the estimates of influence are somewhat less than those derived from the bivariate analyses. The other three hypotheses are also supported, and no doubt it is this which depresses slightly the previous estimates of committee influence.

Many readers may not be familiar with probit analysis and therefore uncertain how the results should be interpreted. Probit equations are

---

previous writings on the subject to guide the development of the nonpolitical portion. The few nonpolitical variables I included in the multivariate model are simply those I suspected bureaucrats might employ and for which I could conveniently assemble data.

17. I have identified changes in the relative importance of various military functions by charting changes in total employment at installations with the same principal function. Eight functional categories were examined for the Air Force: strategic (bombers), air defense (fighters), training, transport, research and development, depot, reserves, and headquarters. Those found to be contracting functions from 1952 to 1974 were air defense, training, and depot, as was the strategic function from 1962 to 1974 (before that it was expanding rapidly). I discovered no important changes in the functional makeup of the Army which might affect the probability of installations being closed.

analogous to regression equations. Unfortunately, their coefficients do not have the same straightforward interpretation that makes regression coefficients so attractive. A probit coefficient describes the impact of a particular variable on the probability of an event's occurrence, with its sign indicating whether the variable increases or decreases the probability and its magnitude indicating the extent of the effect. However, the impact of a particular variable is not constant across all cases as it is for regression; instead, it varies according to the values that the other variables take, principally because the underlying relationships are assumed to be nonlinear. Although probit coefficients are not themselves probabilities, the effects they describe can be converted to probabilities. For an individual case, one can calculate the expected probability by multiplying the value of each variable by its coefficient, summing across all variables, and using a table of the cumulative normal distribution to convert the resulting value to a probability. A probit value of zero corresponds to an expected probability of .50. Since the normal distribution is symmetrical, a probit value of plus one corresponds to a probability of .84, while a value of minus one translates into a probability of .16. Similarly, a value of plus two corresponds to a .98 probability, while a value of minus two corresponds to a .02 probability. One can determine the marginal impact of a single variable by setting all other variables to their sample means (or some other typical values) while varying the value of the selected variable and studying how the expected probability changes.

The probit analysis of Air Force decisions, summarized in table 6.3, supports both the committee hypothesis and the three alternative explanations of closing decisions. As expected, small installations were more vulnerable than were large ones; those performing functions that were declining in importance were more likely to be closed than others; and every installation was more vulnerable during periods of retrenchment. However, even controlling for these three variables, representation on the military committees was still associated with closing decisions. The probit coefficients for both committee variables are negative, and significance tests indicate that the probability of such relationships arising purely by chance is low (about 10 percent). The second part of the table contains a marginal analysis of the committee variables, with other variables controlled by setting them at their sample means. The typical installation with no committee representation had about a 4 percent

Table 6.3. Probit Analysis: Effects of Committee Membership on Decisions to Close
            Major Air Force Installations

Variable	Probit Coefficient	Standard Error	Significance Level	Sample Mean
a Military Subcommittees of Appropriations Committee	− .791	.448	.08	.058
b Armed Services Committee	− .367	.233	.11	.135
c [Rest of Appropriations Committee]	.128	.220	.60	.073
d Base size	− .061	.016	.0001	8.424
e Total base closings	.065	.013	.0001	6.354
f Military function	.351	.148	.02	.243
Constant	−1.907			

$$n = 1304 \text{ decisions}$$

Analysis of Committee Variables:

Installation Represented on	Calculated Probability	Observed Probability
Military Subcommittees of Appropriations Committee*	.005	(.013)
Armed Services Committee†	.017	(.023)
Neither committee‡	.040	(.059)

Notes: *Variable a = 1; variables b, c = 0; variables d, e, f = means.
        †Variable b = 1; variables a, c = 0; variables d, e, f = means.
        ‡Variables a, b, c = 0; variables, d, e, f = means.

chance of being closed during any two-year period, while those on
Armed Services had a 1.7 percent chance, and those on the military
subcommittees of Appropriations had a 0.5 percent chance. Each of
these probabilities is less than the observed probabilities in table 6.1, but
the relationship among them is unchanged. Installations without representation on the military committees are still more than twice as likely
to be closed as the others, even with such alternative explanations as
base size controlled.

The probit analysis of Army decisions (table 6.4) provides further
support for the committee hypothesis. In fact, the equation is structur-
ally identical to the one developed for Air Force decisions, with each
relationship's direction the same and its magnitude approximately
equal.[18] Once again, the probability of an installation being closed was

18. Some readers may be uneasy about the significance levels for the committee
variables. One of them is incalculable (because the computer approximation routine

Table 6.4. Probit Analysis: Effects of Committee Membership on Decisions to Close
            Major Army Installations

Variable	Probit Coefficient	Standard Error	Significance Level	Sample Mean
a Military Subcommittees of Appropriations Committee	−3.136	NA	NA	.038
b Armed Services Committee	− .304	.249	.22	.131
c [Rest of Appropriations Committee]	.118	.246	.62	.058
d Base size	− .034	.010	.001	11.131
e Total base closings	.096	.021	.0001	5.575
Constant	−1.990			

n = 1175 decisions

Analysis of committee variables:

Installation Represented on	Calculated Probability	Observed Probability
Military Subcommittee of Appropriations Committee*	.001	(.000)
Armed Services Committee†	.017	(.026)
Neither committee‡	.034	(.055)

Notes: *Variable a = 1; variables b, c = 0; variables d, e = means.
        †Variable b = 1; variables a, c = 0; variables d, e = means.
        ‡Variables a, b, c = 0; variables d, e = means.
    NA = Not available because the estimation routine used for probit breaks down when no
installations with a given attribute are closed.

at least twice as great for installations not represented on the military
committees (.034) as it was for those represented either on Armed Services (.017) or the military subcommittees of Appropriations (.001).

The conclusion is inescapable: bureaucrats *do* take into account
committee members' preferences when deciding which Army and Air
Force installations should be closed. The only other conceivable explanation for the relationship is that bureaucrats employ some other objective criteria (besides those already included in the multivariate analysis)
which are themselves correlated with committee membership.

If one accepts the fact that congressmen influence bureaucrats' deci

breaks down when *no* installations sharing a particular attribute are closed), while the
other is considerably larger than that with which one ordinarily feels comfortable. Actually, there are good reasons to feel quite confident about the results, for they correspond
very closely to the results from the Air Force analysis. The probability of two independent
analyses yielding identical results solely as a consequence of chance is not very great.

sions, how important is this influence? Consider, for example, a newly elected congressman with a major installation in his district who wonders what value a seat on a military committee might have for his district (and his career). If he contemplates a long career in Congress (say, twenty years), a committee seat could significantly reduce the chances of his installation being closed. Over twenty years, a typical installation with no committee representation would have almost an even chance of being closed (34 to 59 percent depending on whether one extrapolates from the bivariate or multivariate models); if it were represented on Armed Services, the prospects would be far better (17 to 26 percent); and if it were represented on the military subcommittees of Appropriations, the prospects would be excellent (1 to 13 percent). Committee membership has considerable value for a district's well-being (and conceivably for a congressman's career).[19]

One can also ask how extensive is committee members' influence? How frequently do bureaucrats adjust their decisions to conform with committee members' preferences? Some simple calculations indicate that between 9 and 14 percent of the 125 closing decisions would have been made differently in the absence of committee influence; in other words, between eleven and seventeen installations represented on the military committees would have been closed and a corresponding number without such representation would have been more fortunate.[20] Bureaucrats appear very responsive to committee members' preferences, but because these committees are relatively small, bureaucrats need adjust only a small fraction of their decisions.

SITE SELECTION FOR NEW INSTALLATIONS

Measuring committee members' influence over decisions about the location of *new* installations is slightly more difficult than measuring

19. The value for a congressman's career is less certain. Elsewhere I suggested that constituents might blame committee members for adverse decisions more than they would blame nonmembers, since the former are popularly thought to be in influential positions. If so, a congressman might be better off as a nonmember, risking a 59 percent chance of an important installation being closed, than as a committee member with a 13 percent chance of having one closed.

20. The estimates are straightforward. I merely calculated how many installations represented on the military committees would have been closed if there were no dif-

influence over closing decisions, both because the Pentagon built considerably fewer installations than it closed between 1952 and 1974 (thirty-eight opened, 125 closed), and because no natural agenda exist for opening decisions as they do for closing decisions. Although it still makes sense to conceptualize decision making as a two-stage process, one can, without doing too much violence to the facts, combine agenda setting and choice for purposes of analysis, particularly since bureaucrats dominate both stages. Initially they prepare a list of potential sites, and then they select one or more of these for construction.

Pentagon officials use a long list of objective criteria for evaluating potential sites. These include climate, population density, proximity to other installations, and various strategic factors. Although districts differ enormously in their suitability for specific installations, I make the assumption that, at least prior to 1963, these differences were uncorrelated with committee membership. In other words, districts represented on the military committees were neither more nor less suitable for new installations than were other districts (the evidence being that they in fact contained neither more nor fewer *old* installations than other districts). This assumption might not be tenable after 1963, when the military committees became increasingly unrepresentative of the House.[21] However, prior to 1963, when thirty-four of the thirty-eight new installations were constructed, districts represented on the committee were not much different from the rest.

If one assumes that districts represented on the military committees were inherently no more attractive as sites for new installations than were other districts, one can easily test for committee members' influence simply by examining the frequency with which installations were constructed in their districts. Disproportionate construction activity will be taken as evidence of disproportionate influence. The evidence from this period is suggestive, but not conclusive. In part this is a conse-

ferences in closing rates. The calculations were performed both with the probit estimates and with the observed probabilities, which accounts for the range from 9 percent (probit) to 14 percent (observed).

21. It is not clear whether districts with above-average military employment are more or less attractive as sites for new installations. On the one hand, there may be a tendency to build new installations in close proximity to existing ones so that certain facilities may be shared. On the other, dispersal is sometimes advocated (especially for Air Force bases) because close proximity in a nuclear age creates fewer targets. Additionally, some districts are thought to be saturated with installations and thus unable to absorb additional ones.

quence of the small number of base openings available for analysis (thirty-two Air Force and six Army). If the thirty-eight new installations were distributed randomly among districts, one should expect 33.5 would have no committee representation, 3.2 would be represented on Armed Services, and 1.2 would be represented on the military sub-committees of Appropriations.[22] In fact, thirty-one were represented on none of the committees, seven were on Armed Services, and zero were on the military subcommittees. Districts represented on Armed Services were clearly getting more than their share of new installations (more than twice their share, in fact). Furthermore, there was only about a 4 percent chance that a difference this large could have arisen purely by chance.[23] Districts represented on the military subcommittees of Appropriations were getting slightly less than their share, but given the subcommittees' small size, this could easily be just chance variation (probability $= .29$).

The evidence clearly supports the hypothesis about the value of Armed Services membership, but it is inconclusive about whether membership on the Appropriations subcommittees has any value for attracting new installations. Maybe this and the previous analysis demonstrate some real differences between the two committees. Recall that the closing rates associated with the Appropriations subcommittees were considerably lower than those associated with Armed Services. Now it appears that the reverse may be true for opening decisions, with Armed Services the more advantaged committee. The Appropriations subcommittees may provide better opportunities for protecting installations because they have a greater impact on the defense budget than Armed Services. Conversely, members of Armed Services may be more successful at acquiring installations, not because they occupy inherently more powerful positions but rather because they are more inclined to be entrepreneurs and work to affect bureaucrats' agenda of sites. If there are any entrepreneurs operating in the defense area, they are more likely to

22. The House Armed Services Committee averaged thirty-seven members during this period, while the military subcommittees averaged fourteen (counting only once members of both subcommittees).

23. The problem is the familiar one of drawing (with replacement) seven or more red balls in thirty-eight tries from a box containing thirty-seven red balls (districts represented on Armed Services) and 398 white balls (those not on Armed Services). See William L. Hays, *Statistics* (New York: Holt, Rinehart, and Winston, 1963), pp. 140–43.

be on Armed Services than on the Appropriations subcommittees, which, after all, draw members from but a small subset of the House. The best one can do is speculate, for most of the relevant evidence has been exhausted. If one moves backwards in time, one runs into World War II, a time in which many installations were constructed but political influence was probably at an all-time low. Since 1966 there has not been a single major installation opened, and this is unlikely to change for many years to come.

How extensive and how important was the influence of Armed Services members over site selection? Its extent was probably slightly less than that for closing decisions. Bureaucrats adjusted approximately 10 percent (3.8 out of 38) of their opening decisions to take into account members' preferences, whereas between 9 and 14 percent of the closing decisions were so adjusted. Its importance, from the perspective of the congressman, was considerably less. Many committee members benefited from the committee's influence over closing decisions, with some eleven to seventeen installations spared. Few members benefited from the committee's influence over opening decisions. At most only three or four members had installations placed in their districts which otherwise might have been placed elsewhere.

Party and seniority are not part of the theory developed here. In fact, I argued previously (chapter 4) that it would be irrational for bureaucrats to employ such criteria when making allocational decisions. Nevertheless, some readers may wish some empirical evidence demonstrating that party and seniority were not important criteria. Twenty-two of the thirty-eight new installations (58 percent) were built in the districts of Democratic congressmen. Since this proportion is only slightly larger than the proportion of all districts then Democratic, it is obvious that party discrimination was not practiced. Seniority is more a property of committee rank than service in Congress, so the hypothesis is examined at that level. The seven members of Armed Services who had new installations built in their districts had the following seniority (within their own parties) at the time site selections were made: five, ten, thirteen, fourteen, fifteen, sixteen, and sixteen. Since seniority ranks ranged from one (chairman) to about twenty during this period, it is obvious that senior members were not getting more than their share. If anything, it was the newer members of the committee who were reaping the benefits of membership. This *might* reflect a bureaucratic strategy of rewarding committee members early in their careers (when such help would mean the most to them) and then living off their investments throughout the congressmen's careers. The party and seniority hypotheses were also tested in the multivariate models of closing decisions. I discovered no relationships of any importance.

FLUCTUATIONS IN MILITARY EMPLOYMENT

Committee members appear able to affect the level of military employment in their districts by influencing bureaucrats' opening and closing decisions. But can they do more? Specifically, can they induce Pentagon officials to increase employment at the installations already in their districts, or at a minimum, can they prevent them from reducing the employment already stationed there?

Measuring influence over employment changes proves more difficult than measuring the same relations for opening and closing decisions. I should say at the outset that I am not entirely happy with the following analysis, nor do I have complete confidence in the results. Nevertheless, I do not see how the question can better be answered without assembling an entirely different data file. The basic problem is that employment decisions occur in a dozen different ways, shapes, and forms, whereas opening and closing decisions occur in but a single form, easily identifiable by both participants and researchers. Decisions that affect employment include: decisions about which installations should suffer and which should be spared when total military employment declines; decisions about which installations should be expanded or altered to accommodate new or expanding military functions; and decisions about where employees should be transferred when existing installations are closed. Given that data on these decisions are not readily available in time series, I have chosen to analyze fluctuations in each installation's employment. Such fluctuations are the result of the aforementioned unobservable decisions. As before, I assume that Pentagon officials make such decisions at two-year intervals, so that there are eleven fluctuations to explain for each installation. The fluctuations examined do not include the initial two-year surge when a new base opens or the final two-year decline when a base closes.

To make a very long story short, I have found no support for the hypothesis that members of military committees are able to affect employment at installations in their districts, either by promoting their expansion or by slowing their contraction. In fact, the simple bivariate relationship between committee membership and employment fluctuations is *negative*: installations with committee representation suffered greater-than-average losses in employment. This negative relationship fades away in a succession of more elaborate multivariate models, but under no circumstances does a significant positive relationship emerge. The multivariate models consider changes in an installation's employment to be a linear function of:

1. its committee representation
2. its current employment level
3. changes in national military employment
4. changes in national employment for particular military functions
5. changes in the number of installations in existence
6. an installation's age

All except the committee variables prove to be important determinants of change. Even when separate models were tested for employment increases and employment decreases, committee representation was of no importance. Each model was also tested with the standard party and seniority variables, but the results were no different. (Summaries of some of the regression analyses appear in appendix B.)

Why is it that committee members appear influential over opening and closing decisions but uninfluential over decisions that affect employment levels? There are a number of possibilities. One reason may be that opening and closing decisions are more visible than the others, and this visibility creates greater congressional interest, involvement, and influence. What's more, there may be little credit in acquiring small increments in employment as compared with acquiring a new base, both because few will notice these small increases whereas everyone notices the construction of a base, and because claims of congressional responsibility may be less credible for the former, because the ebb and flow of base employment correspond so closely to fluctuations in national military employment. By extension, electoral blame, thought to be significant for base closings, may be nonexistent for mere reductions in employment.

CONGRESSIONAL DISTRICTS

Until now I have examined allocational decisions from the bureau-crats' perspective, with military installations as the basic analytic units. It seems clear that members of military committees are able to affect bureaucrats' decisions about some matters (closing installations and, to a lesser extent, building new ones) but not about such matters as em-ployment levels. But how do these decisions look from the con-gressman's perspective? How, in other words, do these various decisions cumulate by *district?* Do districts represented on the military commit-tees do significantly better than those without such representation? The answer is not as obvious as it may seem, because districts frequently contain multiple installations. A congressman may be able to keep all the installations in his district open during his tenure on the committee, but each installation's employment may be cut so deeply that the net effect would have been no different if bureaucrats had chosen to close one.

In order to see how allocational decisions cumulate across congres-sional districts, I have examined gross changes in military employment for districts represented on either House Armed Services or the military subcommittees of Appropriations. (Gross change refers to *all* changes in a district's employment, whether caused by the reallocation of em-ployees, the closing of an installation, or the opening of a new one.) Of particular interest is a comparison between each district's employment at the time its congressman first joined a committee and its employment when he finally left it. Only thirty-two districts are suitable for this type of analysis, although 170 congressmen served on the military commit-tees between 1952 and 1974. (Those eliminated include sixty-four con-gressmen who sat on a committee for two terms or less, sixty-two who had no bases in their districts, and twelve who occupied districts that were reapportioned so severely that one can hardly chart employment changes within them.) The employment record for these thirty-two districts was not very impressive. After representation on one of these committees, eleven districts increased their employment (mean increase = +1,993; median = +971), while 21 suffered declines (mean de-crease = −6,620; median = −3,359). Of course, this comparison is not entirely fair, for there was a long-term decline in the size of the military during this period (from 2.2 million Army and Air Force employees in the continental states in 1952 to 1.5 million in 1974). Better is a comparison between a district's share of total military employment at the start of its committee representation and its share at the end. Of the thirty-two districts, fifteen had larger shares after being represented on one of the committees, while seventeen had smaller shares—just about what one would expect by chance. Military committee members may be able to affect the status of installations in their districts, but this does not translate into influence over gross employment levels.

COMMITTEE MEMBERS AND MENDEL RIVERS

The picture I have been painting of the military committees is one in which members have disproportionate influence over allocational decisions, but it is an influence limited in magnitude and scope. The image of members using their institutional positions to fill their districts with military booty is greatly exaggerated. More accurate is a picture in which members struggle to hold on to what they already enjoy, and maybe acquire a bit more. It is mostly a conservative influence, though nevertheless an important one. Members have had some success in attracting new installations to their districts, but as far as I can ascertain, no success in acquiring extra shares of employment for existing installations.

This picture does not square with the popular image of Mendel Rivers (D., S.C.) who, according to journalistic accounts, "single-handedly brought Charleston ninety percent of its rich honeycomb of defense activity."[24] Was Rivers the exception to the rule, or was there more myth than influence behind his campaign slogan, "Rivers Delivers"? Rivers was surely an important guardian of his district's interests, but his influence has, in my judgment, been greatly exaggerated (no doubt with his encouragement). When he was first elected in 1940, his district already contained important military installations: a naval base, an Army depot, and a marine training camp. During the next thirty years, while he sat first on Naval Affairs and then on Armed Services,

24. Seymour Hersh, "The Military Committees," *Washington Monthly* 1 (April 1969): 84–92.

other installations were added, but all were built around this central core. One may wish to argue that Rivers was responsible for retaining these three initial installations, but one can hardly give him credit for their acquisition (the Navy yard opened in 1901).

In 1970, a few months before his death, Rivers's district employed 37,548 Army, Air Force, and Navy personnel. An analysis of how they came to be stationed there is the key to understanding Mendel Rivers's influence. As previously mentioned, three large installations were already located in his district when he first entered Congress in 1941. World War II added a few small installations (as it did most everywhere), but all save one were closed at war's end. A few years later a naval hospital and a small naval receiving station were built. In 1952, the first year for which complete employment data are available, the district contained 21,517 military and civilian employees, 20,657 of whom were stationed at installations built before Rivers came to Congress and 830 at installations built after 1940. By 1970 these installations had hardly changed at all, employing 21,508 (a loss of only nine in eighteen years). For these installations Rivers probably had a conservative influence, keeping them open while others were being closed, and maintaining their initial size during a time when national military employment was declining. On the other hand, he may not have affected these decisions at all, for many other installations without committee representation had at least as good records. The problem with a case study is one can never be sure what would have happened in the absence of committee representation.

One is probably on safer grounds crediting Rivers with the growth in military employment that resulted from the acquisition of new installations. The Navy built six new installations there during the 1950s and 1960s, installations that employed 8,076 by 1970. Some of these were built to perform new military functions (e.g., servicing the Polaris submarines), while others were designed to accommodate personnel previously stationed elsewhere. Of course, none of these installations would likely have been located in Charleston if it had not already been a center of naval activity, but there were plenty of other potential sites. That so many did end up in Charleston can probably be attributed to Rivers's influence. The case is not as clear cut for the other installation opened during this period, an Air Force base. This installation, which employed 7,540 in 1970, was essentially an old World War II base reactivated during the early 1950s when the Air Force expanded rapidly. It is not as certain that Rivers influenced this choice, because other installations were also being reactivated at the same time. What's more, it seems perfectly rational to reactivate old installations rather than to build new ones from scratch. Economic rationality may well have coincided nicely with political rationality.

Mendel Rivers comes off as a congressman who did well for his district, but hardly as one who "single-handedly brought Charleston ninety percent" of its defense activity. He probably deserves at least part of the credit for holding on to the 20,000 employees with whom he began, though it would be incorrect to assume that without him none would be left. The responsibility for the other 18,000 employees in 1970 is mixed. Rivers was probably responsible for acquiring some of the new Navy installations (employing about 10,000). On the other hand, it is not certain that he had anything to do with the reactivation and expansion of the Air Force base.[25]

The differences between Mendel Rivers's influence and the influence of other committee members are not as great as one might have thought, although they are still important. But why were there any differences at all? It is tempting to argue that Rivers was able to acquire so many installations simply because of his seniority and his position as chairman of Armed Services. The evidence to support this is weak, for many equally senior members acquired nothing, and what's more, most of Rivers's acquisitions took place during his middle years on the committee. A better explanation is that Rivers was in many respects unique. He was a great entrepreneur, always pointing out to Pentagon officials how important installations and contracts were to his district, and he was certainly one of the best friends the military ever had. He regarded himself as their chief lobbyist in Congress, and there was never a battle he would not fight for them. Pentagon officials quite naturally placed new installations in his district because they knew how much such installations meant to him *and* because they knew how much they needed his continued work on their behalf.

25. Rivers's influence may actually have been greater in the field of defense contracting, which underwent greater expansion at the national level than did direct military employment. Some potential contractors are thought to have built plants in the Charleston area in hopes of having contracts thrown their way. See Peter H. Prugh, "The War Business: Mendel Rivers' Defense of Armed Forces Helps His Hometown Prosper," *Wall Street Journal*, 17 June, 1969, p. 1.

COMMITTEE RECRUITMENT

Most of this chapter has examined the influence of military committee members over allocational decisions. But why do congressmen seek
membership on these committees in the first place? What rewards do
they see for themselves when they join? And how rewarding do they
actually find committee service? Definitive answers to these questions
would require interview evidence that I do not have. What I do have are
some hypotheses and a little evidence both about what attracts congressmen to Armed Services[26] and about how changes in the committee's attractiveness over time have affected its basic composition.

The Armed Services Committee tends to attract two types of congressmen: those interested in defense *policy* and those interested in
defense *benefits.* [27] (Of course, some may be interested in both.) Those
who already have military installations in their districts when they first
join the committee are almost certainly interested in benefits, though
they may also have some interest in policy. Those who have no installations in their districts are more likely to be motivated by policy concerns, though it is also possible that they seek to acquire a new installation. (This, of course, would have been more likely during the 1950s
and early 1960s, when new installations were still being built.) The
proportion of new members who already have installations in their
districts when they join can thus serve as a rough measure of the committee's relative attractiveness for benefit seekers and policy enthusiasts.

During the past two decades, Armed Services has attracted a disproportionate number of congressmen who have installations to protect. Of
the ninety-four congressmen who joined between 1953 and 1975, fifty-
two (55 percent) represented at least one major Army or Air Force
installation, as compared with the 30 to 40 percent of all districts that
contained one or more installations. However, this attractiveness to
benefit seekers has not been constant throughout this period. At times
the proportion of newcomers already having installations has been ex-

26. Congressmen generally have little say about whether or not they will sit on the
military subcommittees of the Appropriations Committee. Members of Appropriations are
usually *assigned* to subcommittees, frequently to those they least prefer. See Richard F.
Fenno, Jr., *The Power of the Purse* (Boston: Little, Brown, 1966), pp. 138–43.
27. Policy and benefits are two of the three goals Fenno ascribes to committee members. The other is influence within the House. See Richard F. Fenno, Jr., *Congressmen
in Committees* (Boston: Little, Brown, 1973), p. 1.

tremely high (83 percent in 1961; 79 percent in 1965) and at times very low (20 percent in 1955; 14 percent in 1971).

Two hypotheses account for the changing attractiveness of the Armed Services Committee for policy-oriented and benefit-oriented congressmen. First, one expects that congressmen with military installations in their districts would be more likely to seek membership on Armed Services during periods in which Pentagon officials have been closing a large number of bases, both because they are more conscious of the risks of closure and because they see committee membership as a way to protect their districts from a very real threat. During periods in which few bases are being closed, the threat seems less immediate. Second, one expects that more policy-oriented congressmen will be attracted to the committee during periods in which defense policy becomes a major national concern (e.g., Vietnam). A somewhat crude analysis of the data from 1953 to 1975 supports both hypotheses. (Better would be an analysis of individual behavior rather than aggregated data.) For a dependent variable I use the proportion of the members joining Armed Services during a given Congress who had at least one major installation in their districts. The independent variables (X_1 and X_2, respectively) are the net base closings during the previous two years (total bases closed less total bases opened), and a dummy variable to represent the peak of domestic conflict over Vietnam, which I take to be from the Tet offensive in early 1968 to the last withdrawal of American troops in 1972. The following regression analysis for the twelve Congresses supports both hypotheses and explains 54 percent of the variance:

$$Y = .429 + .019\ X_1 - .242\ X_2$$
$$\qquad\quad (.007) \qquad (.139) \qquad \text{(standard errors)}$$

Clearly, benefit-oriented congressmen were flocking to the committee during periods of intense base-closing activity with, for example, ten base closings increasing by about 19 percent the proportion of new members from military districts (significance level .01). The reverse was true during the Vietnam period, when the proportion of benefit-oriented congressmen dipped by about 24 percent (significance level = .08) as more policy-oriented representatives (both hawks and doves) scrambled for positions on the committee.[28]

28. Actually, the evidence about who was joining the committee does not allow one to differentiate between changes in the committee's attractiveness and changes in committee

Most members apparently find Armed Services a rewarding place to stay. One study of transfer patterns ranked it fifth out of nineteen committees in its ability to hold members, exceeded only by Rules, Ways and Means, Appropriations, and Foreign Affairs.[29] But some members do choose to leave, and a look at which ones make this choice provides insight into the rewards of committee service. Sixteen of the eighty-six members who joined Armed Services between 1953 and 1973 had transferred to other committees by 1975. Most had no installations in their districts. In fact, whereas ten of the thirty-seven members without installations chose to transfer (27 percent), only six of the forty-nine members with installations made this choice (12 percent). (The probability of a difference this large arising purely by chance is .15.) Clearly, those who had installations to protect found greater rewards in committee service than their more policy-oriented colleagues. That there is a difference between members who do and do not come from military districts is also evident if one examines the committees to which they transferred. Four of the six members from military districts transferred to Appropriations (67 percent), a committee noted as a place where one can do nice things for one's district. Only one of the ten members from districts without installations made the same move (10 percent); the others moved to more policy-oriented committees such as Ways and Means (four), Foreign Affairs (two), Judiciary (one), Rules (one), and Science and Astronautics (one). (There is only a .08 probability of a difference this large arising purely by chance.) Those attracted to Armed Services because of an interest in benefits appear relatively satisfied; they leave infrequently, and then only for the greatest benefit committee of all, Appropriations. Those attracted because of an interest in policy seem less satisfied; they are more likely to transfer, and when they do, they tend to choose the more policy-oriented committees.

All this provides a good explanation for why Armed Services became unrepresentative of the House beginning in the early 1960s and continuing until today. Increased base closing activity prompted more con-

assignment patterns. It may well have been a little of both. Increased base closing activity may prompt more congressmen from military districts to request seats, *and* it may make the committee on committees more receptive to arguments based on constituency interests. Likewise, heightened national interest in defense policy may impel more policy-oriented congressmen to request seats while at the same time making the committee on committees more receptive to these requests.

29. George Goodwin, Jr., *The Little Legislatures* (Amherst: University of Massachusetts Press, 1970), pp. 114–15.

gressmen from military districts to join the committee, and once on the committee, they tended to stay until the end of their careers. Vietnam temporarily increased the number of new members from nonmilitary districts, but many of these members found committee service unrewarding and transferred to other committees. Thus, as the size of the military establishment has diminished, the Armed Services Committee has become more and more dominated by congressmen representing military districts.

7: WATER AND SEWER GRANTS

During the Johnson administration the number of expenditure programs increased dramatically. Every public problem was thought a federal problem, and for each of these the administration designed, pushed through Congress, and implemented a specific program to solve or ameliorate it. Nowhere was this proliferation of federal programs more evident than in the government's approach to helping communities construct water and sewer facilities. At least six major programs, administered by four separate departments, dispensed money for such facilities by 1967. (Four of these were enacted in 1965; the other two predated the Johnson administration.)[1] Communities could apply, depending on their eligibility, for Public Facility Loans (HUD), Basic Water and Sewer Facilities Grants (HUD), Grants and Loans for Public Works and Development Facilities (Commerce), Grants and Loans for Water and Waste Disposal Systems for Rural Communities (Agriculture), Construction Grants for Wastewater Treatment Works (Interior), and Grants for Construction of Sewage Treatment Works in Appalachia (Interior).

In this chapter I examine one of these, the program of Water and Sewer Facilities Grants administered by the Department of Housing and Urban Development from 1965 until 1974. In addition to offering a number of theoretically interesting situations, this program has an advantage over the others in that virtually all communities were eligible for its grants. Furthermore, bureaucrats had almost complete freedom in deciding which of these applicants should be allocated a share of the benefits. The other programs either restricted eligibility according to a community's size or location or else dispensed benefits by formula.

Although the water and sewer program signed into law on August 10, 1965, resembled the one Johnson had proposed the previous winter, its

1. J. Clarence Davis, *The Politics of Pollution* (New York: Pegasus, 1970), p. 11.

basic purpose and rationale had undergone considerable change.[2]
Whereas the draft bill served a presidential purpose, the final bill advanced purely congressional ends. The original program was designed
to assist but a small fraction of all communities, those "expected to
experience significant population growth in the reasonably foreseeable
future."[3] The intent was to help these communities cope with growth,
first by encouraging sound planning and then by subsidizing the
additional costs associated with building oversized water and sewer
facilities. It was thought that such a program would save resources in the
long run by avoiding the duplication that would result from having to
rebuild undersized facilities at a later date.

Not surprisingly, few congressmen were enthusiastic about the program. It provided little in the way of general benefits unless, perhaps, a
handful of congressmen with unusually long time perspectives took
pleasure in the fact that society might, by spending a little more today,
save money ten or twenty years hence. There was not even anything for
the environmentalists, for the program specifically excluded sewage
treatment plants from the lists of facilities to be funded. The program
did offer local benefits of substantial value, but restricted them to a
small fraction of all communities. Those eligible were mostly the newer
cities of the South and West and the suburbs ringing the older cities,
while rural areas, most small cities, and the central cities of the East
were ineligible. A majority coalition could hardly be built on such a
foundation, because only a minority of districts contained eligible
communities.

The solution was simple. Coalition leaders on the House Banking
and Currency Committee merely enlarged the program's geographic
scope to include *all* communities, whether large or small, and whether
growing, stable, or declining in population. A community's growth rate
was removed as a criterion for selection and retained only as a factor to

2. The narrative that follows is based on a reading of the relevant hearings, committee
reports, floor debates, and other public documents, as well as summaries in appropriate
volumes of the *Congressional Quarterly Weekly Report* and the *Congressional Quarterly
Almanac.*
3. The draft bill and the administration's justification for it appear in U.S., Congress,
House, Committee on Banking and Currency, *Housing and Urban Development Act of
1965, Hearings before the Subcommittee on Housing,* 89th Cong. 1st sess. 25–31 March
1965, part I, pp. 14, 44.

be considered in planning a facility's size.[4] Of course, the original purpose for the program was lost along the way, but the program survived. Every district was made eligible for a share of benefits, and consequently every congressman was given a reason to support it. As the bill moved through Congress, both the number and value of these shares were also increased. Whereas the draft bill offered federal funding for up to 40 percent of a project's costs, the final bill provided 50 percent for most projects and up to 90 percent for facilities in small communities. In addition, the program's annual authorization was raised from $100 million in the draft bill to $200 million in the final bill.

The program began as a bill with little congressional support. With a few changes, however, it became a bill that no one could oppose, for it virtually guaranteed each congressman a half million dollars worth of public works for his district every year. What's more, the program funded the most noncontroversial type of public works imaginable— water and sewer lines; unlike programs for building dams or roads, it hurt no one directly and therefore could not possibly offend constituents.

The strategy of broadening geographic scope, increasing the number of shares of benefits, and increasing the value of each share was effective. The revised program sailed through Congress. Although the omnibus bill that authorized this and several other programs encountered some opposition, all was centered on a controversial program of rent supplements. Coalition leaders had done their job well for the water and sewer program, for hardly a voice was raised against it, and a formal vote was never even requested.

The program was enacted with almost universal support in Congress, and during the next few years the supporting coalition held firm. Congress always appropriated at least as much as the administration requested, and no dissents, amendments, or recorded votes indicated that anyone wished otherwise. The program began with an appropriation of

4. Members of the House committee made their wishes known in the committee report, where they wrote: "The expectation of growth is not a prerequisite for this aid but only that in planning a system the plans should take into account future demands as well as present requirements" (U.S., Congress, House, Committee on Banking and Currency, *Housing and Urban Development Act of 1965*, House Report #365, 89th Cong. 1st sess., 1965, p. 38.

$100 million in fiscal 1966 and then received another appropriation of the same amount the following year. In subsequent years, as the demand for grants mushroomed, so too did appropriations. In fiscal 1968 the administration requested and received $165 million; in fiscal 1969 they requested $150 million, but Congress appropriated $165 million.

Word about a new federal giveaway gets around quickly. During the program's first three months, HUD received some 2,400 preliminary inquiries for projects estimated to cost $1.4 billion. Of course, some of these did not meet all the necessary requirements for grants; some were referred to other agencies administering similar programs; and still others were never followed by complete applications. Nevertheless, the number of inquiries indicates the magnitude of local demand for grants. By the end of the year, 741 complete applications had been submitted and 225 (30 percent) were funded, thus exhausting the first year's appropriations. Initially HUD employed an allocational system with little discretion for anyone. In fact, control was actually in the hands of the applicants themselves, though they were probably not aware at the time. Decisions were made, first, by allocating available funds to the ten administrative regions, largely according to population, and then by accepting applications within regions on a first-come, first-served basis until funds were exhausted.[5]

Demand for grants remained strong in subsequent years as nearly one thousand new applications poured in annually. If the system of first come, first served had been retained, each year acceptances would have fallen another three or four years behind applications (with, for example, a twelve-year wait for those applying in the third year). Two changes were made to prevent this. First, annual appropriations were increased, which in turn increased the acceptance rate. Second, HUD instituted a system for ranking applications according to certain standards of merit. Those scoring lowest were rejected immediately, while others were retained for subsequent decisions. The new system gave bureaucrats significant discretion over allocational decisions, in that acceptance was neither automatic nor guaranteed for those applications not rejected at the first stage.[6]

5. U.S., Congress, House, Committee on Appropriations, *Independent Offices Appropriations for 1967, Hearings before a Subcommittee of the Committee on Appropriations*, 89th Cong., 2nd sess., part 2, p. 857.

6. U.S., Congress, House, Committee on Appropriations, *Independent Offices and Department of Housing and Urban Development Appropriations for 1968, Hearings before*

The program was immensely popular among both congressmen and local government officials. Local officials liked the subsidies it provided for facilities that otherwise might have required increases in either local taxes or user charges. Congressmen enjoyed the publicity and credit they received every time they announced another grant for another community in their district. The one hitch was that demand far exceeded supply. Money was available to fund only about one out of five applicants. As a consequence, *most* local officials received nothing, and many communicated their disappointment to their congressmen. Although it is impossible to say precisely how each congressman reacted, it seems safe to say that many favored an expansion of the program. Clues can be found in the records of hearings conducted at that time. One such clue was the attitude of Charles Jonas (R., N.C.), the ranking minority member of the Appropriations subcommittee that handled HUD's budget and a man who spent two decades attempting to restrain federal spending. Throughout a number of hearings Jonas berated administration officials for not requesting *more* money for such an important program.[7]

GENERAL ALLOCATIONAL STRATEGIES

Carefully devised allocational strategies would hardly be necessary if bureaucrats sought nothing more than budgetary security. Support for the water and sewer program on local-benefit grounds was so overwhelming that a nondecreasing budget was a foregone conclusion (unless, of course, bureaucrats systematically denied benefits to large classes of congressmen or otherwise set out to alienate part of their natural supporting coalition). Bureaucrats could, in other words, allocate benefits pretty much as they pleased without much concern with congressional politics. However, if bureaucrats also sought budgetary growth (as I have assumed), then carefully devised allocational strategies would

a Subcommittee of the Committee on Appropriations, 90th Cong., 1st sess., part 3, pp. 345–407. For a flow chart of the decision process, see U.S., Department of Housing and Urban Development, *The Federal Grant Process*, Community Development Evaluation Series, Number 10 (Washington, D.C.: Government Printing Office, 1972), p. 40.

7. See, for example, U.S., Congress, House, Committee on Appropriations, *Independent Offices and Department of Housing and Urban Development Appropriations for 1970, Hearings before a Subcommittee of the Committee on Appropriations*, 91st Cong., 1st sess., part 4, pp. 713–15.

serve an important purpose, for they would permit bureaucrats to cope with congressmen's differing attitudes toward growth.

Many congressmen are cross-pressured on the issue of budgetary growth for a public works program such as this. On the one hand, growth seems desirable because a larger program would mean more benefits for their districts. On the other hand, growth implies certain costs, and some congressmen may find unacceptable the associated trade-offs. These costs include less funds for other programs, increased taxes, or a larger deficit (with its resulting economic effects). Of course, if the proposed increase is small (say $10 million), the associated costs would be negligible for most congressmen. However, if the increase is quite large (say $1 billion), congressmen would have to evaluate seriously the trade-offs to determine if the additional local benefits are worth the costs. All congressmen will not evaluate the trade-offs in the same way, for some fear deficits more than others, some place higher priorities on other programs, and some are more philosophically opposed to growth in federal spending.

In addition, some congressmen will feel cross-pressured whenever the administration voices opposition to a program's growth. Both Republican and Democratic administrations tend to oppose growth in public works programs such as this because they see substantial costs but few collective benefits of any magnitude. If the administration does oppose increased appropriations, congressmen from the president's party will be cross-pressured. Party loyalty and a wish to stay on the right side of the president pulls them one way, while the desire for additional local benefits pulls them the other. How much they are influenced by the administration's position will, of course, depend on whether the administration chooses to use its instruments of persuasion.

Bureaucrats can, to a certain extent, counterbalance congressmen's differing attitudes towards growth by allocating extra benefits to those reluctant to sanction growth. These reluctants, after all, are not really opposed to the program itself; their opposition stems from an evaluation of the costs and benefits associated with a larger program, an evaluation that, in their view, shows the expected costs greater than the expected benefits. Bureaucrats can affect some congressmen's evaluations by increasing the shares of benefits for their districts. If congressmen see more local benefits coming their way, the costs will begin to look smaller by comparison. They may decide that although economy in government is important, *this* program is not the place to begin such economies.

The allocational strategies I have chosen to examine are those used in calendar years 1970 and 1971, for in many ways this was the most interesting period for the water and sewer program. In previous years the Johnson administration had accepted moderate expansion of the program in response to the growing backlog of applications. Although this expansion was less than many congressmen might have hoped, it nevertheless provided some relief. Probably most congressmen and bureaucrats did not really expect much more, for the combination of Vietnam and increasing rates of inflation made the expansion of any domestic program extremely difficult during this period. By 1970 the prospects for substantial growth in the program looked better. American involvement in Vietnam was declining, a recession made increased public works spending attractive to many, and the backlog of grant applications was so great that some regional offices had stopped accepting any new ones. Everything seemed favorable *except* for the attitude of the new Nixon administration, which was, as we shall see, cool.

When the strategic situation in Congress changes, different allocational strategies become necessary. As I shall demonstrate later in this chapter, the situation confronting bureaucrats in 1971 was considerably different from the one they faced in 1970, and consequently different allocational strategies were appropriate. For convenience I assume bureaucrats adopted one allocational strategy in January 1970 which guided all their allocational decisions throughout that calendar year, and then, after reassessing the situation in early 1971, adopted a second strategy which guided all their allocational decisions during calendar 1971. The assumption that bureaucrats adopted an allocational strategy at the beginning of a calendar year to govern all their decisions during that year allows one to analyze two processes that actually unfolded at the same time: the budgetary process in Congress and the allocational process in HUD. Essentially I have assumed that bureaucrats devised a general rule at the beginning of the year in anticipation of certain broad congressional actions, rather than readjusting every one of their allocational decisions during the course of a year in response to every problem that developed in Congress as their budget moved through its maze. The assumption that bureaucrats selected a new strategy in January of each year, rather than a couple of months before or after, is admittedly arbitrary. Unfortunately, empirical research requires many such arbitrary assumptions, and this date is as justifiable as any other.

ALLOCATIONAL STRATEGIES, 1970

Increasing the budget for the water and sewer program in 1970 required three things: a majority in Congress to support legislation authorizing such an increase, a majority to support increased appropriations, and either the president's approval of both bills or a two-thirds majority willing to override his veto. A sound allocational strategy would have to address all three problems. Rational bureaucrats seeking budgetary growth would, I suggest, allocate benefits as follows. First, some preference would be given to applications from districts represented either on the Banking and Currency Committee or on one of two subcommittees of the Appropriations Committee, either its Subcommittee on Independent Offices or its Subcommittee on Agriculture. Second, some preference would be given to applications coming from districts represented in Congress by conservatives, particularly Republican conservatives. Third, bureaucrats would tend to accept applications for small or medium-sized projects in preference to those for very large ones.

The reasons for allocating extra shares to committee members were discussed in detail in chapter 4. Banking and Currency was the legislative committee with jurisdiction over the water and sewer program and would have to approve any legislation increasing its authorized spending. Extra shares for committee members could speed such approval, increase the margin of victory at the committee stage, and induce members to act as coalition leaders on the floor. The situation with the Appropriations Committee was more complicated, for jurisdiction over the water and sewer program was being transferred from the Subcommittee on Independent Offices to the Subcommittee on Agriculture.[8] Although the actual transfer did not occur until early 1971, one might

8. This and other programs were transferred to the Subcommittee on Agriculture in an effort to maintain a majority coalition in support of agricultural appropriations. Maintaining coalitions for such programs became increasingly difficult in the late 1960s as the proportion of rural districts diminished and fewer urban congressmen chose to assist their rural colleagues. The solution, contrived by George Mahon (D., Texas) and Jamie Whitten (D., Miss.), two rural congressmen who were, respectively, chairmen of the Appropri-

expect cautious bureaucrats to reward members of both subcommittees, the first for services currently needed and the second in anticipation of services needed in the future.

Conservative congressmen would also be logical candidates for extra allocations, because they were most likely to have serious misgivings about rapid expansion of the program. Extra allocations would give them a greater stake in the program and might even persuade them to support budgetary growth. Republican conservatives were a special case, not because they were any more reluctant to support growth than Democratic conservatives or any more crucial to the coalition than others, but rather because they might be able to persuade Nixon not to veto new authorizing legislation or additional appropriations. The administration had made clear its opposition to growth in this program, but it had not made known how far it would go in opposing growth. If conservative Republicans were to support expansion, Nixon might be more reluctant to veto the legislation than he would if they all had supported his position on the issue.

Finally, if bureaucrats were in fact allocating benefits in a way calculated to maintain a supporting coalition, they would attempt to minimize the expenditure of scarce resources on each individual congressman. Specifically, rational bureaucrats would select small and medium-sized projects in preference to large ones, because the latter rapidly deplete available funds and preclude a broad distribution of benefits among districts. Political considerations make it wiser to allocate four hundred shares of $250,000 each rather than one hundred shares of $1 million each, the assumption being that, in general, four hundred moderately happy congressmen are more valuable than one hundred ecstatically happy congressmen.

---

ations Committee and its Agriculture Subcommittee, was to add to the subcommittee's jurisdiction programs of interest to urban congressmen, such as environmental and consumer protection programs. The effect was to create an appropriations bill that had something for everyone. It was a clever way of assembling majority coalitions for programs of interest to but a minority of districts, far easier than arranging complicated trades between blocs of congressmen when such programs are contained in different bills. The Mahon-Whitten story is recounted in a number of places, including Gerald S. Strom, "Congressional Policy-Making and the Federal Waste Treatment Construction Program," (Ph.D. dissertation, University of Illinois, 1973), chapter 1. Four years later Mahon removed environmental assistance from the subcommittee's jurisdiction, this time to forestall a movement in the Democratic caucus to strip Whitten of his position as chairman. See Michael Barone, Grant Ujifusa, and Douglas Matthews, *The Almanac of American Politics, 1976* (New York: Dutton, 1975), p. 458.

DATA BASE

The data I use throughout the remainder of this chapter are derived from a computer listing of all 8,246 applications for water and sewer grants received between January 1, 1966 and October 7, 1971.[9] The listing includes information about each project's location, the type of project planned, the project's cost, the size of the grant requested, the date an application was received, the date it was accepted or rejected, the current status of the application, and the congressional district in which the project would be located.[10] Using the application, acceptance, and rejection dates, I have reconstructed the file of applications available for bureaucratic action during calendar years 1970 and 1971. As best I can determine, there were 1,647 applications in the active file during 1970, not counting those involving multiple districts or those for which data were missing.[11] Of these, 309 were accepted.[12]

9. The computer output was reprinted in two volumes of congressional hearings. The one I used was U.S., Congress, House, Committee on Banking and Currency, *Emergency Community Facilities and Public Investment Act of 1972, Hearings*, 92nd Cong., 2nd sess., 23 May 1972. An earlier version is contained in U.S., Congress, House, Committee on Banking and Currency, *To Amend Title VII of the Housing and Urban Development Act of 1965, Hearings*, 91st Cong., 2nd sess., 12 and 15 June 1970. The taxpayer took quite a beating, with over 1,600 pages of computer output printed as part of the hearing record (estimated cost, $46,000). But the organization of the material made clear its true purpose. Applications were sorted by state and congressional district so congressmen could easily determine what communities in their districts had applied for funds and how few had been successful. (Printing costs are estimated in U.S., Congress, Commission on the Operation of the Senate, *Senate Administration*, 94th Cong., 2nd sess., 1976, p. 90.)

10. The evidence on congressional districts was in some cases inaccurate. For each application I have checked the district information and revised that which was in error. Most of the errors stemmed from either obvious mistakes in coding or recent reapportionment decisions. There are good reasons to believe that the bureaucrats who made allocational decisions were not victims of the erroneous district information but rather that it was assembled specifically for the public report. One clue is that *all* applications were sorted according to the districts of the Ninety-first Congress, including those received and rejected during the Eighty-ninth and Ninetieth Congresses, when, in many cases, the projects would have been located in completely different districts.

11. During a given year, an application is either accepted, rejected, or carried over into the next year. Each application is assumed to be under active consideration until it is eventually accepted or formally rejected.

12. The figures contained in this chapter do not always agree with those provided in HUD's publications. For example, HUD reports that 318 applications were accepted in 1970, not 309. Such differences stem from the fact that HUD used the complete data set, whereas I have deleted some applications from the file either because they involve multiple districts or because data were missing.

The data set for the water and sewer program is similar to the one used for the analysis of base closings. The basic analytic unit is the *application*, which is, of course, precisely the unit for which bureaucrats make their decisions. For each application I have assembled information about whether it was accepted, rejected, or carried over into the following year, information about various objective attributes, and information about the locality's congressman, including his party, seniority, committee assignment, and ideology.

BIVARIATE ANALYSIS, 1970

My analysis of water and sewer acceptances parallels the previous one of base-closing decisions. First I examine each of the hypotheses individually with some simple bivariate tests. Then I develop and test a more elaborate multivariate model which incorporates certain structural elements from the actual process that bureaucrats constructed for reviewing applications. Throughout, the dependent variable is the probability of an individual application being accepted.

The evidence in table 7.1 provides strong support for the hypothesis that bureaucrats would select applications in part according to their committee representation. Whereas applications from areas without committee representation were accepted less than 18 percent of the time, those represented on either the Banking and Currency Committee or the Appropriations subcommittees enjoyed acceptance rates of 28 to 31 percent, a difference far too large to reflect mere happenstance. The committee advantage was substantial. By chance one would expect approximately twenty-eight applications would have been accepted from committee members' districts; in fact, forty-eight were accepted, or 72 percent more than the laws of chance would predict.

Table 7.1. Effects of Committee Membership on Project Selection, 1970

Applicant Represented on	Application Accepted	Application Not Accepted	Total Decisions	Probability of Acceptance
Subcommittee of Appropriations Committee	21	46	67	.313
Banking and Currency Committee	27	69	96	.281
Neither committee	261	1223	1484	.176
Total	309	1338	1647	

Chi-Square = 13.80   Significance level = .001

The expected advantage for conservative congressmen, particularly Republican conservatives, is also supported by the evidence, though it is considerably weaker than the committee advantage and not in complete agreement with my prediction. (Here I define a conservative congressman as one who supported the position taken by the Americans for Constitutional Action at least 70 percent of the time during the previous year.) As table 7.2A demonstrates, applications from areas represented by conservative congressmen enjoyed acceptance rates about 3 percent higher than those from other areas (21 vs. 18 percent). Although the difference is in the expected direction, there is a relatively high probability (.17) that it reflects nothing but chance. However, if one partitions applicants according to both the party and the ideological position of their congressmen (tables 7.2B and 7.2C), it becomes clear that there was a definite advantage given to conservatives, but it was wholly confined to Republican conservatives. The acceptance rate for applications from areas represented by Republican conservatives was nearly 23 percent, a full 5 percent higher than the acceptance rates for applicants

Table 7.2.   Effects of Congressman's Ideology (and Party) on Project Selection, 1970

Applicant's Congressman	Application Accepted	Application Not Accepted	Total Decisions	Probability of Acceptance
A. Conservative	107	405	512	.209
Moderate/Liberal	202	933	1135	.178
Total	309	1338	1647	
Chi-Square = 2.03		Significance level = .17		
B. Conservative, Republican	79	268	347	.228
Conservative, Democrat	28	137	165	.169
Moderate/Liberal, Republican	69	351	420	.164
Moderate/Liberal, Democrat	133	582	715	.186
Total	309	1338	1647	
Chi-Square = 5.50		Significance level = .15		
C. Conservative, Republican	79	268	347	.228
All others	230	1070	1300	.177
Total	309	1338	1647	
Chi-Square = 4.30		Significance level = .04		
D. Republican	148	619	767	.193
Democrat	161	719	880	.183
Total	309	1338	1647	
Chi-Square = .21		Significance level = .65		

represented either by more liberal congressmen or by conservative Democrats. (There is only a .04 probability that a difference this large would have arisen purely by chance.)

It seems clear that bureaucrats did allocate benefits strategically. Conservative Republicans were, at the same time, both the most reluctant supporters of budgetary growth, given their ideologically based predispositions against federal spending and their sense of loyalty to the administration, and the most important members of any supporting coalition, for they, more than anyone else, might be able to influence Nixon's decision about whether or not to veto increased funding for the program. The evidence allows the inference that bureaucrats recognized their strategic importance and, in an effort to win them over, allocated extra benefits to their districts. The inference can also be drawn that bureaucrats did not perceive conservative Democrats as occupying an important strategic position, for contrary to my expectation, bureaucrats did not give preference to applications from their districts. Finally, in accordance with the argument I have been presenting throughout this work, it is obvious that bureaucrats did not discriminate among applicants strictly on the basis of party (with the exception of the advantage given to conservative Republicans on account of their peculiar strategic importance). As table 7.2D demonstrates, the acceptance rates were not significantly different for applications from Republican and Democratic districts.

The hypothesis that bureaucrats would accept applications for smaller, less expensive projects in preference to those for larger ones is supported by the evidence, though the difference is not overwhelming (table 7.3). The average size of the applications accepted was about 10 percent smaller than the size of those rejected, a difference not quite large enough to be statistically significant. Nevertheless, even a difference this small, assuming it does reflect more than happenstance, means that bureaucrats were able to accept about twenty-six more appli-

Table 7.3.   Effect of Project Size on Project Selection, 1970

	Mean Grant Requested	n
Application accepted	$445,000	309
Application not accepted	$495,000	1338

T = 1.40   Significance level = .16

cations (9 percent) than they could have if size were not a criterion for selection. Once again, bureaucrats seem to be acting rationally (i.e., in accordance with the postulated goals) by conserving their scarce resources.

MULTIVARIATE MODEL, 1970

The discussion up until now has completely ignored the *process* of bureaucratic decision making, whereas, in fact, a great deal is known about that process. Bureaucrats constructed an allocational system designed to serve multiple goals, including both their public service goal and their budgetary goals. The system contained an elaborate set of guidelines for appraising applications according to standards of merit, with each application assigned points on the basis of fourteen separate evaluations (for such things as size of the service area, per capita income, financial need, quality of housing stock, proximity of public housing, etc.).[13] At the same time, the system gave bureaucrats the right to make the final selection, for the numerical rankings of applications were meant to be guides, not substitutes for their own judgment. Bureaucrats could, in other words, substitute political criteria for standards of merit.

Under this system, the probability of an application being accepted depended on fourteen objective criteria plus whatever political criteria bureaucrats choose to apply. In addition, an application's chances for acceptance depended on the demand for grants within the administrative region in which it was located and on when the application was first submitted. Region was important, because for equity's sake as well as for administrative convenience, available funds were first assigned to the ten regions according to a formula (based on population and per capita income), and then allocations were made within regions until these ceilings were reached. An applicant's chances for a grant depended on the region in which it was located, because, as we shall see, the demand for benefits varied widely from region to region and in a manner completely unrelated to variations in the allocation of funds among regions.

13. The system for ranking applications is described in Circular MPD 6220.2, located in the files of the Department of Housing and Urban Development.

In 1970, for example, the region with headquarters in Chicago had on file applications for nine times its annual allocation of funds, while the one with headquarters in San Francisco had a backlog of only three times its annual allocation.

In the long run, the date on which an application is filed probably has little effect on whether or not it is eventually accepted. However, if one asks which applications will be accepted during a particular calendar year, this date does become important, for large organizations have their procedures, and procedures take time. An application filed today is unlikely to be accepted tomorrow, simply because the review process is time consuming. As an application ages, however, one expects the probability of its acceptance to increase (up to a point). On the other hand, one expects very old applications to have a lower probability of acceptance, if only because they have been passed over so many times (with repeated declinations suggesting both lack of merit and lack of political importance). A graph of acceptances and age might look something like figure 7.1, with the ordinate representing either the probability of an individual application being accepted or the frequency with which applications of a given age are accepted. Of course, bureaucrats were not prisoners of the procedures they developed; they could, if they wished, reach forward and accept a brand new application or reach backwards and accept a very old one, either because the application was particularly meritorious or because its acceptance was politically useful.

The forces that affect bureaucrats' allocational decisions are well

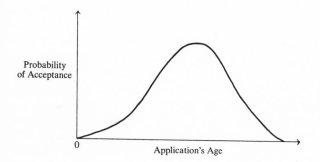

Probability of Acceptance

0   Application's Age

Figure 7.1. Hypothetical Function of Age and Acceptance

known, and one could, at least in theory, construct a multivariate model incorporating all of them. However, testing such a model would be a Herculean task, because the necessary information concerning the fourteen objective criteria exists only on the applications themselves, which, seven years later, are no longer accessible. Age and regional demand can more easily be incorporated into the model, for the appropriate information is readily available. Convenience aside, there is also a real need to include regional demand in the model in order to estimate accurately the impact of the political variables, for region tends to be correlated with such variables as conservatism, and thus the exclusion of the former could lead to biased estimates of the latter. Presumably the fourteen criteria of merit are not significantly correlated with the political variables (or at least there is no reason to expect that they would be), so that their exclusion should not bias the estimates.

The basic structure of the model is as described in chapter 5. I assume that the probability of an application being accepted during calendar 1970 is a quadratic function of an application's age and is a linear function of three committee variables, two variables representing combinations of ideology and party, a variable measuring a project's size, a variable measuring the regional imbalance between available resources and the demand for benefits, and a random error term. Each committee variable is a dummy variable which takes a value of one if an application is represented on a particular committee and zero otherwise. The committees coded are the Banking and Currency Committee, the Independent Offices and the Agriculture Subcommittees of the Appropriations Committee, and the full Appropriations Committee (excepting members of these two subcommittees). Once again, the final category is included not because members of the full committee are thought to influence bureaucrats' decisions but rather to facilitate a discussion in a subsequent chapter. The two ideological variables are also dummy variables. The first takes a value of one if an application is represented by a Republican conservative; the second is similarly coded if it is represented by a Democratic conservative. The remaining variables are continuous. A project's size is represented by the dollar value of the grant requested (in millions, but measured to the third decimal place), while regional demand is the ratio of the total funds allocated to a region and the total grants requested (times 100). An application's time in the queue (measured to one decimal place) is taken to be the number of years between its filing date and the last day of 1970.

Once again, probit analysis is an appropriate method for estimating the model, because the underlying dependent variable is a continuous, bounded probability that happens to have been observed as a dichotomy. The hypothesized curvilinear relationship between an application's age and the probability of its acceptance can be incorporated into the model by including two variables, one measuring its age and the other the square of its age.

The probit analysis of bureaucrats' decisions, summarized in table 7.4, supports most of the hypotheses. Looking first at the probit equation itself, one can see that the first two committee relationships were strong, positive, and highly significant (and, as expected, the third one involving representation on the full Appropriations Committee was minuscule and insignificant). Similarly, representation by a conservative Republican was positively related to the probability of an applica-

Table 7.4. Probit Analysis: Effects of Political Variables on Project Selection, 1970

Variable	Probit Coefficient	Standard Error	Significance Level	Sample Mean
a Subcommittee of Appropriations Committee	.444	.180	.02	.041
b Banking and Currency Committee	.368	.154	.02	.058
c [Rest of Appropriations Committee]	.086	.142	.55	.087
d Conservative Republican	.178	.096	.06	.210
e Conservative Democrat	−.209	.136	.12	.100
f Grant size	−.046	.077	.55	.486
g Regional demand	.025	.006	.0001	18.381
h Time in queue	1.486	.135	.0001	1.515
i (Time in queue)^2	−.230	.027	.0001	3.418
Constant	−3.064			

n = 1647 applications

Analysis of political variables:

Applicant Represented by	Probability of Acceptance $[a = 1]$ Appropriations Subcommittee	$[b = 1]$ Banking Committee	$[a, b = 0]$ Neither
[d = 1] Conservative Republican	.657	.629	.485
[d, e = 0] Moderate/Liberal	.591	.561	.415
[e = 1] Conservative Democrat	.508	.479	.337

Notes: Variables a, b, d, and e take the values given in the appropriate rows and columns. Variables c, f, and g take their sample means. Variables h and i take the value that maximizes the age function (3.24 years).

tion's acceptance. Surprisingly, however, the relationship involving representation by a conservative Democrat was strong, *negative*, and nearly significant (significance level = .12). The hypothesis was that such representation would be positively correlated, the bivariate analysis suggested there was no relationship at all, and now the multivariate analysis demonstrates that with the effects of other variables held constant, conservative Democrats were actually doing worse than their colleagues. Assuming that this is not merely a statistical fluke, it suggests that bureaucrats were allocating fewer benefits to this class of congressmen than to any other class.[14] Unfortunately, I have no explanation for this. Grant size is, as expected, negatively related to acceptance, but the magnitude of the relationship is small, and significance tests suggest that it may reflect nothing more than chance. Finally, the hypotheses about regional demand and applications' age are strongly supported.

In the second part of table 7.4 I have estimated the marginal impact of the committee and ideological variables by varying the values of these variables while setting other variables to their most typical values. (For most variables, this typical value is its sample mean; for the age variable, the appropriate value is the one that maximizes the quadratic age function, about 3.24 years.)[15] The impact of committee representation on acceptance rates is striking. Applications represented on the proper committees enjoyed acceptance rates 1.3 to 1.5 times higher than others. The impact of ideology and party was somewhat less, though still

14. The standard error for the Democratic conservative variable suggests that there was as much as a 12 percent chance that the coefficient was actually no different from zero. However, there was less than a 1 percent chance that the acceptance rates for Democratic and Republican conservatives were the same. The hypothesis that two coefficients are actually no different can be tested with probit analysis (in a manner similar to the one used with regression analysis) by estimating two probit equations, one without any constraints and one with the two coefficients constrained to be equal. Since it is known that minus two times the difference between the logs of the likelihood function for the two models is approximately distributed like chi-square with one degree of freedom, one can easily test the hypothesis of no difference. In this case, minus two times the difference equals 6.68, which suggests that there is less than a .01 probability that the acceptance rates were actually equal. See James Tobin, "The Application of Multivariate Probit Analysis to Economic Survey Data," Cowles Foundation Discussion Paper, number 1 (1955), pp. 9–11.

15. The mean of the age variable represents how long the typical application had been on file. The value that maximizes the age function is the amount of time the typical *accepted* application had to wait before acceptance.

significant. Applications represented by conservative Republicans had acceptance rates of 1.1 to 1.2 times the rate of those represented by their more liberal colleagues, and 1.3 to 1.4 times that of conservative Democrats.

The multivariate model in table 7.4 is actually quite complex, for imbedded in it are two types of curvilinear relationships. First is the quadratic age function, in which, as expected, the probability of acceptance first increases as an application waits in queue and then, after reaching a peak (at about 3.2 years), begins to drop off. Second, as the reader will recall from chapter 5, *all* relationships in a probit model are, by assumption, curvilinear, for the marginal impact of one variable depends both on its value and on the value of all other variables in the model. The nature of all these curvilinear relationships is illustrated in figure 7.2, where the probability of acceptance is plotted against age for various classes of applications. Figure T demonstrates how the likelihood of acceptance varies with an application's age for a typical application—i.e., one neither represented on a committee nor by a conservative Republican, and which took the mean value of every other variable in the model. As one can see, an application received during 1970 had only a tiny chance (less than 10 percent) of being accepted during the same year, whereas those on file for about three years had approximately a 40 percent chance of being accepted.

Figures A and CR plot the same function for two classes of applications, the first for those with representation on the Appropriations subcommittees and the second for those represented by conservative Republicans. The reader will note that figures A, CR, and T are not parallel, for the distances between peaks are far greater than the distances between tails; this is a consequence of the curvilinear relationships inherent in any probit model. (By contrast, in an analogous regression model that also contained a quadratic age function, one would find a whole family of parallel curves nested atop one another, for the marginal impact of one variable is assumed to be independent of the values of others.) Figure 7.2 can be viewed as a graphic representation of influence. The area between figures A and T, for example, represents the influence of members of the Appropriations subcommittees over bureaucrats' allocational decisions, while the area between figures CR and T represents the much smaller influence of conservative Republicans.

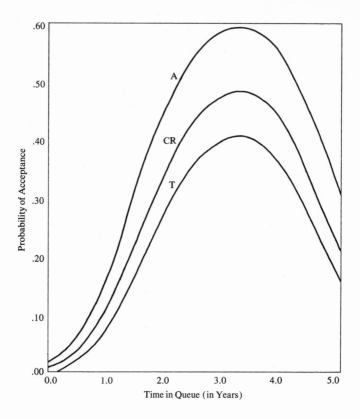

Figure 7.2. Probability of Acceptance as a Function of Age for Three Classes of Applications (1970)

Most of the hypotheses about bureaucrats' behavior during calendar year 1970 are supported by the multivariate analysis. The importance of committee membership is undeniable; bureaucrats accepted applications represented on either the Banking and Currency Committee or the Appropriations subcommittees with much greater frequency than they did other classes of applications. It is also clear that conservative Republicans were favored by bureaucrats, though contrary to expectation, conservative Democrats were not. The special treatment afforded conservative Republicans supports the claim that bureaucrats would see them as the most crucial coalition members. There is weak support for the hypothesis that bureaucrats would prefer small projects to large ones in order to maximize the number of shares allocated.

CONGRESSIONAL ACTION, 1970

While program administrators were allocating benefits, Congress was busy shaping the legislation necessary for the program's expansion. Previous law authorized $500 million for fiscal year 1971, and Democratic leaders on the House Banking and Currency Committee proposed increasing this authorization to $1.5 billion (or more than *eleven* times the actual amount funded for fiscal year 1970). A bill authorizing this amount was reported out of committee in June and was passed by the House in early September (by a 281 to 32 vote). Opposition to the expansion was minimal and came almost exclusively from a few conservative Republicans. Eleven days later the Senate passed the same bill by a voice vote. President Nixon allowed the bill to become law without his signature, although he clearly disapproved of it. He said he had decided not to veto it because it merely authorized increased spending but did not appropriate any funds he might be obligated to spend.

The road to increased appropriations was not so easy. Appropriations politics is a politics of scarcity and thus much closer to a zero-sum game, whereas the politics of authorizations leans towards the symbolic. At the authorization stage congressmen demonstrate all the things they are for; at the appropriations stage their priorities begin to show. They can, without contradiction, authorize all the money in the Treasury for one program today, and then authorize all the money in the Treasury for another tomorrow, and still not deplete it of a single cent. But when it comes to appropriations, they have to make choices. (Of course, to fund all programs fully is to choose either higher taxes or a larger deficit.)

The administration requested $150 million for the water and sewer program, an increase of 11 percent over the previous year's appropriations. The House Appropriations Committee recommended the same amount. On the House floor, however, an amendment was added to increase appropriations to $500 million, which at the time (May) was all the law authorized. The Senate Committee recommended $200 million, but it was overruled on the floor as an amendment was adopted increasing appropriations to $500 million. President Nixon then vetoed the $18 billion bill appropriating funds for the Department of Housing and Urban Development (and various independent agencies), calling inflationary a bill $540 million above his request. Since the only major provisions in the bill which exceeded the administration's request were an extra $350 million each for the water and sewer and urban renewal programs, it should be fair to characterize the veto as a rejection of increased funding for these two programs, though the issue was not framed quite that simply. The House failed in its effort to override the veto by a vote of 204 to 195. Congress then passed a second bill, identical to the first except for cuts of $150 million each for the urban renewal and water and sewer programs. Nixon signed the bill into law on December 17.

The water and sewer program had a good year in Congress during 1970, though it came close to being even better. Its annual authorization was tripled to $1.5 billion, and its appropriated funds were increased from $135 million to $350 million. But by the end of the year, it had become clear that there was sentiment in Congress for even greater increases, though the intensity of support was still insufficient to overcome a presidential veto.

Unfortunately, it is not possible to determine if the allocational strategies that bureaucrats employed during 1970 affected congressmen's actual voting decisions. One thing is certain: extra allocations to conservative Republicans did not contribute much to the maintenance of a winning coalition. Although most of them supported an increase in the authorization level and many supported increased appropriations, they did not persuade Nixon to sign the original appropriations bill, and they were unwilling to override his veto.

ALLOCATIONAL STRATEGIES, 1971

The situation that bureaucrats faced at the start of calendar 1971 was somewhat different from the one they faced at the start of 1970. In 1970 they had little experience to guide them, for during the previous four years of relatively stable appropriations, the program had not an enemy in Congress. Bureaucrats could only guess how various classes of congressmen might react to proposals for expansion or what the administration might do to block it. By 1971 the lines had been drawn more clearly. On a number of occasions congressmen had been forced to stand up and be counted as either for or against budgetary expansion, and the administration had demonstrated its eagerness to veto major increases. In addition, after a year's experience, it became clear that increasing the program's authorization was no hurdle at all; it was the appropriations bill that drew the fire.

Given these changes, one should expect that bureaucrats would alter their allocational strategies in order to take into account the failures of 1970. The principal failure was that Nixon had vetoed the original appropriations bill, a veto the House was unable to override. Bureaucrats apparently anticipated the administration's opposition, for they channeled extra benefits into the districts of conservative Republicans; however, the strategy failed, for these congressmen neither persuaded Nixon to sign the bill nor joined the effort to override his veto. Reacting to their 1970 experiences, bureaucrats would, I think, orient their allocational strategy for 1971 towards overriding a presidential veto, not preventing one.

The question, then, is how would bureaucrats allocate benefits in order to create a congressional coalition large enough to override a presidential veto? Bureaucrats began the task with excellent knowledge of where congressmen stood, for most had established voting records on the program during the previous year (excepting freshmen and a few absentees). The list of 204 congressmen who had voted to override Nixon's veto the previous year constituted the core of the program's supporters, while the 195 who voted to sustain it were the ones in need of a little persuasion. In fact, however, bureaucrats needed to convert only about a third of the latter group in order to override a presidential veto, assuming that the support of the first group held fast. So the question becomes, which third? In general, one expects it would be easier to convince the Democrats in this group to override a Republican president's veto than it would be to persuade the Republicans. If benefits were unlimited, one might be able to bring the Republicans around too; but since the benefits available for distribution were in fact scarce, it made sense to concentrate them where they had the greatest chance of producing the desired effects.

Bureaucrats seeking to build a coalition capable of overriding a presidential veto would, I suspect, allocate generous shares of benefits to those Democratic congressmen who previously had voted to sustain such a veto, the logic being that if they were given a greater stake in the program, they might decide to reverse themselves and support increased appropriations (just as they had supported even larger increases in the program's authorizations). Generous shares would also be allocated to core supporters, whether Democrats or Republicans. Their support, it will be recalled, stemmed not from any fundamental attachment to the program, but rather was contingent upon constituency benefits. On the other hand, bureaucrats would have no reason to provide special allocations for those Republican congressmen who had voted to sustain the veto, since it was unlikely they would reverse themselves anyway. In fact, it was by cutting back on acceptances for Republican opponents that bureaucrats could afford to allocate extra shares both to core supporters and to Democratic opponents. There was, after all, but a limited stock of benefits to be distributed.

Again one should expect bureaucrats to allocate extra shares of benefits to members of the two Appropriations subcommittees. Although jurisdiction over the water and sewer program was formally transferred from the Independent Offices Subcommittee to the Agriculture Subcommittee at the start of 1971, one might still expect cautious bureaucrats to reward members of both subcommittees, particularly since there was no reason to expect that the transfer would be permanent. (In fact, it was not.) Bureaucrats might also allocate extra shares to members of Banking and Currency to encourage them to continue working as coalition leaders. However, the ease with which authorization legislation sailed through the House the previous year, as compared with appropriations legislation, suggests that members of this committee need not be a high priority. Finally, one still expects that bureaucrats would select small projects in preference to large ones, despite the fact that support for this hypothesis in 1970 was not overwhelming.

BIVARIATE ANALYSIS, 1971

The data base I use is essentially the same as the one used from the 1970 analysis. It consists of the 1,444 applications[16] on file during 1971

16. Of these, 870 were carried over from 1970 (309 had been accepted that year and 468 rejected), while 574 were new in 1971.

Table 7.5.   Effect of Congressman's Position on Overriding Veto on Project Selection,
              1971

Applicant's Congressman	Application Accepted	Application Not Accepted	Total Decisions	Probability of Acceptance
Supported funds*	163	590	753	.216
Opposed funds†	110	581	691	.159
Total	273	1171	1444	

Chi-Square = 7.34   Significance level = .01

Notes: *Voted to override veto in 1970 (or freshman with no record).
       †Voted to sustain veto.

Supported funds, Democrat	134	490	624	.215
Supported funds, Republican	29	100	129	.225
Opposed funds, Democrat	44	170	214	.206
Opposed funds, Republican	66	411	477	.138
Total	273	1171	1444	

Chi-Square = 12.13   Significance level = .01

(excepting those received after October 7, 1971, the cutoff date for the published data). Bureaucrats accepted 273 of these.[17]

The hypothesis that bureaucrats would orient their allocational strategy towards overriding a presidential veto is supported by the evidence. As table 7.5 demonstrates, there was a strong relationship between how congressmen voted on the motion to override the veto in 1970 and the acceptance of applications in 1971. The evidence suggests that bureaucrats favored two groups: those who had supported the override attempt, and the Democratic congressmen who had not. The acceptance rate for applicants represented by members of these two groups was more than 1.5 times higher than the acceptance rate for applications represented by Republicans who had opposed the motion to override (a difference far too large to have arisen purely by chance). The inference can be drawn that bureaucrats were rewarding their core supporters and attempting to "buy off" those members of the opposition who were most likely to reverse themselves. The reader should note that the Democratic advantage over Republicans existed only among congressmen who opposed the override attempt; there was no difference

17. Actually, according to HUD's figures, there were 326 applications accepted during 1971. My figures refer only to those accepted prior to October 7.

between the acceptance rates for Democratic and Republican supporters, and indeed none would have served bureaucrats' purposes.

The evidence in table 7.6 demonstrates once again that bureaucrats
selected applications at least in part according to their committee representation. As expected, applications represented on the Appropriations
subcommittees enjoyed a high acceptance rate (28 percent), one nearly
1.5 times that of applications with no committee representation. However, the relationships between representation on the Banking and Currency Committee and the probability of acceptance was not at all as
expected, for applicants with committee representation had a considerably *lower* acceptance rate than those without any committee representation. Of course, Banking and Currency was not a crucial committee in 1971, given the ease with which authorization legislation sailed
through the House in 1970; but that was hardly a reason for punishing
its members, for they were still in a position to do much harm. A key to
the anomaly is contained in the second part of the table, where committee members are apportioned according to how they voted in 1970 on
the override motion. Banking and Currency members who supported
funding had their applications accepted with about the same frequency
as noncommittee members, whereas Banking and Currency members

Table 7.6.   Effects of Committee Membership on Project Selection, 1971

Applicant Represented on	Application Accepted	Application Not Accepted	Total Decisions	Probability of Acceptance
Subcommittee of Appropriations Committee	18	47	65	.277
Banking and Currency Committee	12	81	93	.129
Neither committee	243	1043	1286	.189
Total	273	1171	1444	
Chi-Square = 5.46		Significance level = .07		
Appropriations Subcommittee, Supported	11	22	33	.333
Appropriations Subcommittee, Opposed	7	25	32	.218
Banking and Currency Committee, Supported	10	41	51	.196
Banking and Currency Committee, Opposed	2	40	42	.048
Total	30	128	158	
Chi-Square = 10.08		Significance level = .02		

Table 7.7. Effect of Project Size on Project Selection, 1971

	Mean Grant Requested	n
Application accepted	$439,000	273
Application not accepted	$523,000	1171

T = 2.05   Significance level = .04

who opposed funding had an acceptance rate less than a quarter of the normal rate. (Only 4.8 percent of such applications were accepted!) Conceivably, bureaucrats were punishing errant committee members who, after receiving extra benefits in 1970, still voted against funding on the crucial override vote.

The hypothesis that bureaucrats would accept small projects in preference to large ones in order to maximize the number of applications that could be accepted is supported by the evidence (table 7.7). Applications not accepted had an average size about 20 percent larger than the size of those accepted, a statistically significant difference. A bias this large means that bureaucrats accepted approximately thirty-seven more applications (16 percent) than they would have if size were not a criterion for selection.

MULTIVARIATE MODEL, 1971

Again I have constructed and tested a multivariate model of bureaucratic decision making, a model that parallels in most respects the one developed for 1970. The model's only changes reflect bureaucrats' adoption of a new political strategy, for the selection process itself was no different. Again I assume that the probability of an application being accepted is a quadratic function of an application's age and is a linear function of four committee variables, two variables representing combinations of a congressman's party and position, a variable measuring a project's size, and a variable representing regional demand. The committee variables are the same as before, except that there are now two dummy variables for representation on Banking and Currency, one for members who supported the override attempt, and one for those who opposed it. The party-position variables were also dummy variables, one of which took a value of one if an application was represented by a

Republican who had opposed the override attempt, while the other was similarly coded for a Democrat who opposed it. All other variables were defined and coded as they were in the 1970 model.

The probit analysis of bureaucrats' allocational decisions (table 7.8) provides exceptionally strong support for the various hypotheses. As before, applicants represented on the Appropriations subcommittees were accepted with greater frequency than others, though the size of the difference was slightly smaller in 1971 than it was in 1970. In contrast, applicants represented on Banking and Currency enjoyed differential

Table 7.8. Probit Analysis: Effects of Political Variables on Project Selection, 1971

	Variable	Probit Coefficient	Standard Error	Significance Level	Sample Mean
a	Subcommittee of Appropriations Committee	.295	.180	.10	.046
b	Banking and Currency Committee, Supported	.103	.220	.65	.035
c	Banking and Currency Committee Opposed	− .495	.327	.12	.030
d	[Rest of Appropriations Committee]	.032	.135	.80	.104
e	Republican, Opposed funds	− .221	.098	.03	.332
f	Democrat, Opposed funds	.141	.122	.25	.148
g	Grant size	− .180	.085	.04	.508
h	Regional demand	.026	.005	.0001	19.862
i	Time in queue	1.515	.158	.0001	1.538
j	(Time in queue)²	− .277	.035	.0001	3.392
	Constant	−2.784			

n = 1444 applications

Analysis of political variables:

	Applicant Represented by	Probability of Acceptance		
		[a = 1] Appropriations Subcommittee	[b or c = 1] Banking Committee	[a, b, c = 0] Neither
[f = 1]	Democrat, Opposed funds	.560	.263	.443
[e, f = 0]	Supported funds	.504	.429	.388
[e = 1]	Republican, Opposed funds	.417	.159	.307

Notes: Variables a, b, c, e, and f take the values given in the appropriate rows and columns. Variables d, g, and h take their sample means. Variables i and j take the value that maximizes the age function (2.73 years).

success depending on how their representatives had voted on the override motion. Those applications represented by supporters had a slight advantage, though it was far too small to be statistically significant; nevertheless, they were doing no worse than average. However, those represented by opponents of the motion did considerably worse than any other class of applicants (with a significance level of .12, which was, if anything, surprisingly large given that less than 3 percent of all applicants belonged to this class). It seems plausible that bureaucrats were, in effect, punishing committee members who had opposed the motion. Among rank-and-file congressmen it appears that Republican opponents were also denied their fair share of benefits (a difference that was highly significant), while Democratic opponents were doing slightly better than average (a difference that was not significant). Finally, as expected, bureaucrats accepted applications for small projects in preference to those for large ones (a relationship that was both stronger than the corresponding one for 1970 and statistically significant).

In the second part of table 7.8 I have estimated, using the probit equation, the probability of acceptance for nine classes of applicants, depending on a congressman's party, position, and committee assignment. As one can see, the disparity in acceptance rates for the nine classes of congressmen was considerable, ranging from 16 percent for applicants represented on Banking and Currency by Republican opponents to 56 percent for those represented on the Appropriations subcommittees by Democratic opponents. In general, the disparity was far greater in 1971 than in 1970 (tables 7.4 and 7.8). Whereas in 1970 the highest acceptance rate was only about 1.9 times greater than the lowest, in 1971 the highest was 3.5 times greater than the lowest. This change may suggest that bureaucrats' allocational decisions were much more politically oriented in 1971 than they were in 1970. This would hardly be surprising, for after a year's experience, bureaucrats had a much better sense of who their friends were and what was standing in the way of budgetary expansion.

The contention that bureaucrats' decisions in 1971 were increasingly political is also supported by the fact that bureaucrats were much more likely to select applications for smaller, less expensive projects in 1971, a decision that increased the number of shares of benefits to be allocated. In fact, the relationship between project size and the probability of acceptance was nearly four times greater in 1971 (compare the probit coefficients in tables 7.4 and 7.8). A plausible reason for bureaucrats' marked preference for smaller projects in 1971 is that they were then certain that they needed to build a two-thirds coalition, whereas in 1970 they could only guess as to whether Nixon would veto an increase in their budget.

CONGRESSIONAL ACTION, 1971

While bureaucrats were allocating benefits, Congress was again acting on proposals to expand the program's budget. In early 1971 many congressmen were surprised to learn that the administration was requesting no additional appropriations for the water and sewer program for fiscal 1972 (July 1971 to June 1972). In fact, the administration had no intention of spending the $350 million appropriated for the current year. Although President Nixon had signed the appropriations bill containing that amount, he quickly impounded $200 million; program administrators had thus been given only $150 million, precisely what they had been spending the previous years. The administration then proposed that the remaining $200 million be carried over into fiscal year 1972, with no new appropriations required.

Needless to say, congressmen who had worked for the program's expansion during the previous year were displeased (so, presumably, were program administrators, though their reactions are not part of the public record). The House Appropriations Committee reacted by proposing an additional $150 million, which, combined with the $200 million carryover, would fund the program at the level that Congress and the president had approved for the current year. On the floor an amendment was adopted by voice vote to raise the total to $500 million, the level that Congress had approved the previous year but which the president had vetoed. The Senate also approved $500 million. In early August, when the entire bill appropriating funds for agriculture, environmental assistance, and consumer protection reached Nixon's desk, he signed it, despite the fact that it was $1.2 billion (about 10 percent) over his request and contained $500 million for the water and sewer program.

Given the nature of the program, it is not surprising that Congress had approved annual appropriations more than triple what they were only two years before. But it is surprising that Nixon eventually accepted the tripling when he so obviously disliked the program. Why did he not veto the bill as he had done the year before? Conceivably he might have thought that Congress would override his veto in 1971, although it could not the previous year. Indeed, Congress might well have, for the water and sewer program was now part of an agriculture, environmental assistance, and consumer protection bill, a bill that catered to every regional and ideological taste, whereas before it was part of a housing and urban development bill, a bill that disproportionally benefited certain types of districts. Alternatively, Nixon's failure to veto the bill may simply reflect cyclical changes in his propensity to veto bills. Almost all (twenty-five of twenty-eight) of his vetoes of public bills during the first term took place in the election years 1970 and 1972 (presumably to demonstrate how a frugal administration was battling against a spendthrift Congress).[18] Finally, it could be that Nixon had found selective impoundment far superior to the blanket veto for controlling the growth of unwanted programs. Whatever his motivation, he signed the bill. For my purposes that was unfortunate, for without a veto one cannot determine if bureaucrats' allocational strategy in 1971 had any effect on congressmen's voting decisions.

ALTERNATIVE EXPLANATIONS

I have made the case that bureaucrats allocated benefits in a way calculated to maintain and increase the size of the program's supporting coalition. But could other explanations equally well account for the observed relationships between project selection and such variables as project size, committee representation, party, ideology, and roll-call votes? Specifically, in making allocational decisions, did bureaucrats employ some objective criteria that were themselves correlated with these political variables, such that the relationships which I have been describing between these variables and project selection were actually spurious? An argument along these lines might well be made for the

18. The breakdown of vetoes is as follows: 1969 (0), 1970 (9), 1971 (3), and 1972 (16). All five vetoes of appropriations bills took place in election years. See *Congress and the Nation, Volume III,* 1969–1972 (Washington, D.C.: Congressional Quarterly, 1973), pp. 101a–105a.

relationship between project size and project selection, for small projects usually come from small communities, and such communities are both less likely to have adequate facilities and more likely to have a compelling need for outside financial assistance. Making a similar case for the other political variables is considerably more difficult, particularly because of changes in the pattern of allocational decisions between 1970 and 1971. These shifts can easily be explained in a political framework, but it is difficult to imagine how objective variables could produce such reversals as the one in which representation on the Banking and Currency Committee was first positively and then negatively associated with the acceptance of a particular class of applications.

Alternative explanations for the advantage given to applicants represented on the Appropriations subcommittees cannot be so easily dismissed, for the relationship was, as expected, essentially the same in both years. Perhaps applications from such districts just happened to be particularly worthy of federal assistance (the spuriousness problem), or perhaps congressmen from especially needy areas sought and gained seats on the committee (the causal direction problem). Such alternative hypotheses can easily be tested with a time-series analysis of allocational decisions. As I discussed earlier, bureaucrats had good reason in 1970 and 1971 to reward with extra benefits members of the Agriculture Subcommittee of House Appropriations; before 1970, however, there was no reason at all to reward disproportionally congressmen from these same districts, for they did not yet occupy institutional positions of strategic importance. Table 7.9 demonstrates that, in fact, the acceptance rate for applications from these districts jumped from 21 percent (1966–69) to 38 percent (1970–71) when the subcommittee first gained jurisdiction over the water and sewer program. Such a dramatic shift supports the political explanation, for it is unlikely that the general

Table 7.9. Probability of Acceptance for Applications Located in Districts that Were, Either in 1970 or 1971, Represented on the Subcommittee on Agriculture of House Appropriations

Applications on file in	Application Accepted	Application Not Accepted	Total Decisions	Probability of Acceptance
1966–69	25	96	121	.21
1970–71	16	29	42	.38
Total	41	122	163	

Chi-Square = 4.16   Significance level = .04

Table 7.10.   Probability of Acceptance for Applications Located in Districts Represented
              on the Independent Offices Subcommittee between 1966 and 1971

A. *Applications from Districts*	*Application Accepted*	*Application Not Accepted*	*Total Decisions*	*Probability of Acceptance*
On subcommittee throughout 1966–71	34	72	106	.32
Never on subcommittee during 1966–71	1642	5149	6791	.24
Total	1676	5221	6897	

Chi-Square = 3.12   Significance level = .08

B. *Applications from Districts on Subcommittee during Portion of 1966–71 Period*				
Action while on subcommittee	38	69	107	.36
Action while off subcommittee	17	70	87	.19
Total	55	139	194	

Chi-Square = 5.26   Significance level = .02

C. *Applications from Districts on Subcommittee during All or Part of 1966–71 Period*				
Action while on subcommittee	72	141	213	.34
Action while off subcommittee	1659	5219	6878	.24
Total	1731	5360	7091	

Chi-Square = 9.98   Significance level = .001

merit of applications within the same districts changed substantially
over time.

A similar story emerges from a time-series analysis of the Independent
Offices Subcommittee of House Appropriations. According to the
theory, members of this subcommittee would be given extra allocations
both between 1966 and 1970, when it had exclusive jurisdiction over
the program, and in 1971, for the reasons discussed previously. For
purposes of analysis, I have sorted according to congressional district[19]
all applications on file between 1966 and 1971, and then aggregated
them into three classes: applications from districts never represented on
the Independent Offices Subcommittee; applications from districts represented on it throughout the period 1966 to 1971; and applications
from districts represented on it for only part of this period. Table 7.10A

19. For the analysis in tables 7.9 and 7.10 I employ districts of the Ninety-first Congress, with all applications assigned to one of these districts even if, at the time it was filed,
accepted, or rejected, it was located in another (because of reapportionment).

compares the acceptance rates for applications in the first two classes.
The evidence supports the conclusion that throughout the period 1966
to 1971, districts represented on the subcommittee were doing better
than average, with an acceptance rate about 1.3 times larger. Apparently subcommittee members' influence was not confined to the years
1970 and 1971, when bureaucrats were battling for budgetary expansion
(though the magnitude of that influence does appear greater during
these two years).

Table 7.10B addresses itself to the question of whether the relationship between subcommittee membership and project selection was
spurious. The table focuses on applications from but a few districts
(those represented on the subcommittee for less than the entire six years)
and seeks to determine if the probability of acceptance was higher when
applications enjoyed subcommittee representation. In fact, the acceptance rate was nearly twice as great (36 vs. 19 percent), thus putting to
rest any fears of a spurious relationship. Finally, table 7.10C combines
the previous two tables to demonstrate the magnitude of subcommittee
influence for the six-year period. The conclusion is inescapable:
throughout the period 1966 to 1971 bureaucrats adjusted their allocational decisions to take into account subcommittee members' preferences.

EXTENT OF INFLUENCE

Elsewhere in this chapter I have attempted to measure the influence
of particular classes of congressmen over bureaucrats' allocational decisions in 1970 and 1971. But how extensive was this influence? How
frequently did bureaucrats adjust their decisions in an effort to affect the
size of their supporting coalition? As best I can estimate, program administrators for the water and sewer program adjusted a larger proportion of their allocational decisions than did Pentagon officials. Using
the same basic method as I did in the previous chapter, I estimate that
approximately 17 percent of the favorable decisions in 1970, and approximately 27 percent of those in 1971, would have been made differently if program administrators had not been constrained by the
allocational strategies I have attributed to them.[20] (Recall that Pentagon

20. I prepared these estimates using the observed probabilities only, whereas in the

officials adjusted approximately 10 percent of their site selection decisions and between 9 percent and 14 percent of their closing decisions.)
That program administrators adjusted more of their decisions than Pentagon officials is consistent with theory, for their strategies encompassed
both committee members and rank-and-file congressmen, whereas Pentagon officials could, because of the nature of their supporting coalition,
deal with committee members alone.

PROGRAM DEATH

Old programs never die, or so it is thought.[21] However, the water and
sewer program did expire, and it is important to show how, particularly
because I have been arguing that it was one of the most popular programs in Congress. It died not for lack of congressional support but
rather because the administration used powers (later declared unlawful)
to thwart the will of Congress.[22] In 1972 the administration again
impounded most of the appropriated funds, releasing only $150 million
for the program. Then, in January 1973, the administration ordered a
complete halt in all new commitments for this and several other HUD
programs. At the same time they proposed that about ten categorical
grant programs (including water and sewer) be consolidated into a single
program of block grants for community development, a formula program. The administration argued that it was pointless to spend money
on programs "scheduled for termination." In fact, the impoundment of
all program funds was simply a way of pressuring congressmen to support the new block-grant program. Although litigation was in process to
force the administration to release the funds, communities were mean-

---

previous chapter I calculated them separately from the probit and observed values. About
half of the 17 percent (and about half of the 27 percent) can be attributed to the committee, party, and position variables, while the other half stems from the preference given to
small projects. Of course, these two streams are not necessarily independent. Bureaucrats
may have allocated to committee members only those funds saved by selecting small
projects. To the extent that this is true, my method results in a biased estimate of the
extent of congressional influence, because it counts such decisions twice.

21. The literature on program termination is limited, but see "Termination of Policies,
Programs, and Organizations," special issue of *Policy Sciences*, volume 7, number 2
(1976); or Herbert Kaufman, *Are Government Organizations Immortal?* (Washington,
D.C.: Brookings, 1976).

22. The story is recounted in greater detail in Louis Fisher, *Presidential Spending
Power* (Princeton: Princeton University Press, 1975), pp. 192–94.

while denied any benefits under either the old categorical programs or the new formula program. As time wore on, pressure built up for *some* program, and in August 1974, Congress approved the new block-grant program, formally terminating the water and sewer program. At about the same time, a United States district court ruled that the secretary of Housing and Urban Development had no authority to suspend the program, but by then it was too late.

8: MODEL CITIES GRANTS

The story of the model cities program parallels in many respects the water and sewer story. Both were originally designed to benefit but a limited number of communities and as such had little congressional appeal. Both were completely redesigned in the process of coalition building. In each case eligibility criteria were broadened to encompass a large proportion of all communities, and the number of projects to be funded was increased so that at least a majority of congressmen could share in the benefits. But there were also substantial differences between the two programs; and, as a consequence, different allocational strategies were required.

Model Cities was, from the start, a controversial program. There was neither agreement that the federal government should be involved in rebuilding cities, both physically and socially, nor that the model cities program would be an effective means of doing so. By contrast, the water and sewer program was relatively noncontroversial, for the federal government had a long history of assisting state and local governments in performing state and local functions. What's more, public works have a greater inherent appeal to congressmen than social programs.

The model cities program had its origins in a presidential task force organized in October 1965 and given the mission of developing new programs for the Department of Housing and Urban Development, then in its first year.[1] The nine-member task force worked quickly, for the new programs had to be ready for the president's State of the Union

1. For detailed accounts of its legislative history, see Edward C. Banfield, "Making a New Federal Program: Model Cities, 1964–1968," in Allan P. Sindler (ed.), *Policy and Politics in America: Six Case Studies* (Boston: Little, Brown, 1973), pp. 124–58; Bernard J. Frieden and Marshall Kaplan, *The Politics of Neglect: Urban Aid from Model Cities to Revenue Sharing* (Cambridge, Mass.: The MIT Press, 1975), pp. 1–66; *Congressional Quarterly Almanac, 1966* (Washington, D.C.: Congressional Quarterly, 1967), pp. 210–30; and Robert B. Semple, Jr., "Signing of Model Cities Bill Ends Long Struggle to Keep It Alive," *New York Times*, 4 November 1966, pp. 1, 44.

address in January, and completely in secret, without consulting either the agencies concerned or the Congress. It was composed mostly of academics and interest-group leaders, with no one from the bureaucracy itself and only one congressional representative, Senator Ribicoff (D., Conn.), who was only an occasional participant.

Members first attempted to determine why previous programs had not produced better results. Although various explanations were advanced, attention was focused on three. Members were receptive to a suggestion from Charles Schultze, then director of the Bureau of the Budget, that federal assistance had been spread too thinly in urban areas to have had much impact. Second, some members thought that previous programs had paid excessive attention to physical reconstruction and insufficient attention to social issues. Finally, they agreed that there had been little coordination among all the federal programs then in existence, each of which had been designed to ameliorate but a single, narrow problem. The solution proposed was a "demonstration cities program" which would concentrate resources in a few urban communities to demonstrate what saturation spending could accomplish. Such a program would, the task force thought, show the nation how sufficient money properly spent could transform existing urban complexes into new cities.

Originally it was to be an experimental program. Schultze favored selecting five or ten cities in order to evaluate carefully the impact of saturation spending.[2] Others proposed even fewer.[3] But as the task force deliberated, the number kept expanding. The first draft of their report proposed thirty-six cities: six with populations over 500,000, ten with populations between 200,000 and 500,000, and twenty with populations below 200,000. Senator Ribicoff suggested that fifty cities would be more appropriate, so that each senator would have grounds for expecting his state would share in the program. Their final report proposed sixty-six cities: six large, ten medium, and fifty smaller ones. Expansion was necessary to make it politically attractive to Congress, but expansion was contrary to the goal of an experimental program.

The task force's deliberations lasted about two months, and in late December it submitted a report to the president recommending the

2. Banfield, "Making a New Federal Program," p. 132.
3. Frieden and Kaplan, *The Politics of Neglect*, p. 47.

model cities program. Two weeks later, in his 1966 State of the Union address, Johnson formally announced it, and by the end of January draft bills were introduced in both House and Senate. The reaction in Congress was cool. There was, of course, the predictable opposition from conservatives to yet another urban spending program, but such opposition was hardly a serious impediment in the overwhelmingly Democratic, leftward-leaning Eighty-ninth Congress. Others, however, argued that if the present urban programs were defective they should be reformed, rather than creating another new program which would then have to coexist with all the defective ones. But by far the greatest concern was that only a limited number of cities could participate in the program, and consequently only a limited number of congressmen could share in the benefits. Moreover, cities participating in the program were supposed to obtain preferential access to other grant programs such as urban renewal, and thus nonparticipating cities might suffer real declines in federal assistance as funds were diverted to the fortunate few.

Although the bill was eventually enacted, it was a long, ten-month struggle in which, as one reporter put it, "the measure endured as many perils as Pauline, required frequent rescue, and on two occasions was pronounced stone dead, beyond even the resuscitative powers of the President."[4] Its final passage can be attributed to three factors. First, a series of compromises defused controversial sections of the bill. Desegregation provisions were softened to make it more palatable to southern Democrats.[5] The role of federal coordinators, one of the program's principal innovations, was reduced to practically nothing in order to counter charges that federal officials would wield great power over local officials.[6] The program's funding authorization was reduced from $2.3 billion spread over five years to $900 million for two years, a move designed to appease fiscal conservatives.[7] Second, the number of shares of local benefits was increased and their geographic scope expanded. The Senate doubled the number of participating cities by adding money for a second round of competition.[8] In an effort to convince Senator

4. Semple, "Signing of Model Cities Bill," p. 1.
5. Frieden and Kaplan, The Politics of Neglect, p. 47.
6. Banfield, "Making a New Federal Program," p. 138.
7. Semple, "Signing of Model Cities Bill," p. 44.
8. Frieden and Kaplan, The Politics of Neglect, p. 59.

Muskie (D., Maine) to manage the bill in the Senate, the administration incorporated a provision guaranteeing the selection of some small cities.[9] (Senators Douglas [D., Ill.] and Sparkman [D., Ala.], the usual managers of housing legislation, were preoccupied with reelection campaigns.) An amendment was added on the Senate floor limiting any state's share of funds to 15 percent of the national total, thus insuring that plenty of money would be left for smaller states.[10] The administration added $600 million to the urban renewal authorization so that participating cities, with their preferential access to urban renewal funds, would not deny nonparticipating cities their accustomed shares of assistance.[11] Third, the administration lobbied hard in Congress and stimulated lobbying efforts by labor, business, and civil rights groups. Banfield writes that administration officials had

> scores of private meetings with members of Congress to make explanations, listen to objections, and, when absolutely necessary, offer assurances that a place would not be overlooked when the time came to select the "winning" cities. By the end of the summer, this promise had been made to *more than 100 legislators*, which was less than a third of those who asked for it.[12]

These efforts eventually succeeded, and majority coalitions were formed in both House and Senate. The House passed it by a vote of 178 to 141, the Senate by 53 to 22. (The adoption of the conference report was even closer: 142 to 126, and 38 to 22.) But the final program hardly resembled the one conceived by the presidential task force. An experimental program of five to ten cities was transformed into a program benefiting 120 to 150. A program with a powerful federal coordinator now had none, and thus was more like a traditional categorical assistance program. Selection of cities, supposed to be according to the quality of their proposals, had been compromised by assurances of special treatment for certain congressmen. The whole idea of concentrating large amounts of money in a few cities had been replaced by a congressional desire to spread the same funds among many cities.

9. Semple, "Signing of Model Cities Bill," p. 44.
10. Frieden and Kaplan, *The Politics of Neglect*, p. 60.
11. Banfield, "Making a New Federal Program," p. 137.
12. Ibid., p. 138 (emphasis mine).

Everywhere one looks, congressional purposes replaced presidential purposes. But the program survived.

The supporting coalition in the House was primarily liberal, Democratic, and urban. Most northern Democrats were supporters (141–11) while most southern Democrats were opposed (21–49). Republicans were overwhelmingly opposed (16–81), with only members from the liberal wing, most representing metropolitan districts in the Northeast, voting for it on final passage. The opposition was, by congressional standards, intense. Congressional Quarterly characterized the floor debate as one of the most acrimonious of the session.[13] Opponents first proposed dozens of crippling amendments and then worked to kill the entire bill, first with a recommittal motion (which failed by twenty-six votes), then on final passage (which passed by thirty-seven votes), and finally on adoption of the conference report (which carried by a margin of sixteen votes). Model cities was enacted amid extreme ideological and partisan conflict, with divisions made even deeper by the administration's intense lobbying effort. The result was a polarized distribution, similar to the one characterized in chapter 4.

The program survived the tests of the Eighty-ninth Congress, but the victory proved short-lived. A mere five days after the bill was signed, Republicans staged a comeback at the polls, gaining forty-seven seats in the House. The fragile model cities coalition of the Eighty-ninth Congress was no longer a majority coalition (assuming that most of these new members would, like the rest of their Republican colleagues, oppose the program). Such changes threatened the program's very existence. Although the Eighty-ninth Congress had appropriated $11 million for planning grants just before it adjourned, the major appropriations requests would require the approval of the Ninetieth Congress.

THE YEAR OF DECISION, 1967

The signing of the model cities bill set in motion two interrelated decision-making processes: the selection of cities and the appropriation of funds. Each required nearly a year to complete. The Department of Housing and Urban Development announced the competition for

13. *Congressional Quarterly Almanac*, 1966, p. 227.

model cities funds in December 1966, just a few weeks after the Eighty-ninth Congress had appropriated $11 million for the program (an amount sufficient to fund a year's planning grants for sixty to seventy cities). Applicants were given until May 1, 1967 to submit complete applications, a deadline 193 cities met. Throughout May and June HUD reviewed these applications and by mid July was ready to make its selection. But, as we shall see, appropriations politics in Congress dictated that they delay their selection until the appropriations bill was approved, not because further appropriations were necessary for city selection but rather because delaying city selection helped secure the bill's approval.

The appropriations battle, which ran concurrently with the selection of cities, began in January 1967, when President Johnson requested $662 million for model cities, including $12 million for a second round of planning grants, $400 million for project grants for first-round cities, and $250 million for associated urban renewal expenses. Hearings were held in April, and serious consideration of the budget began in May. The first test came in the Independent Offices Subcommittee of House Appropriations, where opponents defeated (four to eight) a motion to approve the administration's full request of $662 million. Opponents then attempted to eliminate all but the $12 million in planning funds; their motion failed on a tie vote. Subsequently the subcommittee voted unanimously to approve a compromise figure of $237 million: $12 million for planning, $150 million for projects, and $75 million for urban renewal. The full committee concurred. On the House floor opponents again attempted to delete all but the $12 million in planning funds; the recommittal motion containing these instructions was defeated, 193 to 213. After this crucial vote, all was downhill (and predictable). The House passed the bill containing $237 million, the Senate increased it to $537 million, and the conference committee settled on $312 million. On November 3, 1967, a year to the day after signing the initial model cities authorization and nearly ten months after first requesting funds, President Johnson signed into law a bill appropriating less than half the amount he had requested.

The appropriations battle was a continuation of the original battle over creating the model cities program. Opponents, unable to defeat it in the waning days of the Eighty-ninth, saw better prospects at the start of the Ninetieth—and they very nearly succeeded. In subcommittee the

Table 8.1.   Comparison of Freshman's Position on Funding in 1967 with Predecessor's
             Position in 1966

| | | Position in 1967 | | | Proportion |
		For	Against	Total	Who Switched
Predecessor's	For	16	26	42	.62
Position in 1966	Against	0	18	18	.00
	Total	16	44	60	

program was saved by a tie vote, while on the floor a switch of only
eleven votes (out of 406) would have denied it operating funds. The
program survived because the attractions of local benefits for some
congressmen counterbalanced the changes in Congress caused by the
1966 election.

The election did have a significant impact on the model cities coalition. Fifty-one of seventy freshmen (73 percent) voted against funding
on the 1967 recommittal motion. Table 8.1 compares the positions of
freshmen on this motion with their predecessors' positions on the 1966
authorization vote. Whereas only eighteen of their predecessors (30
percent) opposed authorization, forty-four freshmen (73 percent) opposed funding.[14] The 1966 election alone can account for a shift of at
least twenty-six votes from the supporting to the opposing coalition.

But there were also forces working in the opposite direction, forces
pushing incumbents from the opposing to the supporting coalition.
Ordinarily one expects individual congressmen to vote the same way
from year to year as long as issues remain unchanged.[15] The basic issues
involved in the model cities votes were essentially the same in 1966 and
1967, with but one exception. In 1966 congressmen were voting on a
prospective program; their districts were not yet filled with eager applicants waiting for shares of benefits. In 1967 congressmen were voting on
an existing program, that had attracted 193 applications in just four
months. If, as I have argued, congressmen were interested in acquiring
benefits for their districts, one should expect that at least some would
modify their positions in 1967 as a response to this change. Specifically,

14. There were actually seventy-three freshmen in 1967. Table 8.1 compares the
positions of only sixty because three freshmen and ten predecessors did not take positions
on the issues, either with a floor vote or with a "pair."
15. See John W. Kingdon, *Congressmen's Voting Decisions* (New York: Harper and
Row, 1973), pp. 254–57.

Table 8.2.   Opponents in 1966 Who Became Supporters in 1967 When Their Districts
             First Applied for Benefits

District Contained Applicant	Opponent Became Supporter	Opponent Remained Opposed	Total	Proportion Who Converted
At least one	16	19	35	.457
None	10	83	93	.108
Total	26	102	128	

Chi-Square = 17.10   Significance level = .001

one expects that those who opposed the program in 1966, only to
discover a few months later that their own districts were competing for
benefits, would reverse themselves in 1967 and support the program. In
fact, as table 8.2 demonstrates, that is exactly what they did. Nearly half
of those who opposed the program in 1966 but who had applicants in
their districts in 1967 became supporters, whereas only about one-tenth
of those without applicants reversed themselves.[16] The evidence supports my contention that congressmen will adjust their voting decisions
in pursuit of local benefits.

The impact of local benefits was even greater within the Appropriations subcommittee. Recall that the effort to eliminate all operating
funds failed in subcommittee on a tie vote (six to six). The crucial vote,
according to most reports, was that of Louis Wyman (R., N.H.), the
only Republican to support funding on the subcommittee.[17] Wyman
was an unlikely convert, for he was extremely conservative; he was the
only New England representative to vote against the 1964 Civil Rights
Act, was a strong supporter of Goldwater's presidential bid, and scored
high on various scales of conservatism. A plausible explanation for his
support was that Manchester, the largest city in his district, had applied
to be a model city, and he was eager to have it selected.

Another force that contributed to the eventual passage of the bill was
the natural tendency of Appropriations members to support on the floor
the recommendations of its subcommittees.[18] As table 8.3 demon-

16. Table 8.2 contains only 128 incumbents, whereas 141 voted against model cities in
1966. The difference reflects the defeat of a few opponents in 1966 and the failure of some
to take any position in 1967.
17. See *Congressional Quarterly Almanac*, 1967 (Washington, D.C.: Congressional
Quarterly, 1968), p. 478.
18. Richard Fenno, Jr., *The Power of the Purse* (Boston: Little, Brown, 1966), pp.
160–66, 460–69.

Table 8.3. Appropriations Committee Members' Support for Model Cities in 1966
            and 1967

| | | Position in 1967 | | | Proportion |
		For	Against	Total	Who Converted
Position	For	15	0	15	.00
in 1966	Against	8	19	27	.30
	Total	23	19	42	

strates, most members of Appropriations were opposed to the program
when it was first considered; only fifteen members (36 percent) voted for
it in 1966.[19] But in 1967, when the question was framed in terms of
support for one of their own subcommittees, eight additional members
supported it, raising the committee's support score to 55 percent of all
members. The chairman of the full committee, George Mahon (D.,
Texas), who vigorously opposed funding in subcommittee, was a strong
supporter on the floor.

The 1966 election did contribute to the diminution of the model
cities coalition. But the attractions of local benefits and the loyalty of
Appropriations members produced converts at least as numerous, and
the program survived. Also contributing to the victory were two calculated bureaucratic decisions. The first was to require that all applications be submitted by May 1, just about the time Congress began
consideration of the appropriations bill. As a consequence, congressmen knew before they voted whether their districts were competitors. Second, bureaucrats delayed the selection and announcement of
winning cities from mid July until November, when the bill was finally
approved.[20] This delay was necessary because there were more congressmen interested in acquiring benefits than there were cities to go
around, at least in the first round of competition.

ALLOCATIONAL STRATEGIES, 1967

With the appropriations battle won, bureaucrats faced the problem of
how to allocate benefits. It was no trivial matter. If nothing else, the

19. Table 8.3 includes only members who served in both Congresses and who took
positions in both years.
20. For evidence that the delay was strategic and not accidental, see Banfield, "Making
a New Federal Program," p. 147, and Frieden and Kaplan, *The Politics of Neglect*, pp.
194–95.

previous two years had demonstrated how shallow was support for the *concept* of model cities but how broad was congressional interest in its local benefits. A majority of congressmen eventually joined the coalition, but only after the program had been redesigned in ways calculated to affect their local-benefit evaluations. Now the question was whether bureaucrats could satisfy local-benefit expectations and thus keep the coalition together.

If more cities could have been selected, the allocation problem would have been less severe. In fact, it would have served bureaucrats' interests if at least one city could have been accepted from every congressional district. Such a strategy would both satisfy current coalition members and create local pressures in the districts of opponents, pressures that might convert some to the cause or at least lessen the intensity of their opposition. But bureaucrats could accept at most seventy-five cities in 1967 and another seventy-five in 1968, so giving benefits to all was impossible.

Given the scarcity of benefits, bureaucrats needed to set priorities to insure that the actual distribution of benefits would contribute to the maintenance of the supporting coalition. All distributions of benefits would not be equally productive, because some congressmen were more crucial to the coalition than others, and because some patterns of acceptance would satisfy more congressmen than would others. Bureaucrats seeking to maintain their supporting coalition might adopt four general decision rules.

First, they could be expected to *reward their supporters*. Specifically, they would select applicants represented by model cities proponents in preference to applicants represented by opponents. Some congressmen had obtained assurances of special consideration for their districts as a condition of their initial support in 1966.[21] But even without such promises, bureaucrats would be well advised to reward them, for a share of benefits would guarantee their future support, while denying them a share might alienate them. Reserving benefits for supporters would also serve notice on opponents that they must first alter their basic positions if they expected to share in the benefits. (Obviously, many opponents had not yet made the connection between support and selection. At the same time that some were voting in 1967 to deny the program funds,

21. Banfield, "Making a New Federal Program," p. 138.

they were also writing letters to HUD asking that their cities be selected.)[22]

Second, bureaucrats could be expected to *reward committee members*. Those who deserved such special attention were members of the Independent Offices Subcommittee of House Appropriations, the Banking and Currency Committee, and the full Appropriations Committee. The Independent Offices Subcommittee was by far the most important; it was here that the major battle of 1967 had been fought, and it would be here that any battles in 1968 would begin. Allocating benefits to subcommittee members had to be bureaucrats' first priority. Banking and Currency was the legislative committee that handled the original model cities authorization in 1966, and the following year it would have to reexamine the program and decide whether to reauthorize it. On these grounds alone it would have served bureaucrats' purposes to give special consideration to committee members' needs. In addition, Banking and Currency had, from the very beginning, been a source of coalition leaders for the program. Ordinarily one would not expect members of the full Appropriations Committee to receive special treatment when benefits were being allocated. Model cities, however, was no ordinary program, for committee members had played a crucial role in its funding. After the subcommittee had split evenly on the question of appropriating operating funds, the full committee could easily have decided to resolve the dispute itself. If it had, funding would probably have been denied, for the committee was filled with opponents. But not only did committee members refrain from intervening, nearly a third of the original opponents switched and became supporters on the floor. Bureaucrats might well have wanted to reward committee members on these grounds alone. Even more important, however, a divided subcommittee and a hostile committee make for an uncertain future; a single change in the subcommittee's membership could threaten a program's very existence. Bureaucrats could reduce such uncertainty by working to expand their support both in subcommittee *and* in the full committee (the principal source of new subcommittee members).

Third, bureaucrats could choose to *accept multiple-district cities* in preference to single-district cities. Most applicants were represented by only one congressman; a few, however, either because of their size or

22. 113 *Congressional Record*, p. 13666.

because of redistricters' preferences, spanned two or more districts. Accepting such cities in preference to single-district cities would be considerably more productive in terms of maintaining the coalition, because, given a fixed number of cities to be allocated, more congressmen could be rewarded with an acceptance. For the very largest cities such as New York, this strategy invariably yields diminishing marginal returns (for reasons discussed in chapter 2); but, in general, the argument holds.

Finally, rational bureaucrats would *accept only one application* per congressional district. Awarding more than one city to a district would be equivalent to paying twice for the same vote and would effectively deny benefits to other deserving congressmen.

These four decision rules suggest how bureaucrats would select cities if they had complete freedom in allocational matters and if they worked solely in pursuit of budgetary security and were not at all motivated by a public service goal. But how accurate were these assumptions? Bureaucrats' freedom to make allocations was, in fact, almost complete. It was constrained by only two provisions of law. The first prohibited any state from receiving more than 15 percent of model cities funds, a provision that could have confined bureaucrats' choices in but a few cases. The second required them to give "equal regard to the problems of small as well as large cities." Such a phrase was sufficiently ambiguous and open to alternative interpretations (equal funds, equal number of cities, equal acceptance rates, or equal consideration) that it could hardly be a serious problem. It is also clear that although the four political decision rules restricted bureaucrats' choices in many ways, they were not determinative. They did not preclude bureaucrats from incorporating into their review and selection procedures various standards of merit. Political considerations might dictate that supporters be rewarded, but *which* supporters would be so fortunate could be determined according to standards of merit. Similarly, political considerations might dictate that a particular committee member deserved an acceptance, but standards of merit could be used to select which of two applicants in his district should be chosen.

BIVARIATE ANALYSIS, 1967

HUD selected seventy-five cities in the first round of competition. Among the applicants were 159 single-district cities, thirty-two

Table 8.4. Acceptance Rate for Multiple-District Cities Compared with That for Single-District Cities (Round One)

City contained	Applicant Accepted	Applicant Rejected	Total Decisions	Proportion Accepted
Multiple districts	22	10	32	.69
Single district	51	108	159	.32
Total	73	118	191	

Chi-Square = 13.67   Significance level = .001
Unit of analysis: application.

multiple-district cities, and two cities not represented in Congress (San Juan, Puerto Rico and Washington, D.C.). Both of these cities are excluded from the following analysis, although both were accepted.[23] In this section I compare the actual choices bureaucrats made with the selections implied by the four decision rules. The list of applications was compiled at my request by HUD's Office of Community Planning and Development; the list of acceptances is readily available in various HUD publications.

The proposition that bureaucrats would accept multiple-district cities in preference to single-district cities is supported by the evidence in table 8.4. Although most of the cities selected were single-district cities, the acceptance rate for multiple-district cities was more than twice as great. Nearly 70 percent of such applications were accepted, as compared with 32 percent for single-district applicants. The evidence is consistent with my argument that for political reasons, bureaucrats would select cities in which more than one congressman had a direct interest. But it is also consistent with an argument that bureaucrats favored large cities (since large cities are necessarily multiple-district cities). In a later section I attempt to disentangle these effects.

Testing the other three propositions is more complex, for the various propositions suggest different analytic units. Ordinarily one would use *applications* as the basic analytic units. In this case, however, applications are not the best choice, because the fourth decision rule states that bureaucrats would select at most one application from each congressional district. If, for example, one used applications as analytic units in testing the committee hypothesis, one would count as a "failure" every rejection of a committee member's application, even if that member

23. These two acceptances demonstrate that there were other values besides political ones influencing the selection process.

had another application accepted. Clearly such an event is not a failure of the committee hypothesis but rather a success for the fourth decision rule. The solution is to use *districts* as analytic units, or more precisely to examine those districts containing one or more applicant cities. By focusing on districts one can study the effects of committee membership on selection while controlling for the effects of the fourth decision rule. The question to be examined, then, is which districts containing applicant cities were accepted rather than which applications within these districts were selected. [24]

Of course, such a research strategy is applicable only to the 159 single-district applicants and not to the thirty-two multiple-district applicants. But for the reasons discussed in chapter 2, *any* sound research strategy would have to treat them separately. Actually, in this chapter I concentrate almost exclusively on an examination of single-district applicants. Not only would an analysis of multiple-district applicants be inherently more complex, but the number of cases (thirty-two) is simply too small to fuel such a complex analysis.

The evidence in table 8.5 confirms the proposition that bureaucrats would reward their supporters and deny benefits to their opponents. (A congressman is considered a supporter of funding if he voted against the recommittal motion on the appropriations bill in 1967.) [25] Forty-eight of ninety supporters (53 percent) had applications from their districts accepted, whereas only *one* of forty-one opponents (2 percent) was so fortunate. Although there are other explanations for a bias in favor of supporters (which I will examine later), a bias this large could only reflect a carefully calculated bureaucratic strategy. It is inconceivable that all applicants (but one) represented by an opponent were inferior in quality to all applicants represented by supporters; more believable is

24. Some readers may wonder if, by focusing on districts, I am not repeating the same error that I attributed to previous authors in chapter 5. In fact there is a critical difference. Previous authors examined *all* districts, whether or not they were competing for a particular benefit or even eligible for a share; such a method scores as a failure every instance in which a committee member's district received no benefits, even if it had no application on file. In this study I examine *only* districts containing applicant cities, and thus avoid the general problem.

25. For those congressmen who did not vote on the motion, I have substituted their announced positions (as reported by Congressional Quarterly). Two congressmen did not announce positions. For one of these, Smith of Iowa, I have substituted his position on the passage of model cities in 1966. The other congressman, Thompson of Georgia, a freshman, had to be dropped from the analysis.

Table 8.5.   Effect of 1967 Vote on District Selection (Round One)

District Represented by Congressman Who	At Least One Application Accepted	All Applications Rejected	Total Districts	Proportion with an Acceptance
Supported funds	48	42	90	.53
Opposed funds	1	40	41	.02
Total	49	82	131	

Chi-Square = 29.04   Significance level = .001
Unit of analysis: district containing one or more single-district applications.

that they were rejected on the basis of political inferiority. The identity of the one opponent who received a city provides further support for the notion of a carefully calculated strategy. The city was Charlotte, North Carolina. Its congressman was Charles Jonas, ranking minority member on the Independent Offices Subcommittee of House Appropriations. He was, in other words, the one opponent whose conversion bureaucrats would value most. He had opposed the progam from the very beginning in 1966, and again in subcommittee and on the floor in 1967. If he could be convinced to support the program, the Appropriations subcommittee would no longer be evenly divided. Furthermore, if Jonas supported funding, other conservative Republicans might follow, for many looked to him for advice and voting cues. The acceptance of Charlotte appears as a classic case of buying off an opposition leader (chapter 4).[26] Of course, accepting a city from Jonas's district could not guarantee that he would switch sides. But once funds were flowing into his district's largest city and his district acquired a real interest in the program's continuance, it would be extremely difficult for him to advocate its termination, much less to lead the opposing coalition.

Jonas was not the only committee member awarded a model city. As table 8.6 demonstrates, bureaucrats allocated a disproportionate number of cities to committee members, though with the exception of Jonas, the rewards were reserved for members who supported funding. All five supporters on the Independent Offices Subcommittee of House

26. Curiously, two authors view the acceptance of Charlotte as proof that politics was *not* particularly important in the selection process. They argue that bureaucrats must have been guided by standards of merit to have selected a city represented by such a vigorous opponent. But such a view assumes that "political" explanations must involve payment for past support rather than the purchase of future support. See Neil Gilbert and Harry Specht, "Picking Winners: Federal Discretion and Local Experience as Bases for Planning Grant Allocation," *Public Administration Review* 34 (1974): 567.

Table 8.6.   Effects of Committee Membership (and 1967 Vote) on District Selection (Round One)

District Represented on	At Least One Application Accepted	All Applications Rejected	Total Districts	Proportion with an Acceptance
Relevant committee	16	14	30	.53
Other committees	33	68	101	.33
Total	49	82	131	

Chi-Square = 3.38   Significance level = .07

S* Appropriations Subcommittee	5	0	5	1.00
S Banking and Currency Committee	5	1	6	.83
S Rest of Appropriations Committee	5	6	11	.45
S Other committees	33	35	68	.49
O† Appropriations Subcommittee	1	1	2	.50
O Banking and Currency Committee	0	2	2	.00
O Rest of Appropriations Committee	0	4	4	.00
O Other committees	0	33	33	.00
Total	49	82	131	

Chi-Square = 40.79   Significance level = .001
Unit of analysis: district containing one or more single-district applications.
Notes: *Supported funds.
†Opposed funds.

Appropriations had an application accepted, as did five of six supporters on the Banking and Currency Committee. Although I suspected that members of the full Appropriations Committee would also receive a disproportionate share of acceptances, they actually were awarded no more than average. That bureaucrats rewarded ten of eleven supporters on the Appropriations subcommittee and the legislative committee which together supervised the model cities program is further evidence that political calculations must have guided bureaucrats' decisions.

The evidence is also consistent with the proposition that bureaucrats would accept but one application from each congressional district in order to reward as many congressmen as possible, though the number of districts with multiple applications is too small to permit confident conclusions. (Better evidence is reported later, after the second round of competition.) Although twenty-one congressmen had two single-district applicants in their districts and three congressmen had three, only one of these (Olsen of Montana) had more than one accepted. In other words, only one city was "wasted" in the sense that bureaucrats could have used it to reward an additional coalition member.[27] This should be compared with a model in which each application has an equal chance of selection, a model that forces city selection to be independent of district boundaries (table 8.7). Under these conditions, approximately 3.1 cities would have been wasted.[28] This is more than the actual number, but the difference is too small to be statistically significant. If there is a political explanation for the fact that bureaucrats accepted two cities in Olsen's district (and there may not be), it probably centers on the Senate, not the House. Olsen had supported the program faithfully, but he was neither a member of an important committee, nor did he occupy any other strategic position. On the other hand, Montana's senior senator, Mike Mansfield, was a member of the Independent Offices Subcommittee of Senate Appropriations, as well as majority leader. If anything, the double payment was for Mansfield's services, not Olsen's.[29]

The evidence lends support to all four hypotheses about bureaucrats' behavior. As expected, bureaucrats gave preference to supporters, committee members, and multiple-district cities and, with one exception, awarded no more than one city per district. They acted just as one would expect rational bureaucrats would act if they were attempting to hold together a coalition such as the one then supporting model cities. However, there are alternative explanations for the observed relationships. Here I examine alternative *political* explanations; later I discuss nonpolitical ones. Some observers have argued that partisan politics

27. There were also a few congressmen who represented all of a single-district city and part of a multiple-district city—for example, John Conyers (D., Mich.), who represented all of Highland Park and part of Detroit. For such cases I have not counted a dual acceptance as double payment, since so many congressmen shared the benefits produced by the two acceptances (six in the Detroit case).

28. The calculations are relatively simple and are computed from the three binomial distributions associated with the three types of districts (one-applicant, two-applicant, and three-applicant).

29. For readers interested in accounting for all seventy-five cities in the various tables, bureaucrats accepted a total of twenty-two multiple-district cities and fifty-three single-district cities. In addition to the forty-nine single-district cities represented in tables 8.5 and 8.6, they accepted one city from a district in which the congressman took no position (Thompson of Georgia), one city as a district's second city (Olsen of Montana), and two cities not represented in Congress (San Juan and Washington, D.C.).

Table 8.7.   Number of Cities Accepted Per District (Round One)

	Number of Cities	Number of Districts	"Wasted" Cities
Theory predicts	51	51	0.0
Actual selections	51	50	1.0
Equal chance for each application	51	47.9	3.1

influenced the selections, with Republican congressmen systematically denied their fair shares of benefits. Gerald Ford (R., Michigan), then House minority leader, made such a charge immediately after the selection was announced.[30] On the surface the charge appears true, for a disproportionate number of cities were awarded to Democratic districts. But a Democratic advantage need not be the result of intentional partisan bias; it could equally well arise as a consequence of bureaucrats' preference for cities represented by those who supported funding, a group disproportionately, but not completely, composed of Democrats. Unfortunately, separating the effects of party and position is virtually impossible at this level of analysis; if one were to subdivide each of the entries in the previous tables according to party, the number of cases would become too small for any meaningful analysis. Good multivariate methods, similar to those used in previous chapters, do allow one to separate the independent effects of party and position. Such methods also permit one to make more efficient estimates of the influence of committee membership than did the bivariate methods used until now.

MULTIVARIATE ANALYSIS, 1967

The basic structure of the multivariate model is the same as the one first described in chapter 5 and then used for the analyses of base closings and water and sewer acceptances in chapters 6 and 7. I assume that the probability of a district being awarded a model city in 1967 is a linear function of a congressman's committee assignment, his position on the appropriations bill, his party, the number of applications on file

30. See *Congressional Quarterly Almanac, 1967* (Washington, D.C.: Congressional Quarterly, 1968), p. 485.

from his district, and a random error term. All but one are dummy variables. The dependent variable is coded zero if a district was not awarded a model city and one if it was. The position variable is coded zero if a congressman opposed funding by voting to recommit the appropriations bill in 1967 and one if he supported funding. The party variable is coded zero for Republican congressmen and one for Democrats. The three committee variables are coded one if a district was represented on the Independent Offices Subcommittee of House Appropriations, the Banking and Currency Committee, or the full Appropriations Committee, and zero otherwise. The number of applications on file from a particular district takes the appropriate value, either one, two, or three. (Districts without applications continue to be excluded from the analysis.) I included this variable because I was still a bit uneasy about using districts rather than applications as analytic units. If, in fact, bureaucrats were making decisions strictly on the basis of the quality of applications, it stands to reason that a district containing three applicants would be more likely to have at least one selected than would a district containing only one applicant (assuming that quality was distributed independently of the other variables). Including this variable, therefore, permits an indirect test of the wisdom of a district-oriented model. Once again, the analysis centers on the 131 districts with one or more single-district applications.[31]

As before, probit analysis is an appropriate means for estimating a multivariate model of this type. Table 8.8 displays the probit equation and the usual marginal analyses of individual variables. Examining the

31. For technical reasons, I have been forced to generate one hypothetical district and add it to the 131 real districts with single-district applicants in order for the computer estimation routine to work properly. The problem is caused by the fact that *all* districts represented on the Independent Offices Subcommittee by supporters were awarded a model city. Under these conditions the method employed for estimating the probit model, maximum likelihood estimation, is unable to converge on a solution, no matter how many iterations are permitted. (The estimation routine is built on the assumption that neither rejection nor acceptance is a sure thing for any class of cases.) The hypothetical district is one not awarded a city but represented on the subcommittee; other committee variables take a value of zero, while all other variables (including position) take their sample means. The addition of one false case is not without cost. The principal cost is a slightly biased estimate of subcommittee influence. But the benefits far outweigh the costs. By facilitating the estimation of the probit model, it permits one to test alternative explanations that otherwise would have to remain untested, such as allocation according to party.

Table 8.8.   Probit Analysis: Effects of Political Variables on District Selection (Round One)

Variable	Probit Coefficient	Standard Error	Significance Level	Sample Mean
a Subcommittee of Appropriations Committee	1.820	.720	.01	.053
b Banking and Currency Committee	.926	.589	.11	.061
c Rest of Appropriations Committee	− .049	.415	.90	.114
d Supported funds	2.575	.744	.001	.687
e Party (Democratic)	.072	.335	.85	.626
f Number of applications	.054	.316	.85	1.206
Constant	−2.743			

n = 132 districts

Analysis of political variables:

		Probability of Selection	
		[d = 1]	[d = 0]
	Represented on	Supporter	Opponent
	Subcommittee of Appropriations		
[a = 1]	Committee	.960	.204
[b = 1]	Banking and Currency Committee	.805	.044
[a, b, c = 0]	Other committees	.472	.004

Notes: Variables a, b, c, and d take the value given in the appropriate row and column.
Variables e and f take their sample means.

probit coefficients carefully, one can see that the number of applications a district had on file was completely unrelated to the likelihood that the district would be awarded a model city. Districts with three applicants had no edge over districts with but a single applicant. This further supports my contention that bureaucrats structured decision making according to congressional districts, not applications.

The probit model proves quite effective at separating the effects of party and position on district selection. The probit coefficient for congressman's party was virtually zero, which puts to rest any notion that bureaucrats allocated benefits in an intentionally partisan fashion. On the other hand, the coefficient for congressman's position was both large and highly significant (at better than the .001 level). Consistent with theory, bureaucrats were allocating benefits according to coalition membership, not party membership. True, more Democratic congressmen received benefits, but this reflects the greater number of

Democrats who were members of the model cities supporting coalition. What is important is that the acceptance *rate* for Republican supporters was identical to the acceptance rate for Democratic supporters.

The analysis of the multivariate model confirms all committee relationships first uncovered with bivariate tests (with the added advantage of standard errors for each committee coefficient). The strongest relationship is the one involving representation on the Independent Offices Subcommittee of House Appropriations. The probit coefficient for this subcommittee is both large and statistically significant (at the .01 level), despite the fact that it is based on only seven cases.[32] The influence of members of the Banking and Currency Committee was somewhat less, and significance tests indicate a greater probability that this relationship could reflect nothing more than chance (.11). Contrary to my expectation, but consistent with the bivariate tests, representation on the full Appropriations Committee was unrelated to district selection.

ONE LAST BATTLE, 1968

In early 1968 the appropriations and selection processes began once again. As in 1967, the two were closely interrelated, and each required nearly a year to complete. HUD announced the second round of competition in January and set April 15 as the deadline for complete applications. Unsuccessful applicants from the first round were encouraged to reapply. Throughout May, June, and July, HUD officials reviewed these applications, and by July was ready to select and announce the winners. But, once again, appropriations politics in Congress required that they delay selection until the bill was approved. In early September, with most congressional action completed, they announced thirty-three cities. After the bill was finally passed and signed into law in early October, they announced seventeen additional cities, with twenty-two more in November, and three in December, for a total of seventy-five second-round cities.

The appropriations process also began in January, when President

32. Actually eight cases. The eighth was the hypothetical case, described in note 31, which had the effect of depressing the real coefficient and increasing the real standard error; both effects are conservative in that they work against acceptance of the subcommittee hypothesis.

Johnson submitted a request for $650 million in model cities funds for fiscal year 1969.[33] This time the program attracted little opposition either in committee or on the floor, though there were differences over how much should be appropriated for it. The House Appropriations Committee recommended $500 million, and the House accepted this figure. A single amendment was offered on the floor to reduce appropriations to the previous year's level ($312 million), but only two congressmen spoke in support of it, and it failed on a voice vote.[34] The Senate Appropriations Committee then recommended $1 billion, which the Senate approved. House and Senate conferees finally settled on $625 million (exactly twice the previous year's appropriations), and in early October the bill was signed into law.

Why was there so little opposition in 1968 as compared with the year-long battles of 1966 and 1967? One explanation is that opponents had simply worn themselves out. They became passive because they had lost twice before and saw no better prospects for success in 1968. Another explanation is that the pressures of local benefits were continuing to affect congressmen's voting decisions, just as they did in 1966 and 1967. I have already demonstrated how some opponents in 1966 became supporters in 1967 after learning that their districts contained applicant cities. In 1968 there were seventy-six brand new applications as well as many carry-overs. Presumably those opponents who represented these applicants felt the same pressures that had affected their colleagues in 1967. If anything, the pressures were probably greater in 1968, for bureaucrats had effectively demonstrated in the previous year that a congressman's support of the program was practically a precondition for the award of a model city. Since 1968 was known to be the last year in which model cities were to be awarded, congressmen could remain opposed only if they were willing to sacrifice their cities' chances for benefits for many years to come.

ALLOCATIONAL STRATEGIES, 1968

Again bureaucrats faced the problem of how to select model cities. As before, the demand for cities far exceeded the supply. In addition to the

33. *Congressional Quarterly Almanac, 1968* (Washington, D.C.: Congressional Quarterly, 1969), pp. 465–72.
34. 114 *Congressional Record,* pp. 12254–56.

118 cities not chosen in 1967, seventy-six new applications were submitted.[35] Of these, bureaucrats could select but seventy-five, or less than 40 percent.

In general, the four decision rules adopted in 1967 were also appropriate strategies in 1968. Bureaucrats would contribute to the maintenance and expansion of the model cities coalition if they gave preference to applicants represented either by supporters or by committee members, accepted multiple-district cities in preference to single-district cities, and accepted only one application per congressional district. The one difference between 1967 and 1968 was that virtually *all* congressmen supported funding in 1968 (or at least did not actively oppose it), whereas previously the question had split Congress deeply. Thus, a decision rule to "reward supporters" was not very discriminating. Though most congressmen supported funding, all were not equally fervent in their support. Some were backing model cities for the third straight year, and presumably the intensity of their support had increased a bit each year. Others had opposed it strenuously for two years; their support in 1968 was doubtless tentative. A well-orchestrated opposition campaign could probably push them right back into the opposition camp. Although it would serve bureaucrats' purposes to reward both core supporters and converts, the former should take priority. In a sense, core supporters "deserved" a city the previous year but were denied one because there were not enough to go around. It would be difficult for HUD to exclude its most loyal supporters two years in a row, particularly since 1968 was known to be the last year in which allocations would be made. On the other hand, it was also important for bureaucrats to reward a substantial number of converts and thus give them good reason for remaining converts. Former leaders of the opposition were particularly attractive targets. Placing cities in their districts would insure that they would never again lead the opposing coalition.

In addition to the question of which cities should be chosen, there was a question of when those choices should be announced. In 1967 bureaucrats delayed announcement from July until November while

35. In fact, bureaucrats considered only 168 applications in 1968, not 194, because twenty-six of the 118 cities rejected the previous year did not reapply. Unfortunately, HUD was unable to identify these twenty-six cities for me, and consequently my analysis includes all 194 cities. The inclusion of these extra cities should not seriously bias the estimates of influence, unless, for some reason, a city's decision not to reapply was somehow correlated with the other political variables.

waiting for Congress to approve the appropriations bill. As I have already noted, delay was necessary because, with demand far exceeding supply, premature announcement could alienate those supporters not awarded cities. But the four-month delay also played into the hands of opponents, who charged that it was politically motivated—which, of course, it was.[36] In 1968 bureaucrats improved their timing. In early September, after each House had approved funding but before the conference committee had met, they announced thirty-three cities; then, after final congressional approval, they announced the remaining forty-two cities. A memo in the White House files confirms that the timing was not accidental. Barefoot Sanders, one of the president's legislative aides, wrote in a memo to the president which accompanied HUD's recommendation of second-round cities:

> I believe there is an advantage in making two announcements rather than one. In this way we would avoid the criticism which we encountered last year that we were delaying these announcements until after the appropriations bill was voted on. At the same time we would be free to make additions to or deletions from the second group based on any considerations which might be important toward the end of the congressional session.[37]

BIVARIATE ANALYSIS, 1968

In the second round of competition, HUD again selected seventy-five applicants to be model cities. As before, the evidence tends to support all four propositions about how bureaucrats would make those selections. Table 8.9 provides strong support for the proposition that bureaucrats would accept multiple-district cities in preference to single-district cities. In 1968 bureaucrats accepted nearly 71 percent of the former as compared with only 35 percent of the latter, acceptance rates almost identical to the corresponding ones for the first round.

36. *Congressional Quarterly Almanac, 1967* (Washington, D.C.: Congressional Quarterly, 1968), p. 485.
37. Memorandum, Barefoot Sanders to the President, 4 September 1968, Congressional Leadership Folder, Califano Files, Box 1750, Lyndon Johnson Library, Austin, Texas.

Table 8.9. Acceptance Rates for Multiple-District and Single-District Cities (Round
Two and Both Rounds Together)

Round Two:

City contained	Applicant Accepted	Applicant Rejected	Total Decisions	Proportion Accepted
Multiple districts	15	6	21	.71
Single district	60	113	173	.35
Total	75	119	194	

Chi-Square = 9.17   Significance level = .01

Both Rounds:

Multiple districts	37	6	43	.86
Single district	111	113	224	.49
Total	148	119	267	

Chi-Square = 17.99   Significance level = .001
Unit of analysis: application.

Combining the evidence from both rounds demonstrates that in two years bureaucrats accepted all but *six* multiple-district applicants (14 percent) while rejecting 113 single-district applicants (51 percent).

In order to test the other three propositions, I have again focused on *districts* containing single-district applicants rather than on applications themselves. Initially I exclude from the analysis districts that were awarded a city in 1967; this, in effect, allows one to control for the effects of the one-city-per-district proposition while examining in detail the committee and support hypotheses. The evidence in table 8.10 confirms the proposition that bureaucrats would reward core supporters (those who supported funding in 1967) in preference to more recent converts. Thirty-three core supporters (62 percent) had applications from their districts accepted whereas only twenty-three former opponents (36 percent) were so fortunate. The advantage given to 1967 supporters is striking, but not nearly as great as their advantage in 1967, when all but one of the single-district acceptances went to supporters. This shift is consistent with my argument that bureaucrats would reward congressmen who abandoned their active opposition to the program. If the evidence is combined for both rounds of competition, one can see how important the 1967 recommittal motion really was. Eighty percent of those who voted "right" on that motion were eventually rewarded with a city, while only 38 percent of opponents were given shares of benefits.

Table 8.10.   Effects of 1967 Vote on District Selection (Round Two and Both Rounds Together)

Round Two:

District Represented by Congressman Who	At Least One Application Accepted	All Appli- cations Rejected	Total Districts	Proportion with an Acceptance
Supported funds	33	20	53	.62
Opposed funds	23	40	63	.36
Total	56	60	116	

Chi-Square = 6.65   Significance level = .01

Unit of analysis: district containing one or more single-district applications (excepting those with an acceptance in round one).

Both Rounds:

Supported funds	81	20	101	.80
Opposed funds	24	40	64	.38
Total	105	60	165	

Chi-Square = 29.05   Significance level = .001

Unit of analysis: district containing one or more single-district applications.

The committee hypothesis also receives strong support in the second round of competition. Seventy-three percent of the districts represented on relevant committees were awarded a city, compared with 43 percent of those without such representation (table 8.11). As before, bureaucrats differentiated among members of the various committees as well as between supporters and opponents on particular committees. All three core supporters on Banking and Currency received cities (100 percent), as did four of five members who opposed the program in 1967 (80 percent). Seven of nine supporters on the full Appropriations Committee were accepted (78 percent), compared with two of four opponents (50 percent). Members of the Independent Offices Subcommittee of Appropriations were rewarded so well in 1967 that only one district was competing for benefits in 1968, a district represented by Burt Talcott (R., Calif.), an opponent in 1967, whose district contained the small city of Seaside (population 19,000). The application was rejected. The rejection of Talcott's one city suggests that however important political considerations may have been, they were not determinative. Some cities presumably were rejected because they were unable to meet minimal standards, even when their acceptance would have been politically advantageous. Finally, among members of other committees, 56 per-

Table 8.11. Effects of Committee Membership (and 1967 Vote) on District Selection (Round Two and Both Rounds Together)

Round Two:

District Represented on	At Least One Application Accepted	All Applications Rejected	Total Districts	Proportion with an Acceptance
Relevant committee	16	6	22	.73
Other committees	40	54	94	.43
Total	56	60	116	

Chi-Square = 5.35   Significance level = .02

S* Appropriations Subcommittee	0	0	0	—
S Banking and Currency Committee	3	0	3	1.00
S Rest of Appropriations Committee	7	2	9	.78
S Other committees	23	18	41	.56
O† Appropriations Subcommittee	0	1	1	.00
O Banking and Currency Committee	4	1	5	.80
O Rest of Appropriations Committee	2	2	4	.50
O Other committees	17	36	53	.32
Total	56	60	116	

Chi-Square = 15.88   Significance level = .05

Unit of analysis: district containing one or more single-district applications (excepting those with an acceptance in round one).

Both Rounds:

S* Appropriations Subcommittee	5	0	5	1.00
S Banking and Currency Committee	8	0	8	1.00
S Rest of Appropriations Committee	12	2	14	.86
S Other committees	56	18	74	.76
O† Appropriations Subcommittee	1	1	2	.50
O Banking and Currency Committee	4	1	5	.80
O Rest of Appropriations Committee	2	2	4	.50
O Other committees	17	36	53	.32
Total	105	60	165	

Chi-Square = 40.91   Significance level = .001

Unit of analysis: district containing one or more single-district applications.

Notes: *Supported funds in 1967.
†Opposed funds in 1967.

cent of 1967 supporters were awarded a city in the second round, compared with 32 percent of opponents.

The major difference between the two rounds of competition (other than opponents' change in status) was that in 1968 members of the full Appropriations Committee began to receive a disproportionate number of cities, whereas in 1967, contrary to expectation, they did no better than average. Initially this is puzzling. Conceivably bureaucrats were reluctant to allocate too many cities to members of important committees in 1967 and thus deprive rank-and-file supporters of a share of benefits. If so, it would be rational to defer rewards for Appropriations members until 1968, since members of both Banking and Currency and the Independent Offices Subcommittee obviously deserved greater priority in 1967. But this is only conjecture. The final portion of table 8.11 presents the hierarchy of acceptance rates for both rounds of competition. As the reader will note, acceptance rates order themselves in a theoretically pleasing manner, ranging from 100 percent for supporters represented on the Independent Offices Subcommittee or the Banking and Currency Committee down to 32 percent for opponents represented on nonstrategic committees.

Congressmen's committee membership and their positions on the 1967 recommittal motion account quite well for allocational patterns in both 1967 and 1968. But what about the allocations to opponents who were members of no relevant committees? I have already explained why bureaucrats would award some cities to these congressmen—in effect, to reward them for abandoning their previous opposition. But can one say anything useful about how bureaucrats allocated cities within this class of congressmen? *Which* seventeen converts should they choose to reward? Theory predicts that two types of converts would make particularly attractive targets: former leaders of the opposition and fence-sitters (those who had been the weakest of all opponents in 1967). Identifying opposition leaders is relatively easy. Most were members of the aforementioned committees, and most, as I have already demonstrated, were awarded a city. But there were others. Gerald Ford (R., Mich.), then minority leader, is an obvious example. Ford, it will be recalled, had charged that partisan politics dominated first-round selections. Not surprisingly, Ford's hometown of Grand Rapids was selected in the second round. In fact, it was one of the thirty-three cities announced in September, in the middle of congressional consideration of the appropriations bill. One might attribute the selection of Grand Rapids to yet another coincidence if it were not for the September 4 memorandum to the president (cited previously) which discussed the political rationality of the decision. The memorandum stated, "The inclusion of Ford plus a substantial number of Republican districts [in the September announcement] should afford ample protection against any claim of partisanship in the selection of these cities."[38]

Identifying fence-sitters is a more difficult empirical question, for there were no objective measures of intensity to which I could turn. However, sifting through the fifty-three districts represented by former opponents (who were not members of strategic committees) I was struck by the amazing success of freshmen (table 8.12). Ten of thirteen freshmen (77 percent) were awarded cities, as compared with seven of forty nonfreshmen (18 percent). The relationship is surprisingly strong. One explanation is that bureaucrats, lacking good information on the intensity of opposition, decided to place their bets on freshmen. There were, in fact, good reasons to believe that freshmen were less strongly opposed than others when they voted to recommit the appropriations bill in 1967. After all, they were not even around in 1966 when model cities was an intense partisan and ideological issue. They arrived in Congress in early 1967, just when local benefit considerations were beginning to displace ideology in congressmen's voting calculus. True, they voted against funding in 1967; but this probably reflected cue taking from their elders as much as deep conviction. Awarding cities to freshmen was almost certain to make them enthusiastic supporters, whereas awards to nonfreshmen were more risky. Nonfreshmen had previously responded to strong ideological and partisan appeals, and presumably their feelings could be aroused again. A second explanation for the freshmen advantage is that the administration interceded in bureaucratic decision making to improve the reelection chances of marginal freshmen. But this explanation is unlikely, for all ten acceptances were given to *Republican* freshmen, in whom a Democratic administration had little interest.

There is also evidence to support the proposition that bureaucrats would accept but one application per district, though the evidence is not quite as strong as it was in the first round. In round one, a single district

38. Ibid.

Table 8.12.   Acceptance Rates for Opponents of Funding in 1967 (Round Two)

District Represented by	At Least One Application Accepted	All Applications Rejected	Total Districts	Proportion with an Acceptance
Freshman	10	3	13	.77
Nonfreshman	7	33	40	.18
Total	17	36	53	

Chi-Square = 13.34   Significance level = .001

Unit of analysis: district containing one or more single-district applications (excepting those with an acceptance in round one).

was awarded two cities. In round two, four more districts received a second city. The four, all Democrats, were Evins of Tennessee, Kazen of Texas, Mills of Arkansas, and Waldie of California. For two of these there are plausible political explanations. Evins was chairman of the Independent Offices Subcommittee, and thus more important to the program's budget than any other congressman. Mills, chairman of Ways and Means, had no special influence over model cities officials, but the administration was constantly courting him because he controlled the fate of other important legislation. Conceivably the administration intervened in bureaucrats' decision making to obtain extra benefits for Mills as part of a larger legislative strategy.

Five times bureaucrats violated the one-city-per-district decision rule: three times for understandable reasons (Mansfield, Evins, and Mills) and twice for unexplainable reasons. But is five "errors" a large or small deviation from the prediction? Clearly one needs a standard for comparison. One such standard is the number of cities that would have been "wasted" (in the sense of being a district's second model city) if each applicant had an equal chance of being selected. Table 8.13 makes just that comparison. If 112 applications were selected at random from the 224 single-district applications received in both rounds of competition, one should expect that only about ninety-six districts would actually contain model cities.[39] Sixteen cities would be wasted. In this light it

39. The calculations are based on the following distribution of applications for two rounds of competition (plus one additional city selected in 1970 and discussed elsewhere in the text). In all, there were 224 single-district applications from 167 districts, including 123 districts with a single application, thirty-five with two, six with three, two with four, and one with five. The calculations are computed from the five binomial distributions associated with these five types of districts.

Table 8.13. Number of Cities Accepted Per District (Both Rounds)

	Number of Cities	Number of Districts	"Wasted" Cities
Theory predicts	112	112	0.0
Actual selections	112	107	5.0
Equal chance for each application	112	95.8	16.2

appears that bureaucrats actually wasted very few cities, particularly since at least three of the five have plausible political explanations. The fourth proposition is confirmed.

MULTIVARIATE ANALYSIS, 1968

Again I have constructed and tested a multivariate model, both to eliminate alternative political explanations (such as allocation by party) and to make more precise estimates of the influence of particular committees. The model is practically identical to the one constructed for the first round of competition. Deleted is the variable for representation on the Independent Offices Subcommittee, since only one district of this type was competing in round two. Added is a dummy variable for representation by a freshman who opposed funding in 1967. Again the analysis centers on the 116 districts containing one or more single-district applications (excepting those with an acceptance in round one).

The probit equation for this multivariate model (table 8.14) offers the reader nothing startling, but it does provide further evidence to confirm the hypothesized decision rules. As before, a congressman's position on the 1967 recommittal motion was important in bureaucrats' calculations, while his party affiliation was unrelated to district selection. The coefficient for freshmen congressmen opposed to funding was both large and highly significant (.001 level), suggesting that bureaucrats may have favored cities from these districts. The acceptance rate for this class of districts (77 percent) was as high as that for districts represented on important committees. The two committee relationships were essentially the same as those reported before. The coefficient for representation on Banking and Currency was large and significant (.01 level), while that for representation of the full Appropriations Committee was somewhat less and the estimate subject to greater uncertainty (.09

Table 8.14. Probit Analysis: Effects of Political Variables on District Selection (Round Two)

Variable	Probit Coefficient	Standard Error	Significance Level	Sample Mean
a Banking and Currency Committee	1.780	.665	.01	.068
b Rest of Appropriations Committee	.684	.407	.09	.120
c Supported funds	1.078	.307	.001	.462
d Freshman opposed funds	1.714	.473	.001	.128
e Party (Democratic)	.085	.306	.80	.513
f Number of applications	.114	.226	.60	1.291
Constant	−1.140			

n = 116 districts

Analysis of political variables:

		Probability of Selection		
		$|c = 1|$ Supporter	$|c, d = 0|$ Nonfreshman Opponent	$|c = 0; d = 1|$ Freshman Opponent
$|a = 1|$	Banking and Currency Committee	.971	.795	—
$|b = 1|$	Rest of Appropriations Committee	.790	.393	—
$|a, b = 0|$	Other committees	.551	.171	.775

Note: Variables a, b, c, and d take the values given in the appropriate rows and columns. Variables e and f take their sample means.

probability of no relationship). Apparently bureaucrats were, as hypothesized, giving preference to cities represented on the full Appropriations Committee, though the evidence is too weak for very confident conclusions. Finally, as in 1967, the number of applications a district submitted was completely unrelated to bureaucrats' decisions. Districts with two, three, four, or five applications were no more likely to be selected than those with a single application.

ONE MORE CITY

In all, bureaucrats selected 150 cities to be model cities, seventy-five in round one and seventy-five in round two. They did not plan to select additional cities until these 150 had first received a few years of "action" grants and then HUD and its outside consultants had carefully evaluated the program's impact. But bureaucrats had not anticipated either the persistence of Joseph McDade (R., Penn.) or his new sub-committee assignment in the Ninety-first Congress. In 1969, McDade, for many years a member of House Appropriations, transferred to its Independent Offices Subcommittee, a position that offered him the opportunity to influence bureaucrats' behavior. Within a few months he was using his new position for just that. Throughout the 1969 hearings on model cities appropriations McDade questioned bureaucrats on their decision to limit the program to 150 cities. In page after page of hearing transcript he complained that no city from his district had been chosen and inquired as to what he should be saying to his unfortunate constituents.[40] It was clear that he was not advocating a major expansion of the program but merely wanted to share in the benefits. Over and over he asked, "What is so sacred about 150 that is so unsacred about 151?"[41] Bureaucrats understood the message. About a year later Scranton, his hometown, became the 151st (and last) model city. All was achieved without a new round of competition and without national attention, though presumably with immense local fanfare. Curiously, Scranton did not even begin with planning grants, as did each of the other 150 cities, but instead received the much larger action grants right from the start.[42] Clearly, McDade had used his position to benefit his constituency. Bureaucrats could have resisted the pressures for a while, for there were plenty of other subcommittee members already receiving benefits. But not without risk. Bureaucrats interested in long-term budgetary security would not want a vocal critic sitting on this crucial subcommittee, particularly since other nonbeneficiaries might join in subsequent years until critics again controlled the subcommittee. They responded in the one way guaranteed to please McDade—with a share of benefits.

40. U.S., Congress, House, Committee on Appropriations, *Independent Offices and Department of Housing and Urban Development Appropriations for 1970, Hearings before a Subcommittee of the Committee on Appropriations*, 91st Cong., 1st sess., part 4, pp. 404–409.

41. Ibid., p. 405.

42. U.S., Department of Housing and Urban Development, *1973 HUD Statistical Yearbook* (Washington, D.C.: Government Printing Office, 1973), p. 11.

TWO ROUNDS OF COMPETITION

With one exception, all congressmen who opposed funding in 1967 were denied benefits in that year. In 1968, after abandoning their active opposition, they did considerably better, though still not as well as core supporters. But the substantial differences in acceptance rates for various classes of congressmen persisted over the two rounds of competition. Table 8.15 summarizes the results of a multivariate analysis for both years of competition (with a district competing in both years counted only once). As the reader will note, support of funding combined with proper committee representation practically guaranteed

Table 8.15. Probit Analysis: Effects of Political Variables on District Selection (Both Rounds)

Variable	Probit Coefficient	Standard Error	Significance Level	Sample Mean
a Subcommittee of Appropriations Committee	1.241	.752	.10	.042
b Banking and Currency Committee	1.740	.659	.01	.078
c Rest of Appropriations Committee	.471	.379	.20	.115
d Supported funds	1.621	.283	.001	.615
e Freshman opposed funds	1.758	.468	.001	.090
f Party (Democratic)	.091	.277	.75	.596
g Number of applications	.017	.209	.90	1.277
Constant	−1.016			

n = 166 districts

Analysis of political variables:

	Represented on	Probability of Selection		
		[d = 1] Supporter	[d, e = 0] Nonfreshman Opponent	[d = 0; e = 1] Freshman Opponent
[a = 1]	Subcommittee of Appropriations Committee	.972	.617	—
[b = 1]	Banking and Currency Committee	.992	.787	—
[c = 1]	Rest of Appropriations Committee	.874	.319	—
[a, b, c = 0]	Other committees	.751	.173	.793

Notes: Variables a, b, c, d, and e take values given in the appropriate rows and columns. Variables f and g take their sample means.

selection (acceptance rates of 87 percent, 97 percent, and 99 percent, depending on the committee). Those who supported funding in 1967 but who were not represented on important committees also did well (75 percent selected). At the other extreme, nonfreshmen who opposed funding in 1967 and who were not members of these committees had an acceptance rate of only 17 percent.

Bureaucrats' actual allocational decisions correspond closely to those one would expect rational bureaucrats, seeking to achieve budgetary security and growth, to make. Bureaucrats appear to have differentiated carefully among applicants according to congressmen's committee assignments and their past support for the program. Consistent with theory, they did not discriminate on the basis of party. Table 8.16 demonstrates that, although Democratic districts did slightly better than Republican ones (69 vs. 55 percent), the difference is completely explainable in terms of the fact that more Democrats than Republicans supported funding in 1967. In fact, if anything, bureaucrats gave a slight advantage to Republicans, presumably to defuse charges of partisan allocations. The acceptance rate for Republican supporters was slightly greater than that for Democrats (86 vs. 78 percent), as was the rate for Republican opponents as compared with that for Democratic opponents (40 vs. 32 percent).

In three years the character of the model cities program had changed drastically. When first conceived in late 1965, its multibillion dollar

Table 8.16. Effect of Congressman's Party on District Selection (Both Rounds)

District Represented by	At Least One Application Accepted	All Applications Rejected	Total Districts	Proportion with an Acceptance
Democrat	68	30	98	.69
Republican	37	30	67	.55
Total	105	60	165	

Chi-Square = 2.87   Significance level = .10

Supporter, Democrat	62	17	79	.78
Supporter, Republican	19	3	22	.86
Opponent, Democrat	6	13	19	.32
Opponent, Republican	18	27	45	.40
Total	105	60	165	

Chi-Square = 31.73   Significance level = .001
Unit of analysis: district containing one or more single-district applications.

benefits were intended for only a handful of cities. Three years later 150 cities were sharing less than $1 billion. The absolute size of the program had not increased; in fact, budgetary problems associated with Vietnam had actually reduced the funds available for model cities. Funds were simply spread more thinly across more and more cities. But by expanding the number of cities and skillfully allocating benefits, bureaucrats had built the foundation for a stable majority coalition. Benefits were flowing into 150 cities and 226 congressional districts. (Some cities included more than one district.) Fifty-two percent of all congressmen had a share of the action, and thus had an incentive to support its continuance.

ALTERNATIVE EXPLANATIONS

I have argued that bureaucrats allocated benefits according to a carefully calculated strategy designed to maximize the size of the supporting coalition. But other explanations could also account for many of the empirical relationships that I have asserted support my theory and its derivative hypotheses. One such alternative hypothesis—allocation according to congressmen's party—has already been examined and rejected. In this section I examine other plausible explanations.

One of my hypotheses is that rational bureaucrats would select multiple-district cities in preference to single-district cities because, given a fixed number of cities to be allocated, more congressmen would share in the benefits. The evidence reported previously in tables 8.4 and 8.9 supports the assertion. In the two rounds of competition, 86 percent of multiple-district cities were accepted as compared with 49 percent of single-district cities. An alternative explanation for the observed relationship is that HUD officials merely had a large-city bias. Such a bias could arise because bureaucrats perceived the problems of large cities to be more serious than those of small ones, or because large cities had a greater capacity to develop innovative proposals quickly, or simply because most HUD officials had greater experience with large metropolitan areas. However acquired, such a bias could explain bureaucrats' propensity to select multiple-district cities, since city size and the number of districts are themselves correlated.

Separating the effects of population and district composition on city selection proves difficult. For the twenty largest cities it is impossible; there was simply no variation to decompose. Each was populous; each was required by the courts to have multiple districts; and each was selected as a model city. For medium-sized cities the task of separating the effects of population and district composition is, at least in theory, possible. Cities of less than about 415,000 (i.e., 180 million people divided by 435 districts) could, as far as the courts were concerned, be represented by a single congressman. Frequently, however, those who drew district lines divided these cities into two or more parts, each part represented by a different congressman. Consequently, some medium-sized cities had only one congressman, while others had two or more. A comparison of these two groups of cities allows one to make inferences about whether the higher acceptance rate for multiple-district cities stemmed from their size or from their multiple representation in the House.

Such a comparison is reported in table 8.17. It includes all applicant cities between 100,000 and 415,000 in which at least one congressman supported funding in 1967. With the effects of population controlled, one can see that bureaucrats did give some preference to multiple-district cities. All ten multiple-district cities in this population category were accepted, whereas only thirty-four of forty-two single-district cities (81 percent) were so fortunate. Admittedly, the difference is small and not statistically significant (.30 confidence level), but bureaucrats did accept *all* the multiple-district cities, and one cannot expect much better than that. A larger number of cases would, of course, give one greater confidence in the conclusion, but lacking further evidence to examine, one leans toward a conclusion that bureaucrats did prefer multiple-district cities, and that this preference reflects more than just a large-city bias.

Table 8.17. Acceptance Rates for Cities with Populations between 100,000 and 415,000
(Both Rounds)

Representation	City Accepted	City Rejected	Total Cities	Proportion Accepted
Multiple-district city	10	0	10	1.00
Single-district city	34	8	42	.81
Total	44	8	52	

Chi-Square = 1.03   Significance level = .30

The hypothesis that bureaucrats intentionally allocated first-round cities to coalition members while consciously denying them to opponents is also open to alternative explanations. One such explanation rests on the assumption that cities (and districts) differ in their objective need for model cities benefits. One could argue that congressmen merely voted their districts' interests; those from needy areas supported the program, while those from less needy areas opposed it. Similarly, one could argue that bureaucrats allocated benefits according to the same objective standard, accepting applications from the neediest cities and rejecting those from the more fortunate. It is a good argument. If completely true, the reader could scrawl "spurious relationship" across much of this chapter. At one stroke it would explain away all the observed relationships between congressmen's support of funding and the allocation of benefits. These relationships would reflect not a carefully calculated bureaucratic strategy but rather a close adherence to standards of merit.

I should say at the outset that I think there is some truth to the argument. Districts do differ in their need for programs and such differences do affect both congressmen's voting decisions and bureaucrats' allocational decisions. At the extremes—the least needy and the most needy—the alternative causal mechanism probably works well. If the contest were between Watts and Palm Springs, it would be pretty certain how the respective congressmen would vote and how bureaucrats would allocate benefits. But the model cities' contests were *not* between Watts and Palm Springs, or between Harlem and Scarsdale. Palm Springs and Scarsdale did not even apply, and neither did Chevy Chase, Princeton, Kenilworth, or Beverly Hills. Cities that were obviously unworthy knew enough not to apply. At the other extreme, there probably was not much question that the neediest and most troublesome urban areas in the country, such as Harlem and Watts, or parts of Detroit, Chicago, and Washington, would be selected. Their needs, after all, had prompted the development of the whole program. All the real competition was among the two hundred or so cities in the middle—those worthy of assistance but lacking such compelling problems that selection was almost certain. They were a varied bunch. Old New England mill towns (Lowell, Chicopee) competed against southern growth cities (Atlanta, Miami); midwestern cities built around heavy industry (Akron, Youngstown) competed against the newer western cities filled with light industry (Seattle, San Jose); and small towns everywhere lined up for their shares. (Plains did not apply, but there were applications from other tiny towns in Georgia: Alma (population 3,515), Camilla (4,573), and Douglas (8,736).)

Although the alternative causal mechanism may function well for cities at the extremes, it does not work well for the vast majority in the middle. It is difficult to imagine how minor variations in the objective needs of these cities could spell the difference between a congressman's active support and his opposition, particularly since voting decisions are generally the result of multiple forces (chapter 3). A few empirical examples demonstrate that party and ideology explain model cities support better than objective need. Rochester, New York is a useful place to begin. For years this city has been split on a north-south axis into two districts. Since the division does not separate the city into rich and poor areas, one would expect that the objective needs of each half would be nearly equal and, therefore, according to the alternative causal mechanism, the two congressmen would have similar voting records. Yet one was a consistent supporter of model cities and the other a consistent opponent. The difference was ideology. The supporter, Frank Horton, was a liberal Republican (1969 ADA score of 80), while the opponent, Barber Conable, was a more conservative Republican (ADA score of 22). Other examples could be cited.

Alternatively, one can examine pairs of cities. On the surface, two New Jersey cities, Trenton and Camden, appear similar. Both are old, rundown, industrial cities of about the same size, and both live in the shadow of Philadelphia. Nevertheless, their congressmen took opposite positions on model cities. Trenton's Frank Thompson, a liberal Democrat, supported it from the start; Camden's John Hunt, a conservative Republican, was strenuously opposed. (Trenton was accepted in round one; Camden was twice rejected.) These are not isolated examples. In fact, wherever one looks in this middle group of cities, differences in model cities support are more easily explained in terms of party and ideology than in terms of objective criteria.

One of the principal problems with an explanation of congressmen's voting behavior which is based solely on objective need is that most congressional districts are heterogeneous. A typical district might include a few modest-sized cities, some suburbs from a nearby large city, a collection of small towns, and perhaps some rural areas. How would a congressman from such a district even conceptualize his district's "need" for benefits? Is it a weighted average of each community's need, and if so, how should need be measured and weighted? The point is not that congressmen do not evaluate their districts' needs when making decisions, but rather that each congressman will make such evaluations differently. Furthermore, these evaluations are only a small part of a congressman's voting calculus.

If congressmen's support for model cities was only tenuously related to objective need, then the alternative causal mechanism could not have functioned very well (and certainly not well enough to explain how forty-eight of forty-nine first-round cities were awarded to supporters). It is also doubtful that objective need was as important in bureaucrats' decision making as the alternative explanation would imply. Recall that model cities was supposed to be an experimental program. Certainly it was important that bureaucrats select applicants with genuine problems, but it was also crucial that they select innovative proposals by applicants who demonstrated the commitment and capacity to implement them. Need was a necessary, not a sufficient, condition. In fact, if one examines the press releases and other justifications issued by HUD at that time, need is hardly mentioned. According to Secretary Weaver, applicants were judged according to how well they had analyzed their own problems, how innovative were their proposed solutions, how committed were local governments and private groups, and whether they had the capacity to carry out their proposed remedies.[43] Since it is highly unlikely that all these criteria were also correlated with congressmen's voting decisions, the alternative causal mechanism appears even less plausible.

My argument is not that objective need had no effect on congressmen's voting decisions and on bureaucrats' allocational decisions, but rather that its effects were far too limited to account for the amazingly strong relationships reported earlier (forty-eight of forty-nine first-round cities awarded to supporters, and the one exception to the most crucial opponent). Such relationships could only be the result of a carefully calculated bureaucratic strategy designed to maintain (and eventually expand) a fragile coalition.

The evidence used to support the committee hypotheses is also open

43. Weaver's statement is reprinted in 113 *Congressional Record*, pp. 33012–13.

to alternative explanations, and particularly to a variant of the causal mechanism just examined. I have argued that bureaucrats gave special attention to members of certain committees because they occupied such strategic positions. An alternative explanation is that congressmen from especially needy areas tended to join these committees, and that it was this overrepresentation rather than any special consideration that accounts for their above-average acceptance rates. The evidence to support this interpretation is not very strong. The alternative explanation is almost certainly invalid for the full Appropriations Committee, one of the most attractive House committees. Long lines of congressmen wait for a seat on this committee, and there is no evidence that those from needy urban areas (or areas with any other special problems) have an edge in the competition. According to most measures, Appropriations is one of the most representative of all House committees. [44] Similarly, the Independent Offices Subcommittee did not overrepresent needy urban areas; if anything, it underrepresented them. The fifty largest American cities send approximately 140 representatives to the House, nearly one-third of the total. Exactly *one* (Cleveland) was represented on the twelve-member subcommittee that reviewed appropriations for all urban programs. This should make even more plausible my political explanation for the extremely high acceptance rates enjoyed by subcommittee members' cities.

The Banking and Currency Committee did overrepresent major urban areas. Congressmen from large cities had long been attracted to it because of its jurisdiction over most urban legislation. In the Ninetieth Congress, 39 percent of its members represented central-city districts as compared with 26 percent of all congressmen. [45] In principle this over-representation of urban areas could account for the above-average acceptance rates of committee members' applications. In practice, it appears unlikely. Readers will recall that most of my empirical analyses focused on single-district cities, not the larger multiple-district cities. Thus, the high acceptance rates reported for committee members are

44. Carol F. Goss, "House Committee Characteristics and Distributive Politics," paper delivered at the 1975 Annual Meeting of the American Political Science Association, pp. 11, 12, 22.
45. Bruce F. Norton, "The Committee on Banking and Currency as a Legislative Subsystem of the House of Representatives," (Ph.D. dissertation, Syracuse University, 1970), p. 116.

for a class of cities that were *underrepresented* on the committee, for if large cities were overrepresented then small ones must have been under-represented. The twelve single-district cities on the committee which were accepted were politically important, but not necessarily known for their severe urban problems. They included such cities as Texarkana (Texas), Athens (Georgia), Rock Hill (South Carolina), and Bradford (Pennsylvania). All three committee hypotheses hold up well against the alternative explanations.

EXTENT OF INFLUENCE

In this chapter I have made no effort to assess the extent of con-gressmen's influence over bureaucrats' allocational decisions (as I did in the other two empirical chapters). Estimating how frequently bureau-crats adjusted their decisions in an effort to maintain their supporting coalition is considerably more difficult for model cities, largely because of the way I have chosen to test the various hypotheses. For sound reasons I adopted districts rather than cities as analytic units, so that particular hypotheses could be tested properly. But one consequence of this choice is that I have no overall, application-oriented model from which such estimates could be made.

My hunch is that the extent of influence was greater for model cities than it was for military employment or water and sewer grants. The stakes were certainly larger. Model cities officials were fighting for sur-vival, not merely expansion. Conceivably a third or more of all deci-sions would have been made differently if bureaucrats had not had to allocate benefits strategically.[46] But it is also clear that bureaucrats did not use *only* political criteria in their decision making. They assessed applications according to both political and merit criteria, and their final decisions reflected a combination of both evaluations. Political considerations were important, but they were not determinative.

---

46. In another sense, nearly all allocational decisions were political, for it was political necessity that had dictated the program's expansion from a handful of cities to 151. But here I am considering only the selection of these 151 cities.

9: COALITIONS AND PUBLIC POLICY

The evidence presented in chapters 6 through 8 supports, for the most part, the theory developed in chapters 2 through 4. At least for the three programs examined, bureaucrats appear to allocate benefits strategically in an effort both to maintain and to expand their supporting coalitions. When it furthers their purposes, they broaden their program's geographic scope and increase the number of shares of benefits so that more congressmen can be brought into their supporting coalitions. When necessary, they allocate extra shares of benefits to leaders and to those who are crucial coalition members. But the allocational strategies that bureaucrats select are not the same for all programs. Each is specially tailored to fit a program's peculiar situation in Congress, to compensate where general-benefit strategies have proven weak, and to reward those congressmen who are especially important to a particular coalition's success. Though the differences between bureaucrats' strategies for various programs are considerable, they are not inexplicable. They are, I believe, readily understandable in a rational choice framework.

Committees play a prominent role in the politics of geographic allocation. Ordinarily, bureaucrats choose to allocate disproportionate shares of benefits to members of those committees that have jurisdiction over their programs. But these extra shares do not come automatically. They accrue to members who have performed important services, who control resources that bureaucrats desire, or who threaten in some way the achievement of bureaucrats' goals. Committees that merely have the *potential* to threaten bureaucrats' fortunes but that fail to develop that potential do not ordinarily obtain extra benefits for their members. The Appropriations Committee is an obvious example. This committee has delegated almost complete authority over agencies' budgets to its subcommittees. As a consequence, bureaucrats generally single out subcommittee members for special treatment, while providing nothing extra for members of the full committee. The one case in which full committee members were advantaged (model cities) is the exception that proves the rule. In this case, with a subcommittee evenly divided on the question of funding, conflict spilled over into the full committee and then onto the floor. Bureaucrats responded in a way designed to strengthen their hand in the full committee, giving preference to applications from committee members' districts. On the other hand, no such subcommittee advantage exists in most legislative committees, simply because these committees do not grant autonomy to their subcommittees. If there are extra benefits to be distributed, members of the entire legislative committee have claims on them.

But bureaucrats' allocational strategies do not revolve around committees alone. Although committee members provide the nuclei for most winning coalitions, no program could survive without a far broader base of support. At times winning coalitions are built on a foundation of positive general-benefit evaluations (e.g., national defense). When such a consensus does exist, bureaucrats need not allocate benefits strategically among rank-and-file congressmen. More frequently, however, there is no consensus on a program's general benefits. In such cases, strategic allocations of local benefits among rank-and-file congressmen prove useful, both in persuading proponents to continue their support and in enticing those predisposed against a program to switch sides. But contrary to the expectations of some, strategic allocations are rarely partisan allocations. Such allocations would be contrary to bureaucrats' interests, for programs' supporting coalitions are themselves bipartisan.

THE POLITICS OF GEOGRAPHIC ALLOCATION

Congressmen and bureaucrats have together developed a mutually advantageous system of geographic allocation. Since Congress itself is far too large and cumbersome an institution to make the thousands of allocational decisions required each year, it has delegated to bureaucrats the authority to make most such decisions (and has written statutory formulas for most of the rest). But this delegation of authority does not reflect a diminution of congressional interest in allocational matters. In fact, Congress keeps program administrators on a short leash, first with single-year authorizations and then with single-year appropriations. Although in the short run bureaucrats are free to allocate benefits as they see fit, those who seek long-term budgetary security and growth must pay careful heed to congressmen's allocational preferences. If they expect Congress to approve their budgetary requests in subsequent years, they have little choice but to allocate benefits in a manner pleasing to at least a majority of congressmen.

It is a mutually rewarding system. Congressmen can claim credit for whatever benefits flow into their districts, but at the same time they have insulated themselves from their constituents' anger when certain benefits can not be secured. If Congress itself allocated benefits, constituents might well blame their congressmen for failing to acquire benefits, but as long as bureaucrats have the final say, congressmen are partially protected from their wrath. Bureaucrats also profit from the system, for their control of allocational decisions gives them the ability to influence congressmen's voting decisions on budgetary matters. Congressmen such as Gerald Ford and Charles Jonas opposed the model cities program for two years, but once program administrators named their respective home towns as model cities, they abandoned their active opposition.

Chapter 1 examined two alternative theories of geographic allocation—Buchanan and Tullock's exclusive-coalition model and Barry's universalistic model—and then inquired which theoretical model offered the more accurate representation of the American system. It now appears that neither provides a good approximation. The American system of allocation occupies the middle range of the continuum that runs from Barry's universalistic model, where objective criteria are the only determinants of allocation, to Buchanan and Tullock's exclusive-coalition model, where criteria of coalition membership completely determine allocations. Most allocational decisions are made according to a mix of objective and political criteria, though the precise mix varies from program to program. Those that enjoy broad support on general-benefit grounds (such as national defense) lie closer to the universalistic end of the spectrum, while those with either slender or polarized general-benefit support (water and sewer grants, model cities) are closer to the exclusive-coalition end. Undoubtedly there are a few programs for which allocational decisions are made without reference to political criteria, but these are surely the exception. Grants for cancer research come to mind. Allocations for such programs are non-political because support for the potential collective benefits is so widespread that political allocations would not only be unnecessary but, in fact, might prove counterproductive to coalition maintenance. Conversely, there may be a few programs for which political criteria are determinative (though examples do not occur to me). Most programs, however, lie in between these extremes, where bureaucrats make both political and public interest calculations.

But to say that most programs fall in between these extremes is not to say that the politics of geographic allocation is the same or even similar for all such programs. Adherents of the distributive theory would have one believe that a single set of simple hypotheses can adequately explain allocational decisions for these diverse programs. In fact, congressional politics and bureaucratic decision making are far more complex than that. Ignoring the very real differences among congressmen, committees, programs, and allocational processes leads to a conception of the political world which is vastly oversimplified and in many cases incorrect. Taking into account such differences allows for a better understanding of how and why the politics of geographic allocation varies from program to program.

COALITION BUILDING IN CONGRESS

There has been a disturbing tendency in recent Congresses (the last ten or so) to build separate coalitions for each new expenditure program, rather than to assemble a single umbrella coalition for a whole collection of diverse programs. Model cities and the water and sewer programs are examples. In each case, the administration proposed a program to benefit a restricted set of communities and then, in response to congressional pressures, broadened the program's geographic scope until virtually all communities were eligible. Although this strategy of inclusion is obviously effective in building winning coalitions, it frequently destroys the entire rationale for a new program, and it most certainly results in an inefficient allocation of scarce resources. Water and sewer grants were not concentrated in rapidly growing suburbs as program designers had intended, but rather were spread thinly among many communities. The program became nothing but a massive federal subsidy of local investment, much of which probably would have occurred anyway, rather than an incentive for more rational planning in growing communities. Similarly, model cities lost its character as an experimental program the moment the decision was made to fund 150 cities.

Broadening a program's geographic scope is a very effective coalition-building strategy, for it plays on congressmen's weakest spot—the desire for local benefits. However, alternative strategies also exist which do not require that programs be disfigured. One such alternative is the support-trading strategy discussed in chapter 3 in which congressmen from dissimilar districts agree to support each other's· most preferred program. For example, such a strategy might be used to assemble a single umbrella coalition for such diverse activities as a program to rejuvenate declining central cities, a suburban-oriented water and sewer program, and a program of assistance to small farms, *without* having to divert urban redevelopment funds from central cities to small towns, or public facility planning funds from rapidly growing suburbs to old, established cities, or agricultural assistance funds from farms to urban vegetable gardens. If such a strategy were used, each program's resources would be concentrated where they were most needed rather than spread around evenly as a foundation for three separate coalitions. Of course, the *total* funds from the three programs would be dispersed widely, but each program's funds would be concentrated.

Though I do not have firm evidence on the point, there appears to be a trend away from coalitions built with multiple-program logrolls and towards single-program coalitions that rest on wide distributions of benefits. I am not prepared to document systematically the assertion, but scattered evidence is consistent with it. Take for example the urban renewal program, which is interesting because its coalition structure appears to have shifted in this manner during the past two decades. When first passed in 1949, it was essentially a slum-clearance program for large cities. Its initial supporting coalition consisted of urban congressmen (from both parties) and of rural Democrats who were then accustomed to exchanging support with their urban colleagues on various urban and rural issues.[1] However, over time, program adminis-

---

1. David R. Mayhew, *Party Loyalty Among Congressmen: The Difference Between Democrats and Republicans, 1947–1962* (Cambridge, Mass.: Harvard University Press, 1966), p. 88.

trators broadened the coalition by allocating benefits to communities of all sizes. (Fifty-five percent of all communities participating in the program by 1973 had populations less than 25,000, and 14 percent had less than 5,000.)[2] With benefits flowing into most congressional districts, it was easy to sustain a broad coalition in support of the program's expansion without any cross-policy logrolls. Similarly, many programs first passed in the 1960s (besides model cities and the water and sewer program) were enacted by expanding their geographic scope rather than by arranging cross-policy logrolls. The poverty program, for example, was originally conceived as an experimental effort, with benefits to be concentrated in pockets of poverty rather than spread thinly across the entire country. By the time it was enacted, there were shares of benefits for everyone.[3]

Assuming for a moment that there has, in fact, been a shift away from cross-policy logrolling and toward single-program coalitions built on broad foundations of benefits, two questions arise. First, why has this shift occurred? Second, what consequences has it had for public policy?

One explanation for the shift rests on the declining importance of party in American politics and the diminished role of party leaders in Congress. Much of the cross-policy logrolling in the 1940s and 1950s took place within the Democratic party and under the guidance of party leaders. Democratic congressmen from farm, city, labor, and western districts stood together in support of each other's favorite program.[4] But the days of Lyndon Johnson and Sam Rayburn passed, and their successors, Mike Mansfield and Carl Albert, were much less inclined to function as coalition leaders. Yet party leaders were really the only ones who *could* arrange and enforce the complex series of trades necessary to assemble an umbrella coalition for diverse programs that were administered by different agencies, handled by different committees, and considered by Congress at different times. In the absence of central leadership, committee leaders and bureaucrats moved to enlarge the geographic scope of the programs under their jurisdiction, for *that* was something they could accomplish on their own.

---

2. U.S., Department of Housing and Urban Development, *1973 HUD Statistical Yearbook* (Washington, D.C.: Government Printing Office, 1973), p. 32.

3. James L. Sundquist, "Origins of the War on Poverty," in his *On Fighting Poverty* (New York: Basic Books, 1969), pp. 21–29.

4. Mayhew, *Party Loyalty Among Congressmen.*

Whatever the cause of this shift in general strategies, it is a shift with potentially serious consequences for public policy. It means that a substantial proportion of federal funds is devoted to coalition maintenance rather than to solving the most urgent national problems. Yet it need not be so. If an umbrella coalition were built for a diverse set of programs, then benefits could be concentrated where they were most needed. Individual communities would, in general, be better off. Instead of receiving small shares of benefits from many different programs (some genuinely important to them, but many of only marginal interest), they would receive large shares from programs in the first category and nothing from those in the second.

A related problem is the growing tendency in program design for the tasks of policy analysis and political analysis to be separated and performed by different individuals at different times. In both the model cities and water and sewer cases, one group of policy specialists was charged with devising a solution to some public problem, while a second group of political specialists was assigned the task of developing a political strategy for enacting it.[5] The results were disastrous. The policy specialists developed programs that directly addressed the assigned problems and that had excellent chances for success, either in solving these problems (water and sewer) or in encouraging the development of innovative solutions through social experimentation (model cities). However, both programs were politically naive and had little chance of congressional approval. The political specialists then took over and completely redesigned them into forms more acceptable to Congress. Unfortunately, they accomplished this by compromising away each program's most essential features. In the end, the programs enacted failed to address the problems for which they were intended and had little chance of success.

The obvious solution is to integrate political analysis with policy analysis. Those who design programs should be encouraged to pay as much attention to the politics of enacting and implementing their ideas

5. Frieden and Kaplan note the lack of early political analysis for the model cities program. "At an early task force meeting in the White House, members asked whether they should consider the prospects for congressional acceptance when they recommended new programs. Presidential aide Jack Valenti brushed aside any doubts on political feasability, urging the task force to come forward with its best ideas and 'leave the driving to us'" (Bernard J. Frieden and Marshall Kaplan, *The Politics of Neglect* [Cambridge, Mass.: The MIT Press, 1975], p. 39).

as they do to devising effective, efficient solutions to public problems. Surely the latter task is important, but without equal attention to the former, innovative ideas may never see the light of day. Furthermore, such political calculations should be made from the very start, not merely as an afterthought. If "ideal" programs must be redesigned to fit political realities, it is better for the major portion of that task to be entrusted to policy specialists who are well acquainted with the intricacies of the programs they have created rather than to White House aides or congressional staff members whose priorities and expertise lean in the direction of passing programs (in some form or other) once their political superiors have adopted them as their own.

EXTENT OF INFLUENCE

Finally, I return to the question of how extensive is congressional influence in the geographic allocation of benefits. At the stage in which decisions are first made about a program's geographic scope, congressional influence can be enormous. Broadening eligibility criteria so that all communities can apply for benefits or multiplying many times the number of shares to be allocated can completely change both a program's basic character and its potential for success. At the stage in which specific allocational decisions are made, congressional influence, though still considerable, has less impact on a program's basic character. Depending on the program, between 10 and 30 percent of allocational decisions may be adjusted in accordance with particular congressmen's preferences.[6] From the perspective of one interested in the

6. The extent of congressional influence over allocational decisions would undoubtedly be greater if one also took into account the preferences of senators. (In this work I have focused exclusively on the influence of House members.) But it would probably be only slightly greater, and certainly not as much as twice that which one sees looking at House members alone. Senators, as a group, tend to be less involved in acquiring constituency benefits, in part because they can choose from a wider range of electorally useful activities and thus can afford to be more detached from this particular activity, and in part because local communities (particularly those in large states) are likely to turn first to their congressmen for assistance rather than to their senators, whose constituencies may span up to forty districts and include hundreds of communities. Additionally, clever bureaucrats can generally reward strategically placed senators with the same benefits they use to reward congressmen, unless an important senator's state is completely filled with unworthy congressmen.

The question remains as to whether my failure to examine senators' influence over

making of good public policy, neither of these twin effects is to be applauded. Both result in less than optimal distributions of government resources. Nevertheless, the former has the more perverse consequences for public policy, not the latter, which is the more frequent subject of journalistic and scholarly discussion concerning how congressional politics adversely affects public policy. It is certainly regrettable when bureaucrats adjust 10 or 20 percent of their allocational decisions in an effort to maintain their programs' supporting coalitions (though it would be incorrect to equate this with a complete waste of 10 or 20 percent of a program's resources, for these less worthy projects do produce *some* benefits). But if my estimates of the extent of influence are approximately correct, it is a relatively small cost of doing business the democratic way. By comparison, the growing need to design programs with broad standards of eligibility and with hundreds of shares of local benefits constitutes a very large cost indeed. The end result is that a very large proportion of programs' benefits (much larger than 10 or 20 percent) are essentially political allocations. Government becomes unable to target funds in areas of greatest need or even to create experimental programs, which must, by their very nature, benefit only a few carefully chosen areas. Ultimately government may lose the ability to tackle the hard economic and social problems of the day.

A MORE GENERAL THEORY

The theory of congressional influence developed in this book has been tailored to explain but one type of bureaucratic decision, those concerning the geographic allocation of expenditures. Can the theory

---

allocational decisions has produced biased estimates of House members' influence. Probably not. First, such a bias would result if, and only if, the various Senate variables that might be included were themselves correlated with the House variables. Such intercorrelations seem unlikely, at least for the House variables used in this work. (Such intercorrelations would be a real problem for such geographically concentrated benefits and committee memberships as Agriculture or Interior.) Second, I have, in fact, introduced a whole collection of Senate variables into the equations that explain bureaucratic decisions about military employment. The results were sufficiently unrewarding that I did not report them, but there was absolutely no indication of any bias in the coefficients for the models discussed in chapter 6. Since there seemed to be even less chance of such House-Senate intercorrelations for the model cities and water and sewer cases, I did not bother to compile the necessary information.

be extended to include a broader range of bureaucratic decisions? In principle, I believe it can, but a host of problems interfere with a straightforward extension and test of such a general theory of congressional influence. My basic assumption is that whenever bureaucrats suspect that their decisions might affect the size or shape of their supporting coalitions in Congress, they will be responsive to congressmen's preferences regarding those decisions, particularly to the preferences of coalition leaders and other strategically situated congressmen.

The problems inherent in extending and testing the theory stem from two sources. First, one cannot assume that each congressman is interested in every other type of bureaucratic decision, as one can for allocational decisions. Since bureaucrats need respond only to the preferences of interested congressmen, one must have a way of identifying those interested in specific decisions. Second, one cannot assume how congressmen's preference orderings regarding other bureaucratic decisions will look, as one can for allocational decisions. The assumption that each congressman prefers that benefits be allocated to his own district is a relatively safe one. But no such simple assumption can be made for most other bureaucratic decisions; instead, one needs detailed knowledge of each congressman's policy preferences.

These problems are not insoluble, but they do make the task of building and testing a more general theory considerably more difficult, for two crucial assumptions must be replaced with detailed knowledge about the interests and policy preferences of 435 congressmen. It is a task best left for another time, another place, and perhaps another writer.

APPENDIX A: METHODOLOGICAL PROBLEMS IN FIVE PREVIOUS STUDIES

STROM'S STUDY OF FORMULA GRANTS

Strom's study of the waste treatment construction grant program presents some startling conclusions about congressional influence.[1] I should say at the outset that I simply cannot believe that they are true. On the surface, Strom's study is similar to the other six. He tests the same basic hypotheses about the effects of committee membership, subcommittee membership, party, and seniority on constituency benefits, and finds evidence to support most of them. The principal difference is that Strom studied a program of *formula* grants to states, whereas the others examined programs for which *individual* decisions must be made about the funding of each and every project.

In theory it is possible for Congress to write a formula that seemingly allocates benefits according to objective criteria (e.g., per capita income) but that actually allocates them according to political criteria. In practice it is very difficult. Congress would first have to select objective criteria that were good surrogates for all the political criteria, and then would have to devise a complicated weighting scheme capable of differentiating between states on the basis of their congressional representation. Not only would it be difficult for Congress to write such a formula, it is clear that they did *not* for the particular program Strom examined. The statutory formula was quite simple: it allocated half the appropriated funds according to state population and half according to a state's per capita income.[2] No exotic variables and no elaborate weight-

1. Gerald S. Strom, "Congressional Policy-Making and the Federal Waste Treatment Construction Grant Program" (Ph.D. dissertation, University of Illinois, 1973), with excerpts published as "Congressional Policy Making: A Test of a Theory," *Journal of Politics* 37 (1975): 711–35.
2. 70 *U.S. Statutes* 502; 76 *U.S. Statutes* 206; 79 *U.S. Statutes* 906.

ing schemes were adopted. In fact, the formula resembled those used for dozens of other federal programs.

If the formula is so simple, why did Strom find such strong support for his hypotheses about congressional influence? Apparently his study suffers from the same ailment as Ferejohn's, for both his independent and dependent variables are highly correlated with state population. His independent variables are the same as Ferejohn's, and the reasons why they tend to be correlated with population have already been discussed. His dependent variable is "grant funds relative to demand," which is essentially the difference between a state's demand for benefits (according to his calculations) and its actual allocations (according to the statutory formula). It too is correlated with population, because it has been constructed from two variables that are themselves dependent on population.[3] As a consequence, the relationships Strom finds between his independent and dependent variables are largely a reflection of the underlying differences in state population, *not* of substantial congressional influence.

RAY'S STUDY OF AGENCY EXPENDITURES

Ray's work is the most ambitious of all, for he seeks to explain the geographic distribution of spending for seven of the largest federal agencies from 1969 to 1975.[4] The hypotheses that he tests are essentially the same as those examined by others, but his tests are considerably different and his conclusions largely negative. His unit of analysis is the congressional district; his thirty-eight independent variables are the usual committee, subcommittee, party, and seniority ones; his dependent variables are each agency's total spending by districts as well as its year-by-year changes in district spending; and his method of estimation is multiple regression analysis. Ray finds that his independent variables are associated with the *level* of agency spending but not with *changes* in

3. The relationship between population and his dependent variable is obvious in his table 6 (p. 731). The five states that ranked highest on his dependent variable during the Eighty-seventh Congress, beginning with the highest and with their population ranks in parentheses, were: California (1), New York (2), Pennsylvania (3), Texas (4), and Ohio (6).

4. Bruce A. Ray, "Investigating the Myth of Congressional Influence: The Geographic Distribution & Federal Spending," paper delivered at the 1976 Annual Meeting of the American Political Science Association.

spending; he concludes that congressmen are "protectors" of existing spending rather than "promoters" of new spending.

The principal problem with Ray's study is his aggregation of expenditures by agency, a technique that cannot help but deflate one's measures of congressional influence. Most agencies administer scores of programs, each of which has a different allocational system. Some programs give benefits directly to individuals; some provide formula grants to states; some give project grants to local governments; and still others build, staff, and maintain extensive federal facilities. The opportunities for congressional influence differ considerably for these four classes of programs, because the allocational processes themselves differ (see chapter 1). Congressmen seldom have opportunities to influence allocational decisions for the first two classes, whereas such opportunities occur frequently both for the third class and for some decisions in the fourth class. If opportunities for influence differ, one should analyze such programs separately.[5] Combining those programs for which one does not expect to find disproportionate influence with those for which one does expect such influence adds considerable noise to one's data, noise that can easily mask actual influence relations. This is particularly likely, for programs in the first two classes tend to be much larger than the others. Furthermore, although it makes sense to measure influence over *changes* in spending for those programs that involve extensive federal facilities (because large investment costs make spending patterns stable over time), it makes no sense to analyze changes for programs that involve project grants, because grant recipients acquire no preferential rights to benefits in subsequent years. Each year is a new ball game for programs that dispense project grants. In short, ignoring differences in allocational processes makes more difficult the identification and measurement of influence relations.

A second problem is that approximately a third of the 222 districts in Ray's sample are big-city districts, districts that cover only portions of cities represented by three or more congressmen. Such districts should be analyzed separately, both for the theoretical reasons discussed in chapter 2 and for sound methodological reasons. I am not even sure that it is possible to devise good measures for the influence of individual

---

5. Ray does analyze separately "controllable" and "uncontrollable" expenditures, but these categories reflect differences in budgetary processes not allocational processes.

congressmen over allocations to entities as large as New York City, which encompasses nearly twenty districts; but I am sure that Ray's method is inadequate. His approach is to apportion a city's benefits (according to population) to each of its congressional districts, and then to analyze these districts as if they were no different than any others. Note, however, that such an approach assumes that a congressman who single-handedly acquires a $1 million grant for New York City is only one-twentieth as influential as a congressman who acquires the same grant for Schenectady. The grant may be twenty times as *important* to Schenectady, but that does not make its congressman twenty times as *influential*. The only way to get around this problem is to analyze decisions rather than constituencies (though a decision-making approach for big-city districts is not as simple as one for ordinary districts). For now, it is probably best to delete big-city districts from one's analysis, for their inclusion increases the difficulty of measuring influence.

A third problem is that the models Ray tests for each agency's district-level expenditures contain thirty-eight independent variables, even though theory suggests that only a few would be important for any given agency. Thus, a model for the Department of Agriculture contains separate variables to represent membership on the Veterans, Internal Security, and District of Columbia Committees, despite the fact that such committees provide no opportunities for influence over this agency. The inclusion of so many extraneous variables results in extremely inefficient estimates of congressional influence. (This is admittedly a less serious problem than Ferejohn's exclusion of relevant variables, which results in biased estimates.)[6]

There is also a problem with Ray's measure of committee seniority, a measure based on a member's seniority rank. Such a measure assumes that the top man on a forty-man committee is forty times as influential as the bottom man, an assumption with which I think few congressional scholars could be comfortable. (It is not surprising that he finds no relationship between his seniority measure and constituency benefits!) Finally, Ray employs R-square to answer questions for which it is unsuited. In order to determine if congressmen are "protectors" rather than "promoters," he compares the R-squares for models that have

6. J. Johnston, *Econometric Methods*, 2d ed. (New York: McGraw-Hill, 1972), pp. 168–69.

expenditure levels as dependent variables with the R-squares for models based on changes in spending.[7] It makes absolutely no sense to compare R-squares for models based on different dependent variables because the *amount* of variation to be explained varies considerably both from variable to variable and from sample to sample. R-square is useful only for comparisons between models that contain the same dependent variable and were tested with evidence from the same sample.

RITT'S STUDY OF AGENCY EXPENDITURES

Ritt's study is almost identical to Ray's in its scope, methods, and conclusions. (Apparently both were written at about the same time.)[8] Each analyzes the geographic distribution of agencies' expenditures with district-level data and finds very little support for the hypothesized influence relations. There is no need for me to recount all the problems inherent in this approach, for I have previously discussed them in detail (chapter 5). The problems include an inappropriate analytic unit, an inability to test for causal direction, a failure to separate the processes of agenda setting and choice, an absence of tests of statistical significance, the aggregation of expenditures by agency, and the identical treatment of big-city districts and all other districts.

In many ways these two studies are reminiscent of the state-policy-making literature of the 1960s, for they are atheoretical and completely ignore the *process* of decision making.[9] For years students of state policy making attempted to determine whether "politics" caused states to adopt different public policies. They accumulated endless variables representing political "inputs," collected endless measures of policy "outputs" (principally expenditures), and calculated endless correlation coeffi-

7. Ray, "Investigating the Myth of Congressional Influence," pp. 12, 14–15.

8. Leonard G. Ritt, "Committee Position, Seniority, and the Distribution of Government Expenditures," *Public Policy* 24 (1976): 463–89.

9. I have in mind studies such as Richard E. Dawson and James A. Robinson, "Inter-Party Competition, Economic Variables, and Welfare Policies in the American States," *Journal of Politics* 25 (1963): 265–89; Thomas R. Dye, *Politics, Economics, and the Public: Policy Outcomes in the American States* (Chicago: Rand McNally, 1966); and Ira Sharkansky and Richard Hofferbert, "Dimensions of State Politics, Economics, and Public Policy," *American Political Science Review* 63 (1969): 867–79.

cients.[10] The results were largely negative: policy differences were better explained by socioeconomic variables than by political variables. Most studies ignored process; they penciled in a black box to connect inputs and outputs, but it was usually blank. Ray and Ritt have produced studies in the same tradition. They have their political inputs and their policy outputs (and their socioeconomic variables too), but nowhere is there a sense of the policy-making process at work. The effects of inputs on outputs are assumed to be identical no matter what policy is being considered, no matter how decisions happen to be made, and no matter how institutional arrangements may vary among programs, agencies, and committees.

RUNDQUIST'S STUDY OF MILITARY CONTRACTS

Rundquist attempts to determine if members of military committees were able to obtain disproportionate amounts of prime military contracts for their districts in 1960.[11] He concludes that they were not. There are many things about this study which I like, for Rundquist is both sensitive to a number of methodological problems and aware of the limitations of his analysis. Although districts are his basic analytic units, he carefully separates big-city districts from the rest. He uses significance tests wisely and thus avoids confusing minor differences in the distribution of contracts for influence over allocation.[12] He examines separately contracting patterns for fifteen categories of contracts—e.g., aircraft, electronics, and petroleum. He attempts to construct a measure of districts' manufacturing capability in order to estimate how contracts would be allocated in the absence of congressional influence.

Nevertheless, I think the research design is poorly conceived. In fact, I would have been surprised if such a design confirmed any of the hypotheses. For a study of military contracts it is absolutely essential

10. Dye holds the record with more than five thousand correlation coefficients in his book *Politics, Economics, and the Public*.

11. Barry S. Rundquist, "Congressional Influences on the Distribution of Prime Military Contracts" (Ph.D. dissertation, Stanford University, 1973).

12. In an earlier version of the study, Rundquist did not use significance tests and concluded that certain classes of congressmen were more influential than others. See Barry S. Rundquist, "The House Seniority System and the Distribution of Prime Military Contracts," paper delivered at the 1971 Annual Meeting of the American Political Science Association.

that the decision rather than the constituency be adopted as the basic analytic unit, because only a handful of districts are in competition for any given contract. It can only be meaningful to ask whether a congressman influenced an allocational decision when a firm in his district has submitted a bid for a specific contract; this occurs infrequently. Suppose that five firms compete for a typical military contract (a reasonable assumption given the oligopolistic nature of most industries). Then there is only a 1 percent chance that a congressman is even interested in the awarding of a contract, and only a 40 percent chance that any of the competing firms are represented on House Armed Services. If one makes the further assumption that only half the competing firms meet bureaucrats' minimum performance standards,[13] there is only a 20 percent chance that any of the qualified firms would be represented on House Armed Services. In other words, 80 percent of the time bureaucrats could not, even if they wanted, reward members of House Armed Services. Rundquist's constituency-oriented approach combines cases for which committee influence is at least possible with those for which it is impossible; since the latter are much greater than the former, the inevitable result is to mask genuine influence relations. My decision-making approach overcomes this problem, because it begins with an agenda of bids and thus allows one to focus on the process of choice.[14]

PLOTT'S STUDY OF URBAN RENEWAL

Plott's analysis of the location of urban renewal projects, part of his larger study of urban renewal decision making, was the first formal test of the hypothesis that committee members influence bureaucrats' allocational decisions.[15] In many respects it was one of the best, both for its careful attention to process and its development of a basically sound

13. Military officials have performance standards both because of their public interest goal (they want planes to fly) and because of their sensitivity to congressmen's general-benefit preferences (congressmen may evaluate military programs negatively when planes cannot fly).

14. Information about agenda may be more difficult to obtain, but it is not impossible, as I demonstrate in chapters 6 through 8.

15. Charles R. Plott, "Influences of Decision Processes on Urban Renewal" (Ph.D. dissertation, University of Virginia, 1966) with portions published as "Some Organizational Influences on Urban Renewal Decisions," *American Economic Review* 58 (May 1968): 306–21.

research design. Initially he tested the hypothesis with data from states and found strong support for it. Later, recognizing the problem of unequal state populations, he examined it with district-level data and found somewhat weaker support for it. His principal discovery was that the 5 percent of all congressmen who happened to sit on the House Banking and Currency Committee in 1964 (not including those from large cities) received 9 percent of all urban renewal projects and 10 percent of all expenditures. Plott, unlike most other authors, was careful to remove big-city districts from his analysis. He also attempted to test for causal direction, though his tests were inconclusive (as he recognized). It would have been preferable to test for causal direction by studying actions on actual applications for urban renewal projects rather than by assuming how such applications might be distributed among districts over time.

APPENDIX B: FLUCTUATIONS IN MILITARY EMPLOYMENT

This appendix contains the multivariate models that explain employment fluctuations and demonstrate that military committee members do not affect these fluctuations. Although the appendix includes only a few of the models tested, I have actually examined dozens of variations, some with transformed dependent variables and some with different sets of independent variables. None provide any support for the committee hypothesis. The coefficients for the committee variables behave much as one would expect if there were nothing but random variation; some are positive, some are negative, but almost all are *less* than their standard errors.

Table B.1 summarizes three regressions of employment fluctuations at Army installations. Although the committee variables prove unimportant, many of the other variables are associated with employment changes. Definitions and discussions of the variables follow. The dependent variable is change in employment (in thousands) at an Army installation during a two-year period. The committee variables are the standard dummy variables used in chapter 6, with installations represented on a committee coded 1 and others coded 0. Base size refers to an installation's employment (in thousands) at the start of a period. As expected, larger installations received greater increases in employment in good times and suffered larger decreases in bad times. The next four variables measure changes in employment at the national level for four Army functions: training, arsenal, depot, and support. An installation that performs a given function is coded with the national change in employment (in thousands) for that function during the current two-year period; others are coded zero. The evidence shows that much of the change in an installation's employment is merely a reflection of national trends. The next variable, change in total employment, measures changes in the total number of Army employees in the continental

Table B.1.   Regression Analysis: Effects of Committee Membership on Employment Fluctuations at Army Installations

Variable	Regression for All Cases		Regression for Cases with Gain*		Regression for Cases with Loss†	
	B	SE	B	SE	B	SE
Military Subcommittees of Appropriations Committee	−.077	.511	.386	.679	.176	.430
Armed Services Committee	−.213	.296	.050	.420	.106	.241
[Rest of Appropriations Committee]	−.117	.437	.409	.621	−.161	.355
Base Size This Period	−.043‡	.010	.201‡	.015	−.177‡	.009
ΔEmployment, Training Function	.031‡	.002	.009‡	.003	.022‡	.002
ΔEmployment, Arsenal Function	.066	.039	.067	.072	.017	.030
ΔEmployment, Depot Function	.033‡	.016	.040	.039	.009	.012
ΔEmployment, Support Function	.052‡	.021	.039	.025	.030	.019
ΔTotal Employment	.003‡	.001	−.001	.001	.001	.001
Total Bases Closed	.023	.027	.080‡	.037	−.015	.023
Constant	.453		−.036		.185	
Number of cases		1117		486		630
R-Square		.198		.309		.549

Notes: *Cases with negative change deleted from file.
†Cases with positive change deleted from file.
‡Significant at .05 level.

United States during the current period. Not surprisingly, as the size of the Army changes, so too does the size of its installations! The final variable is the total number of Army bases closed during the current period. The evidence shows that when bases are closed, the remaining installations benefit by receiving the displaced shares of employment.

Table B.2 summarizes three similar regression analyses for Air Force installations. Most of the variables and conclusions are essentially the same. The "new base" variable is coded 1 if a base was opened during the previous two years, and zero otherwise. New bases, as the evidence shows, are prime candidates for increases in employment. The second additional variable is coded 1 if an installation contains obsolete missiles (Atlas or Titan missiles after 1964) and zero otherwise. Such bases suffered major declines in subsequent years. The third new variable measures the percent change in the number of bases performing the

Table B.2. Regression Analysis: Effects of Committee Membership on Employment Fluctuations at Air Force Installations

Variable	Regression for All Cases		Regression for Cases with Gain*		Regression for Cases with Loss†	
	B	SE	B	SE	B	SE
Military Subcommittees of Appropriations Committee	.085	.185	−.054	.122	.143	.109
Armed Services Committee	− .052	.128	−.048	.084	−.006	.075
[Rest of Appropriations Committee]	− .129	.171	−.060	.112	−.064	.100
Base Size This Period	− .041‡	.007	.044‡	.005	−.085‡	.004
New Base	.878‡	.275	.919‡	.181	—	—
Base with Obsolete Missiles	−1.011‡	.507	—	—	−.675‡	.299
ΔBases with this function	− .012‡	.004	−.004	.003	−.008‡	.022
ΔEmployment, Strategic Function	.007‡	.003	.003	.002	.004‡	.002
ΔEmployment, Defense Function	.019‡	.007	.007	.005	.012‡	.004
ΔEmployment, Training Function	.023‡	.002	.010‡	.001	.013‡	.001
ΔEmployment, Depot Function	.068‡	.010	.038‡	.006	.029‡	.006
ΔEmployment, Transport Function	.030	.020	.020	.013	.010	.011
ΔTotal Employment	.004‡	.001	.003‡	.001	.001	.001
Constant	.425		.262		.155	
Number of cases		1237		1237		1237
R-Square		.146		.120		.297

Notes: *Cases with negative change set to zero.
    †Cases with positive change set to zero.
    ‡Significant at .05 level.

military function associated with a given air base. The evidence confirms that employment fluctuations are, in part, responses to changing military priorities. The next five variables are essentially the same as the ones used in the Army analysis, measuring changes in employment for specific functions. The results are similar.

Fluctuations in an installation's employment are not unexplainable. Among other things, they are responses to changing military priorities and changes in the total size of the military. But as far as I can tell, they do not reflect any congressional influence in bureaucratic decision making.

INDEX

Accommodating strategy, 46
Achen, Christopher H., 78 *n*, 87
Agenda of alternatives, 74, 101–02, 116, 223
Agenda setting, 5, 6–8, 16, 33, 87–89, 223
Aggrandizement, 23
Agricultural programs, 136 *n*
Agriculture Committee, 87
Air Force installations, 102, 107–19, 123–24. *See also* Military installations
Albert, Carl, 212
Allocational process, 4–8, 16, 219, 221–22
Allocational strategies, 42; for new programs, 46–47; for established programs, 55–71; for military employment, 96–102; for water and sewer grants, 130–31, 133–35, 136–37, 150–52; for model cities, 167–68, 173–76, 186–88
Allocation of benefits: by coalition criteria, 9, 13, 209–10; by objective criteria, 12, 13, 60, 209–10; to committee members, 14, 56, 65–68, 69, 207–08; by general-benefit preferences, 56–64; to opponents, 57–58, 64, 208; to opposition leaders, 57–58, 63, 64, 99; to supporters, 58, 64, 208; to coalition leaders, 58–59, 60, 63, 66, 98, 207; without discrimination, 60, 62, 133, 208, 209; according to party, 68–69, 208; according to seniority, 69, 118–19, 120. *See also* Allocation of military employment; Allocation of model cities grants; Allocation of water and sewer grants
Allocation of military employment: to Rivers's district, 95, 122–24; to Appropriations Subcommittee on Defense, 98–99, 108–09, 112–15, 117–18, 120, 121–22, 225–27; to Appropriations Subcommittee on Military Construction, 98–99, 108–09, 112–15, 117–18, 120, 121–22, 225–27; to Armed Services Committee,

98–100, 108–09, 112–15, 117–18, 120, 121–22, 225–27; to Appropriations Committee, 111, 113, 114; by objective criteria, 116, 120, 225–27; by party, 118–19, 120; by seniority, 118–19, 120
Allocation of model cities grants: to supporters, 174, 178, 184–85, 187, 189–90, 195–96, 198–99, 202–04; to Banking and Currency Committee, 175, 180, 184–85, 187, 190–92, 195–96, 198–99, 205–06; to Appropriations Subcommittee on Independent Offices, 175, 179–80, 181, 184–85, 187, 190, 192, 194, 197, 198–99, 205; to Appropriations Committee, 175, 180, 184–85, 187, 190–92, 195–96, 198–99, 205; to multiple-district cities, 175, 177, 187, 188, 200–01; by dispersing scarce resources widely, 176, 180–81, 187, 196; by standards of merit, 176, 202–05, 206; to opponents, 179, 189–90; by party, 181–82, 184–85, 195–96, 198–99; to converts, 187, 189–90; to opposition leaders, 187, 192; to fence-sitters, 192–93; to freshmen, 193, 195–96
Allocation of water and sewer grants: to reluctants, 134; to Banking and Currency Committee, 136, 139, 144–48, 152, 154, 156–57, 160; to Appropriations Subcommittee on Agriculture, 136, 139, 144–48, 152, 154, 156–57, 160; to Appropriations Subcommittee on Independent Offices, 136, 139, 144–48, 152, 154, 156–57, 161–62; by ideology, 136–37, 140–41, 144–49; by dispersing scarce resources widely, 136–37, 141–42, 146–49, 152, 155, 157, 160; by objective criteria, 142–48, 156, 159–60; to Appropriations Committee, 144–45, 156; to supporters, 151–57; to opponents, 151–57

229

Analytic unit: state as, 82, 83–85, 217–18,
  224; congressional district as, 83, 84–85,
  102, 121, 178, 183, 184, 206, 218, 220,
  221, 222, 224; decision as, 83, 85, 87,
  89, 108, 116, 119, 139, 220, 223; constituency as, 83, 86, 223; choice of,
  84 *n*; military installation as, 102, 108,
  116, 119; application as, 139, 177, 183,
  184, 206, 224
Anderson, Jack, 95 *n*
Appropriations, politics of, 149
Appropriations Committee, 54, 127; coalition leaders on, 41, 51; allocations to,
  65; previous studies of, 82, 83, 90; and
  base closing decisions, 111, 113, 114;
  subcommittee assignments, 125 *n*; and
  water and sewer grants, 144–45, 149,
  156, 158; and model cities politics, 170,
  172–73, 186; and model cities grants,
  175, 180, 184–85, 190–92, 195–96,
  198–99, 208; representativeness of, 205;
  subcommittee system, 207–08; and military employment, 225–27
—Agriculture Subcommittee: and water
  and sewer grants, 136, 139, 144–48,
  152, 154, 156–57, 160; expanded jurisdiction, 136 *n*–37 *n*, 152
—Defense Subcommittee: coalition leaders on, 98–99; representativeness of,
  107; and base closing decisions, 108–09,
  112–15; and new installations, 117–18;
  and employment, 121–22, 225–27; assignment to, 125 *n*
—Independent Offices Subcommittee,
  133; and water and sewer grants, 136,
  139, 144–48, 152, 154, 156–57, 161–
  62; and model cities politics, 170, 172;
  and model cities grants, 175, 179–80,
  181, 184–85, 190–92, 194, 197, 198–
  99; representativeness of, 205
—Labor and HEW Subcommittee, 99
—Military Construction Subcommittee:
  coalition leaders on, 98–99; representativeness of, 107; and base closing decisions, 108–09, 112–15; and new installations, 117–18; and employment,
  121–22, 225–27; assignment to, 125 *n*
Area redevelopment program, 45
Armed Services Committee, 31 *n*, 95,
  122, 124; and oversight, 67, 99–100;

previous studies of, 83, 86, 104, 222–23;
  assignment to, 87, 125–28; coalition
  leaders on, 98–99, 124; representativeness of, 104–06, 125–26, 128; and closing decisions, 108–09, 112–15, 126; and
  new installations, 117–18; and employment, 119–20, 121–22, 225–27
Army Corps of Engineers, 5, 103
Army installations, 102, 107–19, 123–24.
  See also Military installations
Ashenfelter, Orley, 78 *n*
Aspin, Les, 99
Authorizations, politics of, 17, 149

Banfield, Edward C., 165 *n*, 166 *n*,
  167 *n*, 168, 173 *n*, 174 *n*
Banking and Currency Committee: as-
  signment to, 87; coalition leaders on,
  130, 149; and water and sewer grants,
  136, 139, 144–48, 149, 152, 154,
  156–57, 160; and model cities grants,
  175, 180, 184–85, 190–92, 195–96,
  198–99, 205–06; and urban renewal
  grants, 223–24
Barone, Michael, 31 *n*, 95 *n*, 137 *n*
Barry, Brian, 10–13, 18, 20 *n*, 209
Base, agency's, 25 *n*
Big-city congressmen, 34
Big-city districts, 103, 219–20, 222, 224
Black, Duncan, 20 *n*
Blocs of congressmen, 48, 49, 54, 137 *n*
Bolton, Roger E., 4 *n*
Brinkley, Jack, 104
Buchannan, James M., 9–13, 18, 69, 209
Budgetary growth, goal of, 21–25, 35, 133,
  199, 209
Budgetary security, goal of, 21–25, 35, 41,
  52, 133, 176, 197, 199, 209
Budget maximization, 21 *n*, 25
Bureaucrat, restrictive definition of, 20,
  23 *n*
Bureaucrat's goals, 20–26; occupational,
  21; alternative assumptions, 21; personal, 21, 22–23; budgetary security,
  21–25, 35, 41, 52, 133, 176, 197, 199,
  209; budgetary growth, 21–25, 35, 133,
  199, 209; public service, 21–26, 176,
  210, 223 *n*; budget maximization,
  21 *n*, 25; hierarchy of, 22, 24; justification of, 22–26

Causal direction, 85–87, 160
Chicago, 35 *n*, 57
Choice, as stage in allocation, 5, 6–8, 33, 87–89, 223
Clines, Francis X., 12 *n*
Coalition leaders, 37, 40; presidents as, 41, 48, 50, 68; congressmen as, 41, 48, 50–51; bureaucrats as, 41, 50–51; committee leaders as, 41–42, 48, 49, 51, 66, 98; party leaders as, 42, 49, 212; strategies of, 42, 50; time perspective of, 44
Coalition size, 43–44, 52
Collective benefits, 38. *See also* General benefits
Committee assignments, 86–87, 125–28
Committee attractiveness, 68, 86–87, 110, 125–28, 205
Committee overrepresentation, 14, 104–07, 125–28, 205–06
Committee recruitment, 14, 87, 125–28
Committee unity, 69
Community development block grants, 163
Conable, Barber, 203
Congressman, restrictive definition of, 26
Congressman's goals, 26–35; constituency service, 17, 26 *n*, 27, 28–35, 39, 68, 125 *n*; reelection, 26 *n*, 27, 28, 30; influence within House, 26 *n*, 41, 51, 125 *n*; public policy, 26 *n*, 28, 125 *n*, 127 *n*; voting records, 27–28, 38; hierarchy of, 27; justification of, 27–35; universality of, 32–33
Consensus distribution, 59–60, 97, 208, 209
Constituency service (as goal), 17, 26 *n*, 27, 28–35, 39, 68, 125 *n*
Construction projects, 5
Consumer protection programs, 137 *n*
Conyers, John, 181 *n*
Core supporters, 152, 187, 189
Coser, Lewis W., 44 *n*
Credit claiming, 29, 34, 120, 209
Cross-policy logrolls, 212–13. *See also* Support trading
Cue passing, 38, 179, 193

Dahl, Robert A., 72, 73 *n*
Davis, Glenn, 31 *n*

Davis, J. Clarence, 129 *n*
Dawson, Raymond H., 100 *n*
Dawson, Richard E., 221 *n*
Deception: as a strategy, 58
Defense contracts. *See* Military contracts
Defense issues, 17, 60, 96–97
Demand for benefits, 55, 88, 132, 133, 142, 144–45, 186
Derthick, Martha, 7 *n*
Dexter, Lewis Anthony, 32
Disperse scarce resources widely (a strategy): for water and sewer grants, 136–37, 141–42, 146–49, 152, 155, 157, 160; for model cities, 176, 180–81, 187, 196
Distributive policies, 13 *n*, 16
Distributive theory, 13–16, 18, 210
Douglas, Paul H., 168
Downs, Anthony, 20 *n*, 23 *n*
Dye, Thomas R., 221 *n*, 222 *n*

Economic approach, 8, 20, 21 *n*, 26 *n*
Economic prosperity (local): affected by allocational decisions, 4, 30, 34; effect on elections, 30–32; effect on congressmen's activities, 31–32, 101
Educational assistance programs, 45, 46, 70
Education and Labor Committee, 68, 87
Entrepreneur, congressman as, 32, 33, 88, 101–02, 117, 124
Environmental programs, 129, 137 *n*
Established programs, 42, 50–54
Evins, Joe, 194
Exchange relationships: between congressmen and bureaucrats, 35, 36, 72, 208–09; among congressmen, 40, 49–50, 54, 211–12; between congressmen and leaders, 40, 48, 49
Exclusive-coalition model, 9–11, 13, 18, 209
Experimental programs, 215

Federal employment, allocation of, 6
Fence-sitters, 192–93
Fenno, Richard F., Jr., 17 *n*, 26 *n*, 27 *n*, 41, 42 *n*, 43 *n*, 51 *n*, 54 *n*, 68 *n*, 69 *n*, 100 *n*, 125 *n*, 172 *n*
Ferejohn, John A., 13–15, 16, 18, 74 *n*, 79, 81–91, 218, 220

Finney, D. J., 78 n
Fisher, Louis, 163 n
Ford, Gerald, 182, 192–93, 209
Ford administration, 8
Foreign Affairs Committee, 127
Formula grants, 4, 6, 7, 13 n, 14, 129,
    217
Frieden, Bernard J., 165 n, 166 n,
    167 n, 168 n, 173 n, 213 n

General-benefit preferences, 39, 56–57,
    223 n; about defense spending, 17, 60,
    96–98; and policy attitudes, 38, 44; and
    roll-call voting, 38, 44–46, 52–53, 130;
    consensus distribution, 59–60, 97, 208,
    209; indifference, 60–62; polarized dis-
    tribution, 62–64, 169, 209; about water
    and sewer program, 130
General benefits: evaluation of, 37, 38;
    and collective benefits, 38; and water
    and sewer program, 130
General-benefit strategies, 42, 44; polariz-
    ing, 44–45, 53; for new programs,
    44–46; issue-avoiding, 45–46; ac-
    commodating, 46; for established pro-
    grams, 52–53, 63
Geographic pattern of applications, 61
Geographic scope broadened: as alloca-
    tional strategy, 47, 61, 62, 207; for water
    and sewer program, 130–31; for model
    cities program, 166–67; perverse conse-
    quences of, 210–13, 214–15
Gilbert, Neil, 179 n
Goals. See Bureaucrat's goals; Con-
    gressman's goals
Goldberger, Arthur S., 78 n
Goldfeld, S. M., 79 n
Goodwin, George, Jr., 17 n, 127 n
Gosnell, Harold F., 57 n
Goss, Carol F., 14 n, 68 n, 79 n, 81,
    82–83, 86, 104, 205 n
Grant system, 6, 7. See also Formula
    grants; Project grants
Gray, Kenneth E., 34 n

Haider, Donald M., 7 n
Harris, Joseph P., 66 n
Harsanyi, John C., 20 n
Hays, William C., 117 n
Hersh, Seymour, 95 n, 122 n

Hierarchy of goals, 22, 24, 27
Hofferbert, Richard, 221 n
Horton, Frank, 203
Hunt, John, 203

Ideological conflict, 44–46, 53, 169, 193
Impoundment of funds, 158, 159, 163–64
Indifference, 60–62
Influence: and Senate, 26 n, 214 n; over
    agenda, 33, 88–89; over choice, 33,
    88–89; and power, 72; defined, 72–73;
    rule of anticipated reactions, 73;
    measuring influence, 74–80, 119; coef-
    ficients as measures of, 77; isolating ef-
    fects of, 86–87; expectations about ex-
    tent of, 101; extent of, 115, 118, 162–
    63, 206, 214–15; problem of employ-
    ment changes, 119
Intensity of preferences, 56–57, 59–64;
    and model cities, 169, 192–93
Interior Committee, 87
Issue-avoiding strategy, 45–46

Jackson, Henry M., 32
Johnson, Lyndon B., 129, 167, 186, 212
Johnston, J., 80 n, 220 n
Jonas, Charles, 133, 179, 209
Judiciary Committee, 127

Kaplan, Marshall, 165 n, 166 n, 167 n,
    168 n, 173 n, 213 n
Kaufman, Herbert, 57 n, 163
Kazen, Abraham, Jr., 194
Kelley, Stanley, Jr., 78 n
Kingdon, John W., 27 n, 38 n, 44 n,
    52 n, 69 n, 171 n
Kirst, Michael W., 65 n
Kramer, Gerald H., 30 n, 78 n

Large-city bias, 200–01
Limited-duration benefits, 69–71, 219
Liske, Craig, 31 n
Local agent, congressmen as, 32, 33
Local benefits: evaluation of, 37, 38–39,
    55, 133, 134, 174, 193; and roll-call vot-
    ing, 38–39, 45, 46–47, 131, 134, 167–
    68, 171–73, 186, 193; preferences
    about, 39, 56, 74; allocational strategies,
    42; limited-duration benefits, 69–71,

219; semipermanent benefits, 70–71, 101, 219
Logrolling, 40 *n*. *See also* Support trading; Support-trading strategies
Lowi, Theodore J., 13 *n*, 16
Lulus, 12

McDade, Joseph, 197
Machine congressmen, 35
Machine politics, 57
McNamara, Robert, 100
Magnuson, Warren, 32
Mahon, George, 136 *n*, 173
Manley, John F., 51 *n*
Mansfield, Mike, 181, 194, 212
Markets, political, 36
Matthews, Douglas, 31 *n*, 95 *n*, 137 *n*
Matthews, D. R., 16 *n*
Mayhew, David R., 17 *n*, 20 *n*, 26 *n*, 27 *n*, 32, 211 *n*, 212 *n*
Merit, standards of. *See* Objective criteria
Military committees. *See* Appropriations Committee, Defense Subcommittee; Appropriations Committee, Military Construction Subcommittee; Armed Services Committee
Military contracts: and local economies, 4, 30, 31, 32; bureaucratic allocation of, 6; previous studies of, 14, 15, 16–17, 81, 83, 222–23; and Rivers's district, 124 *n*
Military employment: bureaucratic allocation of, 6, 95–96; previous studies of, 14, 81, 82–83; as semipermanent benefit, 89, 101; reallocating, 101, 102, 119–20, 225–27; and committee representativeness, 104–07; and committee influence, 119–20, 121–22; and Rivers's district, 122–24; *See also* Allocation of military employment; Military installations
Military installations: and local economies, 4, 30–31, 34, 101; congressional decisions about, 5, 96, 101–02; as semipermanent benefits, 70, 89, 101; previous studies of, 82–83; and Rivers's district, 95, 122–24; closing decisions, 101, 102, 107–15, 120, 123; new sites, 101, 102, 115–19, 120, 123–24; size of, 109–10, 112; functions of, 110, 111 *n*, 112, 119–20; and employment, 119–20,

121–22; and committee attractiveness, 125–28; *See also* Allocation of military employment; Military employment
Miller, Clem, 16 *n*
Miller, Warren E., 29 *n*
Mills, Wilbur D., 51 *n*, 194
Minimum winning coalitions, 9, 11, 43, 44, 52
Model cities program, 62, 208, 209, 210, 213 *n*; origins, 165–69; allocational strategies, 167–68, 173–76, 186–88; supporting coalition, 168–69, 171–73, 187; effect of 1966 election, 169, 171–73; choice of cities, 169–70, 176–85, 188–200; appropriations, 169–71, 185–86, 197; extent of influence, 206. *See also* Allocation of model cities grants
Moyer, Wayne, 17 *n*, 97 *n*
Murphy, James T., 86 *n*
Murphy, Thomas P., 60 *n*, 103 *n*
Muskie, Edmund S., 168

Nagel, Jack H., 72, 73
Naval Affairs Committee, 122
Navy installations, 102–03, 104 *n*, 123–24. *See also* Military installations
New programs, 42; strategies for, 43–50
New York City, 57
New York State Legislature, 12
Niskanen, William A., Jr., 14 *n*, 21 *n*, 25
Nixon, Richard M., 149, 151, 158, 159
Nixon administration, 8, 135, 137
Norton, Bruce F., 205 *n*

Objective criteria, 75; and formula grants, 7, 217; allocation by, 12–13, 60, 209–10; and military allocations, 116, 120, 225–27; and water and sewer grants, 132, 142–48, 156, 159–60; and model cities grants, 176, 202–05, 206
Olsen, Arnold, 181
Olson, Mancur, 20 *n*, 35
Oversight, legislative, 17, 65, 67, 100
Oversized coalitions, 43, 44, 52

Parks, national, 60
Partisan allocation: why unlikely, 68–69, 208; of military employment, 118–19, 120; of water and sewer grants, 136–37, 140–41, 144–49; of model cities grants,

Partisan allocation (*cont.*)
    181–82, 184–85, 195–96, 198–99;
    claims of, 181–82, 193
Party leaders: as coalition leaders, 42, 49;
    and policy trades, 49, 212; declining
    importance of, 212
Party loyalty, 134
Pearson, Drew, 95 *n*
Plott, Charles R., 14 *n*, 79 *n*, 81, 223–24
Polarized distribution, 62–64, 169, 209
Polarizing strategy, 44–45, 53
Policy analysis, 213–14
Policy attitudes, congressmen's, 28, 38, 44
Policy design, 3, 213–14
Policy trades, 49, 54, 137 *n*
Political analysis, 213–14
Political criteria, 75
Poverty programs, 62, 212
Power, 72. *See also* Influence
Probit model, 78–79; interpreting coeffi-
    cients, 111–12, 146 *n*, 147–48; estima-
    tion procedure for, 183 *n*
Program design, 213–14
Program termination, 163–64
Project grants, 4, 6, 7
Prugh, Peter H., 124 *n*
Public interest goal: bureaucrat's, 21–26,
    176, 210, 223 *n*; congressmen's, 26 *n*,
    28, 125 *n*, 127 *n*
Publicity: congressmen's search for, 29;
    from construction projects, 30; in large
    cities, 34; presidential assistance, 48–49
Public Works Committee, 82, 84, 86
Public works programs: voting on, 17, 46,
    165; allocating benefits for, 61, 70; water
    and sewer program, 131, 135, 165; ex-
    ecutive attitudes toward, 134. *See also*
    Rivers and harbors projects
Punishing congressmen, 155, 157

Quandt, R. E., 79 *n*

Ray, Bruce A., 14 *n*, 81, 218–22
Rayburn, Sam, 212
Reelection constituency, 27
Reelection goal, 26 *n*, 27, 28, 30
Regression model, 77, 78, 89–90
Research, medical, 60, 210
Research and development, 60
Ribicoff, Abraham A., 166

Riker, William H., 9 *n*, 43, 69
Ripley, Randall B., 58 *n*
Risk, attitude toward, 24–25
Ritt, Leonard R., 14 *n*, 79, 81, 221–22
Rivers, Mendel, 95, 122–24
Rivers and harbors projects, 5, 14, 15,
    81–82, 84–85, 88, 90
Robinson, James A., 221 *n*
Rohde, David W., 87 *n*
Roll-call voting: on public works, 17, 46,
    165; on defense issues, 17, 96–97; and
    elections, 27–28; and policy attitudes,
    28, 38, 44; and bureaucrats' preferences,
    35, 36; in exchange for benefits, 35–36;
    bureaucratic influence on, 35–36, 209;
    how to study, 37; anticipating, 37,
    136–37, 150–52; and general benefits,
    38, 44–46, 52–53, 130; and cues, 38,
    179, 193; and local benefits, 38–39, 45,
    46–47, 131, 134, 167–68, 171–73, 186,
    193; and support trading, 39–40, 47–50,
    54, 211–12; and ideology, 44–45, 53,
    169, 193; presidential influence on, 48–
    49, 134, 168; and blocs, 49, 54; and
    party leaders, 49, 212; on water and
    sewer authorizations, 131, 149; and
    party loyalty, 134; on water and sewer
    appropriations, 149–50, 158–59; over-
    riding vetoes, 150, 151; and model cities
    authorization, 167–69; and model cities
    appropriations, 170–73, 186; effect of
    elections, 171–72; effect of local ben-
    efits, 171–73, 186, 193; effect of local
    needs, 202–204
Roosevelt, Franklin D., 68 *n*
Rules Committee, 127
Rundquist, Barry S., 13–15, 16, 18, 31 *n*
    68 *n*, 81, 222–23
Russett, Bruce M., 96 *n*

Saloma, John S., 111, 66 *n*
Sanders, Barefoot, 188
Sayre, Wallace S., 57 *n*
Scher, Seymour, 17 *n*
Schneier, Edward V., Jr., 17 *n*
Schultze, Charles, 166
Science and Astronautics Committee, 127
Selective incentives, 35
Selective perception, 38
Semipermanent benefits, 70–71, 101, 219

Semple, Robert B., Jr., 165 *n*, 167 *n*, 168 *n*
Senate: different from House, 26; difficulty measuring influence for, 26 *n*; consequences of exclusion, 214 *n*
Sharkansky, Ira, 221 *n*
Shepsle, Kenneth A., 87 *n*
Significance tests, 91; proper use of, 79–80
Single-program coalition, 210–13
Smith, Neal, 178 *n*
Snowiss, Leo M., 35 *n*
Social security, 8
Space program, 47
Sparkman, John J., 168
Specht, Harry, 179 *n*
Spillover effects, 10, 61
Sputnik, 44, 46
State delegation, 84
Stephens, Herbert W., 67 *n*, 100 *n*
Stokes, Donald E., 29 *n*
Stolarek, John S., 78 *n*, 87
Strategic timing, 187–88
Strategies. *See* Allocational strategies; General-benefit strategies; Support-trading strategies
Strom, Gerald S., 13 *n*, 14 *n*, 79, 81, 90–91, 137 *n*, 217–18
Sundquist, James L., 4 *n*, 7 *n*, 45 *n*, 212 *n*
Supersonic transport, 32
Supply of benefits, 55, 133, 174, 186
Support trading: evaluation of, 37, 39–40; and logrolling, 40 *n*; and policy trades, 49, 54, 137 *n*; and cross-policy logrolls, 212–13
Support-trading strategies, 42; for new programs, 47–50, 211–13; and policy trades, 49, 54, 137 *n*; for established programs, 54; for appropriations, 137 *n*, 172–73; in praise of, 211–13

Talcott, Burt, 190
Taylor, Michael, 20 *n*
Thompson, Fletcher, 178 *n*, 181 *n*
Thompson, Frank, 203
Time perspective: of legislators, 12, 130; of coalition leaders, 44

Time-series analysis, 160
Tobin, James, 78 *n*, 146 *n*
Tonkin Gulf Resolution, 43
Tufte, Edward R., 30 *n*, 80 *n*
Tullock, Gordon, 9–13, 18, 21 *n*, 69, 209
Turner, Julius, 17 *n*

Ujifusa, Grant, 31 *n*, 95 *n*, 137 *n*
Umbrella coalition, 210–13
Universalistic model, 11–13, 18, 209
Urban renewal program: previous studies of, 14, 81, 223–24; and model cities, 167, 168, 170; coalitions for, 211–12
Utility income, 24, 25

Valenti, Jack, 213 *n*
Veto, legislative, 66
Veto, presidential, 150–51
Vietnam War: and conflict over spending, 96; and committee recruitment, 126, 128; and budgetary priorities, 135
Visibility of decision, 120
Voting record (as goal), 27–28, 38

Waldie, Jerome R., 194
Walker, E. S. Johnny, 31 *n*
Waste treatment project grants, 14, 81, 217–18
Water and sewer program, 210; origins, 129–32; allocational strategies, 130–31, 133–35, 136–37, 150–52; appropriations, 131–32, 149–50, 158–59; supporting coalition, 131–33; selection of applications, 132, 139–49, 152–58; extent of influence, 162–63; termination of, 163–64; and model cities, 165. *See also* Allocation of water and sewer grants
Ways and Means Committee, 42, 127
Weaver, Robert, 204
Whitten, Jamie, 136 *n*
Wildavsky, Aaron, 25 *n*, 53
Wright, Gavin, 69 *n*
Wyman, Louis, 172

Zero-sum game, 43, 149

YALE STUDIES IN POLITICAL SCIENCE

1. Robert E. Lane, THE REGULATION OF BUSINESSMEN
2. Charles Blitzer, AN IMMORTAL COMMONWEALTH: THE POLITICAL THOUGHT OF JAMES HARRINGTON
3. Aaron Wildavsky, DIXON-YATES: A STUDY IN POWER POLITICS
4. Robert A. Dahl, WHO GOVERNS? DEMOCRACY AND POWER IN AN AMERICAN CITY
5. Herbert Jacob, GERMAN ADMINISTRATION SINCE BISMARCK: CENTRAL AUTHORITY VERSUS LOCAL AUTONOMY
6. Robert C. Fried, THE ITALIAN PREFECTS: A STUDY IN ADMINISTRATIVE POLITICS
7. Nelson W. Polsby, COMMUNITY POWER AND POLITICAL THEORY
8. Joseph Hamburger, JAMES MILL AND THE ART OF REVOLUTION
9. Takehiko Yoshihashi, CONSPIRACY AT MUKDEN: THE RISE OF THE JAPANESE MILITARY
10. Douglas A. Chalmers, THE SOCIAL DEMOCRATIC PARTY OF GERMANY: FROM WORKING-CLASS MOVEMENT TO MODERN POLITICAL PARTY
11. James D. Barber, THE LAWMAKERS: RECRUITMENT AND ADAPTATION TO LEGISLATIVE LIFE
12. William J. Foltz, FROM FRENCH WEST AFRICA TO THE MALI FEDERATION
13. Fred I. Greenstein, CHILDREN AND POLITICS
14. Joseph Hamburger, INTELLECTUALS IN POLITICS: JOHN STUART MILL AND THE PHILOSOPHIC RADICALS
15. Hayward R. Alker, Jr., and Bruce M. Russett, WORLD POLITICS IN THE GENERAL ASSEMBLY
16. Richard L. Merritt, SYMBOLS OF AMERICAN COMMUNITY, 1735-1775
17. Arend Lijphart, THE TRAUMA OF DECOLONIZATION: THE DUTCH AND WEST NEW GUINEA
18. David P. Calleo, COLERIDGE AND THE IDEA OF THE MODERN STATE
19. Ronald C. Nairn, INTERNATIONAL AID TO THAILAND: THE NEW COLONIALISM?
20. Robert H. Dix, COLOMBIA: THE POLITICAL DIMENSIONS OF CHANGE
21. Sidney G. Tarrow, PEASANT COMMUNISM IN SOUTHERN ITALY
22. Chitoshi Yanaga, BIG BUSINESS IN JAPANESE POLITICS
23. Raymond F. Hopkins, POLITICAL ROLES IN A NEW STATE: TANZANIA'S FIRST DECADE

24. Robert D. Putnam, THE BELIEFS OF POLITICIANS: IDEOLOGY, CONFLICT, AND DEMOCRACY IN BRITAIN AND ITALY
25. Hugh Heclo, MODERN SOCIAL POLITICS IN BRITAIN AND SWEDEN
26. David R. Mayhew, CONGRESS: THE ELECTORAL CONNECTION
27. Lewis Austin, SAINTS AND SAMURAI: THE POLITICAL CULTURE OF THE AMERICAN AND JAPANESE ELITES

66669